HORSE & RABBIT STEW

It's Probably Because I Was a Breech Birth

HORSE & RABBIT STEW

It's Probably Because I Was a Breech Birth

Memoir of a Recovering Baby Boomer

J. GREGORY STREET

ALL RIGHTS RESERVED. All material contained herein is protected under International and Federal Copyright Laws and Treaties. Reprint or other use of any included material is prohibited without the written permission of the author.

Horse & Rabbit Stew © 2014 J. Gregory Street

Author has recreated conversation reflecting his recall, and a few names have been changed in consideration of privacy. All photographs are property of the author and are from his own collection. Interested readers may view the book's original color photographs and several more at the author's website:

www.jgregorystreet.com

Trade Paperback
ISBN-13 978-1499731491
ISBN-10 1499731493

Hardcover
ISBN 978-0-9906756-0-0

eBook
ISBN 978-0-9906756-1-7

Library of Congress Control Number
2014910279

Printed in the U.S.A.

For those who relate.

Acknowledgements

Thanks to my late parents for their measured intolerance of my youthful indiscretions and warm friendship as I matured. Their love, humor, intellect, strength, and manifest goodness forged the mature me.

Thank you to my good friends Jon Laird, Wayne Witwicki, Jack Tinsley, Terry Valentine, and Richie Guerine for visiting and sharing their memories, and, along with so many others, watching out for me during what has been the single most memorable year of my life.

Thanks also to Colonel (Ret) William C. Haponski, Ph.D. for encouraging me to write of my experiences and reading my very raw first draft, and then pointing the way.

Lastly, a special thanks to my wife Chrisanne for her love of over forty years, putting up with my occasional demons, and helping so much with this project.

Horse & Rabbit Stew

A mixture of the crude and delicate in grossly unequal quantities, with the crude overwhelmingly dominant.

Contents

Preface xiii

PART I: Did I Mention I Was a Dumbass?
1. Fugitive from Achievement 3
2. Many Unforced Errors 15
3. The Remedy Compelled 29
4. Liberating Self with Team 43
5. The Sergeant *Is* the Army 55
6. The Best Laid Schemes...WTF? 69

PART II: Rude, Crude and Socially Unacceptable
7. Surviving Danger's Dragoons 91
8. Fake It till You Make It 109
9. The Ominous Reality 127
10. Hardcore Dragoon 141
11. Dustup in the Rubber 157
12. Continued Survival Was Not Assured 171
13. Death a Peril, Dying the Fear 181
14. The Familiar Was Never Routine 199
15. A Painful Fall from Grace 213
16. Respite from that Beastly Business 229
17. Death Loomed Ever Larger 239

PART III: Finding the True Measure of Self
18. Troubles in "the World" 259
19. Celebration of Survival 273
20. Combatant Rehab 285
21. Traditional Priorities 301
22. The Well-Traveled Route 321
23. It's All Good 337
Epilogue 349
Appendix 361

Preface

As I reached adulthood (in age only), I too slowly began to understand that I, alone, was responsible for my life. I had no plans—live for the moment was my mantra. My friends were able to balance preparation for the future with their current fun. Why could I not do the same? My parents and teachers had always told me what to do. They advised me what was, and what was not, in my best interest. I was not motivated by my own best interest. Why? I barely made it out of high school and into college, and college did not tolerate my lack of performance for very long. I lost my student draft deferment, and I expected I would be called to active military duty any minute. There I would certainly have no choice.

Consider all my nonsense in the context of the 1960s social change, where a sizeable population of Baby Boomers questioned the status quo as never before. The Vietnam War was looming large for every draft-age male and was straining President Johnson's Great Society. Many of my friends were questioning everything, and some were even rebelling—I did neither. I failed to grasp that my country provided an exciting opportunity to healthy young American men without a plan. The alternative they offered was the Vietnam War. With that hanging over me, I slowly became aware that I would not be able to float through life. (For some of us to recognize the simplest of concepts, it *does* take a rock to the head.)

I was determined to control as much of the next several years as was humanly possible. In my infinite (and infantile) wisdom, I devised a plan to: 1) avoid the infantry, 2) dodge combat, and 3) remain well clear of Vietnam. My plan was an epic fail, but the resulting military service paid dividends. There certainly was unpleasantness, but there was also a positive outcome: I survived physically unscathed, and I changed for the better.

Why have I written this memoir? One reason is that I was encouraged by fellow combat veterans to put my story to paper. Additionally, while going through old family records, I saw that my forebears' written record lacks detail; there was very little documenting what they had done, much less what their thoughts were, both at the time and upon reflection. I resolved that I would leave my descendants information about me and in my own words. I began writing everything I could remember, and it just poured out. Once my very raw first draft had been finished, but far from a complete work, a friend suggested my story might have therapeutic value for others. I scoffed but gave it a little thought. There must be others like me. I cannot ignore the possibility that those with similar afflictions might derive meaningful benefit, maybe comfort, from reading my story. It is enough for me to gain from the process of writing, but if others do as well, then that is special. This process has been very therapeutic.

My memory has faded the past four-plus decades. (Dad advised me to keep a journal back then, and I regret very much I did not.) Due to memory deficiency, I have chosen to identify some of the people in this work using a pseudonym, respecting their privacy and covering for the fading memory. I remember some people well and mostly name them outright. For a select few, I provide no name at all. I have bordered on unkindness toward several, without malicious intent—it is all in the past for me. Dialogue has been written to convey the moments of interaction as I remember them. The events are portrayed as I recall them, and their impact on me cannot be sugarcoated.

Those who were a part of this long, exciting, strange, at times very frustrating, but always interesting journey may remember some details differently. That is quite fair, however, please note this is *not* a work of fiction. I have been as factual as my memory has allowed me to be. Also note that this is *not* a war memoir, yet there is one sandwiched within. The reader will not find in this work every single event that has been memorable to me, whether military or civilian, nor meet every person or learn each situation that has influenced me.

Certainly, both the Republic of South Vietnam and the U.S. Army are major contributors to my story, but they are not *the* story. Rather, my story is of the much broader view of how my adolescent apathy, enduring immaturity, rebellion, pathetic absence of focus, lack of planning and self-discipline, and reckless, sometimes dangerous, and always hormonally driven tendencies were serving my long-term benefit poorly. This story tells of belated maturation, too-tardy turn-around, and ultimate emancipation from demons, real and imagined.

Later in my life, I determined that I had been just fine all along, merely in step with a different drum. Who knew way back then there was more than one path in life? Who knew that it is OK to follow your own timeline? Who knew that what is important is the measure of yourself, not that offered by others? Evidently, most other people knew it. Not me, though.

I believe Nietzsche was right: "That which does not kill us makes us stronger." I live the idea and at least one more: If you cannot laugh at yourself, then you miss most of the fun. Laugh *at* me or with me as I tell you of my self-discovery.

Part I

Did I Mention I Was a Dumbass?

*The years teach much which
the days never know.*

—Ralph Waldo Emerson

Chapter 1

Fugitive from Achievement

*M*y journey departed the standard and well-worn path when I arrived into this world by way of a breech birth. I was born in Durham, NC, but we were living in Chapel Hill at the time. I challenged my family's expectations that day just as I would continue to do for years. My childhood was mostly an uneventful one with the usual child drama. I did those things young boys did in the fifties: I found myself in trouble occasionally and innocently explored life. When school began, I was a good student. There seemed to be just the right amount of challenge to keep my interest, and my grades reflected the simplicity of those years. School always had my full attention and participation.

The first career aspiration memory I have is wanting to be a police officer; soon thereafter, it was to be a firefighter. Each of those occupations is typically a young boy's first or second choice. Then it was to be a soldier. That was probably because my dad's older brother, Jimmy, had been recalled into service during the Korean War. After seeing pictures of an F-86 Sabre jet in a magazine, I wanted to be a fighter pilot.

A few years after that, when I was a boy soprano in the church choir, my choice for an occupation was—surprise!— the priesthood. When my boyish voice began to lower, I left the church choir and promptly abandoned thoughts of being a priest. (That whole celibacy thing was unknown to me, or that would certainly have been my reasoning.) As the decade of the fifties ended, I read that the Mercury Seven astronauts were test pilots. Because I am usually motivated toward that which is exciting, colorful, new, and aviation-related, I wanted to be a test pilot. That phase lasted only until I was ten and I visited the cockpit of a DC-7B. (My mother was working for Eastern Air Lines.) Thereafter, I wanted to be an airline pilot and nothing else.

After I received my driver's license, I delivered for Dr. Henry King's drug store. Dr. King and some of the other pharmacists allowed me to help them prepare prescriptions, and I found it fascinating. I thought it was due to the private, intimate nature of prescribed medication. More than likely, though, it was because one young pharmacist's wife was just too damn cute, and I fantasized about her often. I wanted to be a pharmacist, but that lasted for only about two months, the young cutie notwithstanding.

See what is in store for this kid?

The indecision that I was demonstrating is normal at a young age, but I was unable to settle into any one thing, *ever*. Most others did, and it seemed to be so very easy for them.

For me, it was difficult. There was too much world for me, too much to explore.

Of the adult jobs that I have been interested in, only two were recurring. My maternal grandfather was a physician and New York City medical examiner, and that led to the brief consideration of medical school at two points in my life. The idea of becoming a doctor was finally *dis*-considered forever, when, in a brief foray into uncharacteristic clarity, I realized I was altogether unprepared for the undertaking, and I was not willing to do what was required.

With Bob at our grandparents' cabin in N.Y.

The second of those two has been a low-level, almost stealth consideration lasting the duration of my conscious memory. My paternal grandfather was a successful writer, and I have always craved to be creative. To begin with only a blank paper and create something others appreciate is a worthwhile goal, I believe. Throughout my education, the very few compliments I received on schoolwork involved writing assignments. Note that I used the word "assignments." I did little on my own, and my thought of creativity drifted off into nothingness. My grandfather, great-grandmother, and both of my godfathers were writers (Uncle Jimmy and Jack Holland).

Jack Holland was old school, a newspaperman for *The Greensboro Daily News*, and was fifteen or so years older than my parents were. I do not mean old school as the kids are saying today, older than that; he was forties and fifties old school. I am a little fuzzy on the role of godfather, but I am certain it was not supposed to include spending quality time in a bar with your five- or six-year-old godson. Yep, I have a clear memory of sitting at a bar with him while he had a drink and I cracked peanuts. I have no clue how or why I was there, but I knew that I was safe with him. He was no doubt there for an after work drink and awaiting the arrival of his wife, June, my godmother. She worked with Dad at Jefferson Standard Life Insurance Company. (It has since become the Lincoln Financial Group.) Jack was a hoot for a kid like me to be around while June was very proper, loving, and tolerant. I loved them both; they took their roles seriously, and I believe they helped mold the kinder, gentler side of me.

It took tremendous personal effort for me to hold still very long, much less lay a framework by which I might learn a thing or two and be a success at something. *Anything.* My imagination has always written fiction but only for my own amusement. In the early eighties, I wrote two short stories and submitted them for rejection. Sure they were; who knew the U.S. Postal Service could move mail so fast? Usually, I merely fantasized about being a writer. Therein is the theme of my life—motivated and dabbling, but never quite going to the depths of anything enough to make any good come of it. I have always been ambitious but have rarely done much for my long-term benefit.

As I matured, my family naturally assumed there would be measurable achievement from me. Many of my relatives were achievers: those whose accomplishments separate them from others that are merely present and attending life. I was blind to it, however; they were too common. My family has included several master's degrees and a Ph.D., entrepreneurs, writers, lawyers, ministers, farmers, a physician, suffragette, nurse, judge, priest, artist, actor, CPA and an actuary. Also, four of my great-great aunts (all siblings) took vows with the Sisters of Mercy order. Sister-*sisters*! My great-grandfather was a chaplain in France in WWI, and my grandmother was a U.S. Navy nurse during the same war. Mom would never let me forget that Dad (infantry officer, Pacific Theater), Jimmy (infantry non-commissioned officer, European Theater), and her father (medical officer, Iran) had volunteered and served overseas in WWII.

College educations in my family were and are the norm. As if to make my achievement path even more challenging, Mom would often remind me that Dad had been regimental commander as a student at Riverside Military Academy—the ranking cadet! He made his living as an actuary, a profession that was virtually unknown during my school years. Yes, my bar was set high, but it was certainly attainable. My younger brothers could reach it. One received his CPA certificate, and the other earned an MBA. So, why did I not similarly achieve? Today, I realize that I have, but in my own non-traditional, non-conformist sort of way. I take full responsibility for my history and blame no one, not even my parents as so many do today. I own it; I lived it; I am better for it.

Whatever I may have said about my family at that time when I was rapidly coming of age (my maturity moved at a much slower pace), I say now and without equivocation that I had two great parents. I told them so years ago after I realized what an absurdity my youth had been. When I did, they smiled graciously and Dad probably commented wittily, each of them knowing that I still had so much to learn. Then parenthood was visited upon me! It did not take me long with children to appreciate my parents even more. All it took was raising my own, no simple task even when they are easy. I found myself repeating behaviors that I previously considered were my parents' limitations, eventually seeing the wisdom and benefit those very same practices offered my children. Go figure. Bringing my own kids into adulthood healthy and safe was a case of their "grandparent's revenge."

Dad was a stutterer, as were his father and his father's mother. My generation broke that chain. Mom told us a story of my younger brother, Bob, stuttering after he began talking. I am sure they were concerned and gave him extra attention. I, noticing that extra attention and not about to allow him to better me at anything, also began to stutter. I continued right up until that day when Dad threw his shoe at me; I ceased all stuttering instantly at that point. Bob stopped his as well shortly afterward. I believe his was an emulation of Dad's stutter and not really an impediment to his speech. Mine was nothing more than an attention grab.

I was twenty-something before I noticed a characteristic of Dad's. Until that time, I had been too self-absorbed and immature to be aware of it. Because of his stutter, there were certain words he had trouble saying. Early in life he learned he could benefit from language. English offers many ways to say the same thing, and as a result, Dad's vocabulary was much better than the average person's. His speech was never stilted, rather, it was rich with powerful and descriptive words as well as the knowledge of when and where to use them. I cannot remember one of my childhood peers being challenged during their evening meal to define words. At my house, we always were. Dad chose words like *foolscap*, *gandy dancer*, *chukker*, *spelunker*, *lagniappe*, and *picayune*. Those and many others have remained with me.

Back to what I noticed about Dad—the memory of my discovery remains with me. He was meeting a few people for the first time, and his speech was almost flawless. There was none of his (from my perspective) trouble: his tongue stayed inside his mouth, his face was not red, and he was not stuck on the word he could not say. I was puzzled. How could he be so smooth with those people when what I saw routinely were his struggles? Then I got it! (A rock to the head, yet again.) When he was with someone he just met or did not know well, he used his stutter-lexicon to put folks at ease. People usually avoid or mock stutterers, but Dad's word skills allowed him to be more social, and he *was* a very social man, never having met a stranger.

All my life people have told me what a nice man Dad was. I never regretted hearing it; then again, I did not fully embrace it until I was older and much more mature. So why did I know that other man so well, the one who struggled with speech? When he needed to, as when one of his kids was to be the recipient of his lecture or when he met new people, Dad's conversation could be very smooth. When comfortable, or in my case when angry, he would battle with his speech, determined to say the problematic word. His tongue would travel forward, with his face becoming bright red, until he would succeed or give up with his favorite quip, "That's easy for you to say."

One of my proudest days occurred in my mid-twenties when I used a word he did not know: "simplistic." Why did he not know such a familiar word? He could not say, but he praised me as if the word had been chukker. There is no doubt that he had been busy learning all those other words he knew, the ones I still did not know. It had been long before then that I found out my Dad did not know everything, but he still knew many more words, and so much more in general, than I did.

My friends and others would often tell me how beautiful my mother was. I never thought about it; she was just my mom. When I look back, I can see she really was a looker. If I think on it too long, it creeps me out, but I have to admit she was beautiful. She had dark brown hair, olive skin, and brown eyes. None of her children has brown eyes, but two of the five share her left-handedness. She was quick to anger, suffered no fool, and equally ready to party, but she could never tell a story very well; she always remembered it wrong. Uncle Jimmy told me he liked my mother a lot because she had honesty about her words, even when confused or being disagreeable. She was always quick with unsolicited opinions and animation, and Dad was serene and measured.

When I was in my late twenties, I was not shocked when

I heard my mother say, "He can put his shoes under my bed anytime." She showed a friend and me how to tap a keg of beer that we had purchased for our high school graduation party. Mom was a feminist when there were not very many organized. Her grandmother was a suffragette, so that is no real surprise. Mom was born twenty-five years too soon; she would have fit perfectly in the Baby Boom generation. I doubt she would have been a hippie, but I have no doubt she would have smoked weed and been some kind of political activist for common sense and good.

Many of my friends thought my parents were cool. Me? Not so much; they were just parents to me. Indeed, my entire family was remarkable and not just for their achievements or humanity. The family humor was ubiquitous; it was ironic, deadpan, usually sophisticated, and often self-deprecating. If you were not paying attention to the vagaries of the fun, you would quickly become the butt of that fun. Exposure to that as a child has given me a perspective I think a minority of people have: I can be in hysterics over something infinitely trivial, induced by the nuance of a spoken word. When I am, many around me question my sanity. It is the DNA. The days leading up to my sixteenth birthday are an illustration of the family humor. I was looking forward to passing my driver's test so I could take my girlfriend out—I would have freedom! I talked about it incessantly to her, to my friends, and to each of my parents.

The day of my driving test came and Dad took the day to take me; I drove. I felt panic as the one-lane bridge across the Chattahoochee was coming into view; there was a car at the opposite end—a standoff. I hit the gas and Dad stopped me.

"Give way, son."

We drove on to the state patrol testing center without incident. I passed my written and driving tests readily.

"Dad, can I borrow the car tonight?"

"Do you mean 'may I', son?"

"Yes, of course. *May* I borrow the car tonight?"

"Sure. However, I have a business dinner at the club

first, with someone I went to school with...Ward Evans...and you need to come, too. Do you remember hearing about him?"

I did not.

"He wants to meet my firstborn. He can't believe I have a kid sixteen and driving...nor can I, for that matter."

Dad smiled at me—it was a touching father and son moment—but it did not last long. I was growing up and he recognized the fact and knew it was time to let me lead a bit.

"Drive your mother and me to the club...then after the meal you may take your leave...Ward will be happy to drive us home. So, yes you *may* have the car tonight. But only if you promise you'll be smart...and careful."

He looked away, then back, feigning sternness.

"Oh, yeah...and your curfew is still midnight. So don't get so carried away with all your friends that you forget how to tell time."

"I promise."

My self-worth was escalating. My life was in a great, if not exceptional, place. I had myself a girlfriend, use of a car and the exuberance (and stupefying ignorance) of youth. My world was good.

"There is just one thing I ask," Dad said.

He looked at me earnestly. I was steeled for his lecture about safety and my responsibility for driving others. I was floored.

"During the war, Ward lost all but one finger. He has just that one finger for the both of his hands. I don't know how it happened...he's never offered details, and we just don't want to ask. But it's a might disconcerting, I must say...when you *first* shake his hand, I mean."

I could feel Dad's eyes locked on me as I stared at the road ahead and wondered what Mr. Evans had in store for me. The more I thought, the worse that very first encounter with him and his hand was imagined.

"It's his middle finger, by the way," he said, chuckling. "That damn thing...it's nearly perfect. But, nope, not the rest of that strange hand. Lumpy, scarred, stretched out...hard to look at, frankly…he doesn't have a single other finger or thumb—just that middle one. Very strange looking. But, please…don't stare. Allow the man some dignity."

I glanced his way.

"Watch the road, son."

"Yes, sir."

My mind began to race and it filled with dread. I feared that my meeting him was going to be very embarrassing—for me. My brain was that of a sixteen-year-old. Dad let me stew again for a few minutes, and then he continued.

"He's a great guy, son, but he's very self-conscious about that one finger that remains. It's very awkward when shaking his hand…so…please, Greg, just look him in the eye, stick out your hand like a grown man, and shake his stub. He'll appreciate that. Don't…under any circumstances…don't even *look* at his hand. It will send you to a place you don't want to go. Don't say anything about it…and don't allow him to see how queasy you really are about it. For cryin' out loud, he's just a man like you and me…a man with only one finger sitting atop a ball of flesh and bone."

Aside from his referring to me as a man—for the first time in my memory—at the same instant he did himself, the rest of my day was agony. I could not get the ever-changing images of that hand out of my head. I needed to get past the first handshake with Mr. Evans, eat immediately, and then go and pick up my girlfriend. I tried desperately to think about her (my usual task was trying *not* to think about her) so I might avoid the mental horror of imagining Mr. Evans' hand. Yet, those images danced around in my head. No matter what I tried, I kept coming back to Dad's friend with a strange hand. I even sketched variations of what it must be like, and I worked myself into a frenzy.

When the time came to leave, I could not concentrate on driving. I repeated to myself: *eyes, handshake, do not look shocked.* Inside the clubhouse, I nervously looked around for "Ward Evans." Across the room, I saw a table full of my friends from school, with my girlfriend seated alone. "Happy

Birthday!" they said in unison.

I was bewildered until I finally made the connection. It was for me. My parents wished me a happy sixteenth and then gave me instructions to join my friends at their table and have some fun. Yes, the car would be mine after dinner. The hand was still playing in my mind, though, and Dad realized it. He seized the moment, giving it an afterthought treatment to disarm me—again—and ensuring its storage in my head for his future use.

"Ward called me just before we left and said he can't make it tonight. I really wanted him to meet you and you, him. He's a very memorable man with that hand. Oops! That finger. Oh my! I should be more careful. There will be another time, very soon. He thinks he can make it in a few weeks. Let's hope so."

It was years before Dad told me the truth.

That is how the fun often went around my house. It can be a quick, witty retort, playful banter, or the slow, steady, deep, head-play, and off-putting type this was. My parents had me so worried about "Ward Evans" and his mangled hand that I saw none of their preparations for the surprise party. Brilliant. That brand of humor is still with me.

For too long, my humor contribution stemmed from my pitiful effort at academics. My family DNA primed me to attain a similar level of performance as others in the family had and would. No one ever said that my achievement must be the same as anyone else's, but they expected that it eventually would be. I did not. I would not. At the time, I could not. It is cliché, but I could not get out of my own way. I was ignorantly priming myself for a monumental awakening, a horrendously crude "rock to the head"—nothing at all delicate about it.

My grandfather launched his writing career as a newspaper reporter in the South and moved to New York City with Associated Press. In the mid-thirties, while researching a fictional story idea, he visited the medical examiner's office in New York City and interviewed one of the examiners. The story that came out of his research launched his novel writing career. Years later, in 1946, he and that very same medical examiner met once again—at the rehearsal dinner for their children's wedding.

Those children became my parents, shown here at my sixteenth birthday party. My mother was the doctor's daughter and Dad the writer's son.

Chapter 2

Many Unforced Errors

---

*P*rior to reaching adolescence, I displayed the usual self-discipline and self-motivation. However, soon after I entered puberty—and thereafter was a teenager—everything changed for the worse. At least some measure of personal motivation and discipline was needed to succeed at anything, much less achieve anywhere near the levels other family members had. I had become entrenched in a pattern of flux with no focus, no goal, and no plan—just my astounding aimlessness. My only concentration was on the pursuit of fun and adventure. My pitiful venture was truly *un*-achieving—not under-achieving. I was exceptional, too, outdistancing all competitors.

The only activity I made an authentic effort with was competitive swimming, but during summers only. I was good, better than most on the team. I swam all individual events in all strokes, and so, too, on the relay teams. The first night that I ever swam the butterfly stroke in competition, I won by a considerable distance. Dad came rushing to the side of the pool and asked, "Where the hell'd you learn that, son?" He was proud, but that was the last occasion he would express it for quite some time. I never gave him reason to. Later, so much later, he would indicate pride in many other ways. Meanwhile, I had some serious growing up to do.

I eschewed all that was remotely academic in favor of fun, and serious problems for me began in junior high school, no doubt complicated by my all-in attraction to girls. My grades plummeted. I often daydreamed about girls and what they were like; not their personalities, their bodies. I liked the way they smelled. They were soft, but I did not know very much about that. I *absolutely* wanted to know much more, and as quickly as I could. Girls made me feel good just to be around them, but many paid me very little or no attention. I joined my junior high school's mixed chorus chiefly because the most attractive and physically mature girls were there. That was fun; I was one of four guys singing bass. Yeah, the same kid that was a boy soprano just a few years prior. My puberty had arrived with a bang.

A few years later, Dad accepted a new job that required our relocation to Atlanta, GA; I was ready for a fresh start. A new school, new friends, and the continuing family influence would put me on a road to academic success. Nah, that was not to be quite yet. Clean slate or not, I continued with my unfocused, undisciplined ways.

The first gym class I had in my new school, Chamblee High School, I was quizzed by the teacher who was also the baseball coach. I was struck by his pencil-thin mustache, and I could not take my eyes off it.

"Welcome to Chamblee," Coach Palma said. "Where do you come to us from?"

"North Carolina."

"Where? What high school?"

"We just moved down here from Greensboro. I was at Kiser Junior High."

"Do they have organized sports? Do you play baseball?" he asked.

"No, sir."

He seemed surprised, almost displeased.

"Football?"

"No, sir"

"Basketball?"

"No, sir."

"Track or tennis?"

"No, sorry."

"What do you play? Tiddlywinks?" he asked.

"I swim."

"Swim? We don't have a pool. No swim team."

He glanced out at his gym class.

"Well...guess there's nothing here for you. If you become

interested in any sport, you'll have the opportunity to try out. For now, just get on out there with the class."

With that, I was summarily relegated to the group that did not include athletes. Given that I was already well on my way to poor grades, it would soon be obvious to all that I was certainly not a scholar-athlete.

My studies suffered; I am surprised I performed as well as I did, which was only marginally better than abject failure. I was never held back, but the truth may be that the faculty pushed me through, just to ensure they would be done with me. I never paid any attention in class, and I disrupted most of my classes with my antics. However, I was not ill-tempered or a surly disrupter. In fact, when teachers would contact my parents—which occurred with great frequency—they would express how polite I was during my disturbances. Maybe I was polite, but I was disruptive and aimless. Today I would be a kid who is prescribed attention deficit medication.

Dad arrived home from work one evening when I was beginning my sophomore year, and we were in the kitchen chatting about nothing in particular. The telephone rang; all I could hear was his side of the conversation.

"Hello," he said cheerfully, as always. "Why, yes, I'm his father. What can I do for you?"

He knew what was coming, because it had occurred too frequently. He listened without looking at me or giving me the slightest indication who the call was from or that it was about me. After a minute, he said, "Oh yes, his mother and I are well aware of that behavior, and you are correct, it's not at all fair to other students. We've been working at this problem for some time now, and it remains a very high priority for us."

He listened to the caller, but within a few seconds, he looked over at me. His look was more like a glare.

"Oh, I *am* sorry for that. I'm embarrassed, too."

My face was getting warm; I was in deep doo-doo, but I could not begin to guess who was on the line. What does that say about my routine behavior?

"Let me ask a question, please...and I'm not trying to be

impertinent," he said as he turned away from me. "Are you young and attractive?"

The response must have been an earful. He was silent for a long time.

"Not at all," he said, "but I do know my son. If you are a young and attractive female, then he'll surely be giving you a lot of attention. On top of that, if you're kind in spite of his poor behavior, he'll only give you more unwelcome attention." He scowled at me and, changing his tone for my sake and for the caller's, said, "You need to make him toe the line. Do *not* accept flirtations...and that's exactly what they are. Be firm with him. Get mean if you have to."

It was then I knew who was calling. Just one of my teachers was under fifty and female. She and my father soon reached an understanding about my behavior and they were united on how to handle me. Dad gave me a lecture, as usual, but never actually gave me the specifics of what I had done to offend her. He was superb at lecturing, assuming his spawn would respond to logic. There were times I wondered if I *were* his biological offspring. He preferred a reasoned approach to a physical approach, but I might have been much better served had he beat me senseless. Back in class, I was thereafter an even greater problem for my young teacher, so she wasted no time in dispatching me to someone else's class, to become their problem. She was unable or unwilling to put up with my nonsense. I do not blame her a bit.

During that time I was delivering prescriptions for Dr. King, and an event occurred that would recur several more times over the next few years. Mr. Ridell, the father of two boys I went to school with, did a good deal of walking around town. My friends and I would see him just about anywhere when we were out cruising. We would honk and wave to him, and he returned our wave with a big smile. He was always friendly to us. Returning from a delivery late one afternoon, I saw Mr. Ridell walking along the roadway. I honked and waved, and he returned the wave with a smile, as he always did. Thirty seconds later, while I was stopped in the line of cars waiting to make a left turn, I was violently rear-ended. The impact caused me to crash into the car in front of me. No one was hurt, and there was only a little car damage. I did not realize it at the time, but this incident was only the first such encounter with Mr. Ridell. He was my jinx, and he would continue to haunt me.

I was busy enjoying my adolescence and so were my friends. Some of them seemed to be older before they needed to be. Was youth not about having fun, being free to express oneself? What was up with all the emphasis on academics? My attitude was that our fun-to-work ratio would invert soon enough, so party-on.

I spent my thought-time fantasizing about being a rock star, a movie director, and, of course, a writer. Why did I need an education immediately? It would always be there for me to grab. Time marched on without waiting for me, and my high school graduation arrived. It was no surprise to anyone that I met the minimum graduation requirements—provided I passed chemistry. I did not.

The chemistry teacher, Mr. Wilson, summoned me.

"How badly do you wish to graduate?"

I was astonished. "I failed?"

"Of course you did. You didn't study at all, nor did you pay attention in class. This isn't that difficult," he offered.

I could not argue with him on its degree of difficulty. I had not the first clue where it was on the difficult-easy scale because I had hardly opened my textbook. To be certain, as always, I was doing something unproductive when I should have been at least paying attention.

"Yes, sir. I *do* want to graduate with my class."

Mr. Wilson thought for a few seconds. He could have failed me right then, and that would have been it; I knew that. I would have accepted just about anything to graduate with my class, and to prevent graduating with my brother's class the following year.

"Okay," he began, "for each of the three remaining days of this school year, you be here every afternoon and wash my board." His eyes pierced mine. "Without fail!"

I thanked him for his consideration and kindness as I darted from his lab, not wanting to allow him a chance to change his mind. The next day when I showed up to wash his blackboard, he told me to wait in the lab supply room for a few minutes while he had a discussion with another student. After about five minutes, he called me out.

"Your grade is already submitted. You may go."

"But did I pass?" I was fearful of a literal setback, having to repeat my senior year.

"Yes, I certainly should *not* have done it, but you might, just might, have learned a lesson. I hope so."

So, that is how I graduated from high school—by not washing a teacher's blackboard. The faculty probably had a conference and made the decision to warm the chair with someone else.

I never shared the news of my near-failure at home. They were already of the mindset that I must have buffaloed someone, somewhere, somehow, and maybe they should just be thankful and just leave well-enough alone. The family joke for the next few years was that I received a standing ovation when receiving my diploma. I do not recall that occurring, nor can I dispute it. There is not a great deal I do remember of graduation day or night. I do recollect a little of the ceremony, seated in cap and gown, hoping my name *would* be called. How embarrassed I would have been to be the only student left, all dressed up with nowhere to go.

Although my teachers would universally decry my poor classroom demeanor, a lack of motivation, and the inability to focus, they never once said I did not "play well with others." I do play well with others. I have always been very social, and that is at the core of my youthful irresponsibility. Repeatedly, teachers warned me either one thing or another thing would become part of my "permanent record." Did we all not get that admonition? I always ignored it. Practicality told me there would be too much paperwork and effort required to maintain such a thing for everyone. In my young, mostly preoccupied mind, I received their message in the metaphorical sense, but I should have regarded it literally. Over time, I have learned there actually *is* a permanent record, but it is not in a single manila folder kept in the permanent record storage file. The real permanent record is written by our achievements, and that is hidden within the minds of those who know us.

My parents continued to preach the individual family accomplishments. One might think with family DNA coursing through my system I would be a natural achiever—one would be mistaken. Maybe I was resentful of the preaching or just being defiant, but I rebelled at having to conform to anything others told me I *should* be doing. I knew I would eventually complete my college education, but I was not ready yet.

For as long as I can remember, my tendencies have been to steer away from the beaten path to avail myself of a trail not so picked over or common. That certainly has often been to my detriment, but I embrace that non-standard route. It is a much more exciting way to travel.

When most of my friends went to college, I went through the motions of going, too, mainly just to satisfy my parents. I was accepted—barely—at a local college with the reputation for allowing anyone in. Staying in became my problem. My earliest class was first period biology, a subject not at all good for me that early. I would arrive at the building's entrance each morning and, almost every day, someone would suggest getting breakfast. "Let's go," was my usual response. Out of four of us in the class who failed to attend regularly, three failed biology, each receiving an "F: failed." No surprise. I was very shocked to receive a "WF: withdrew-failing." By all rights, my grade should have been an unqualified "F," just like the other three. I had not withdrawn; I just did not go to class.

"You'd better get serious about your grades this time or you'll find yourself older and wishing you had," my mother chastised. "I promise you. Life will leave you behind."

As she handed me a check to pay for my winter quarter classes, she did not let up. That was her nature, to drive her point home hoping it would somehow stick.

"No college will let you stay if you don't keep your grades up. Are you listening to me? They'll kick you out and then where will you go? What will you do then? You won't live in this house for very long if that happens."

She held her grip on the check and glared at me as she released it, and I verified the amount was correct. I paid only partial attention to the routine drill since I was accustomed to it. That same old lecture was of no interest.

"This world isn't going to wait for you to grow up," she went on, "and your father and I won't keep paying for you to waste our money."

"I hear ya, Mom, but I really gotta go now...appreciate your confidence in me."

Mom made her standard "pffft" sound as she flipped her hand, something she always did when frustrated. She knew I would not follow the parental plan. Yet, we each continued to go through the motions. I took her money and gave it to the college, knowing I would not be serious. She and Dad must have wondered why I was not like all the successful achievers populating my family. Among them were accomplishments to serve as inspiration to me, but I was not at all inspired.

I made appearances in *some* of my classes over the five quarters I matriculated, but I made virtually no effort at any of the course work. I was not surprised at all when I was placed on academic probation at the first possibility. I still had opportunity to recover my grades and stay in school, thereby keeping my student draft deferment. Despite that, another gift to an undisciplined youth, I made zero effort. I was placed on probation. Although I knew I would eventually complete my formal education, at that point in my very young and immature life I just could not focus on academics, much to my parents' chagrin.

Yep, my focus was still all about the girls, rather, the young women. I was not anywhere near being mature; I was just getting older. "Live for today" was the principle by which I continued to live. I was dumb as a rock. I could have partied *and* gotten an education, but for some reason I saw those things as mutually exclusive. Several friends were getting their education and partying, and they certainly were no smarter than I was. Well, OK, maybe they were!

College was no longer encumbering my partying. After they had warned me that they would if I did not bring up my grade point average, they placed me on probation. Academic probation was their way of suggesting a continuation of my education-deficient ways would result in outright exclusion. That event would preclude my attendance for a year. To bide my time while I waited it out, I spent my days delivering auto parts, my nights dating, and of course, partying.

One morning, I turned out of our parking lot and headed over the slight rise in the road, then on down the hill toward the traffic light. I minded my own business and was not even distracted by loud music—there was no radio in the truck—when I saw Mr. Ridell over on the sidewalk. I honked, and when he looked my way, I waved. As always, he returned my wave with a broad smile. I let the engine slow the truck down for the traffic light and rested my accelerator foot on the brake pedal, ready to stop behind the traffic being held by the light. When I applied the brake pedal, it traveled all the way to the floor. Uh oh! I downshifted to slow the truck more, but since I was going downhill, there was little effect.

I had to make the choice of clobbering the car in front of me, or trying to seize a gap in the oncoming traffic. Since there was a parking lot at the liquor store to my left, I turned left and shot the gap. I avoided the car in front of me with plenty of clearance, but in the oncoming lane was a brand new station wagon prepared to broadside me. In an attempt to avoid what I considered an imminent collision, I stepped on the gas. I almost made it, too, but my delivery truck was clipped in the back by the station wagon. I was at a higher rate of speed, clear of traffic, and without brakes. Staring at me from straight ahead was an eight-foot drop into the Junior Varsity, a restaurant with a much lower parking lot. Uh-oh, again! Thankfully, a liquor store on the higher parking lot had been kind enough to place empty liquor boxes just where I needed them most. A hard left nestled me safe, but comically, in their bosom. Once again, Mr. Ridell had been my jinx.

I once dated a girl attending a local fashion college. Ours was not a romance: ours was a non-exclusive fun thing. I was a few months past my nineteenth birthday, still living at home most nights, and drifting about with no plans other than the next party. I was no longer subject to curfew, as I had been in high school, but my parents called for courtesy. They felt they should always be informed when I expected to arrive home late, or in the event I would not be returning home at all that night. I had no problem with their request; it was the polite thing to do.

One night I was out at a party until about two, and I had failed to let my parents know I would be late. When I walked into the house, I noticed their bedroom light was on. I was surprised to find Dad was sound asleep, and Mom was still awake, a book resting in her lap, cigarette between her fingers—its ash about to fall. She peered over her glasses.

"Where have you been...out with your whore?"

"Don't call her a whore. You don't even know her."

"I've met her...not impressed."

"She doesn't need to impress you. I like her."

Then I turned to go to bed, and she yelled after me, "Yet another failing of my firstborn."

I was dumbstruck and angry, and I wanted to say more; I did not. My friend was certainly not a whore, and my sex life was *decidedly not* my mother's business. It was 1967 and free love was by then becoming the norm among my peers. That concept was foreign to Mom's generation and I knew it.

Why did she lash out as she did? The problem was not with my friend. No, the core problem was my aimlessness and standard lack of consideration toward my parents. Mom's comment was her way to vent—her unique style. That was lost on me at that moment; I was resentful. Dad never stirred.

After that night's bedtime encounter, we never spoke of her outburst again, not even when my friend would visit our house. When face-to-face with her, my mother could not have been nicer. I actually think she liked the girl.

There is one more example I will share of Mom's peculiar style of expressing frustration with me. I had seriously lusted over a gorgeous young woman for several months. She was someone with whom I could have become very serious, very fast. To my frustration, she refused to acknowledge me.

That is, until one glorious night many months after I first met her. It was a night when she did not already have a date, or maybe she was just on the rebound. I will never be convinced she gave in to my incredibly blubbering attempts to get her to notice me. No, I was used that night—but I made no complaints at all. I enjoyed it.

The sun was just setting that warm summer night when I picked her up at her apartment. We went to a friend's party and had a lot of routine fun, then off we went to a party at someone else's house. Theirs was an older, earlier twentieth century home, like so many in Atlanta not then rescued or refurbished, and the rental cost was cheap. Those homes were more commune-friendly than a typical box apartment and they were frequently occupied by groups of hippies, who were beginning to root in Atlanta.

By the middle of the night, we had tired of our hosts and departed. I was enjoying her company and did not want the night to end. Too soon for me, we were at her apartment.

"Would you like to come in?" she asked.

"Yes, thank you...but it's late; I shouldn't stay long."

I did not want to appear too eager, fearing it may quash the entire deal, whatever the deal might become. Casually, I slipped in before she decided otherwise. My mind was racing; I needed to bring up my A-game. Hell, I needed to *invent* an A-game. I decided that laid back, low, and slow was the way to go. Maybe, just maybe, that would work.

"Help yourself to anything. Cold drinks are in the icebox. Make yourself at home," she said. "I'm going to get myself comfortable...I'll be back in a jiff."

Did she really mean it—that old cliché, "something more comfortable," that quaint euphemism for something sexy and stimulating? Oh! Certainly, one could hope.

"Thanks, don't dawdle," I said.

In her kitchen, I saw that she had beer. *In bottles!* What woman kept beer? What person had bottles in those days of aluminum convenience? *This girl may be a keeper*, I thought. She returned in the time it took me to open a beer. (I did not easily find the church key.)

"I'm back."

She bounded into the living room as I was entering from the kitchen. She had slipped into the cliché T-shirt and cutoff jeans. There was something simple, homey and refreshing about that look. Very casual, yet inviting.

"You still look fabulous. Sexy outfit."

"Come sit by me," she said, patting the sofa beside her. I did precisely as instructed.

"So...whatcha wanna do now, huh?" I was being just about as nonchalant as I could, which was not very.

"Do I have to teach you? Do what's natural."

I did—and soon afterward, we were passionately kissing and petting heavily. My confidence grew, feverish in the throes of our mutual lust, hormones coursing through our two young bodies. There was nothing on my mind except for the vision, aroma, and captivating sounds emitting from my real-life desire-of-the-moment girl. I was at one with a fantasy world. Each passing moment was better than the previous, and I was clearly on my way to the highest levels of physical intimacy with the most beautiful creature around.

Could my life get any better? My real life never did, so, emphatically, no, things could not possibly remain that way forever. Her telephone's loud ring shattered my very special moment. It was my standard luck. I very much wished that she would not answer it, but I could not say so. She answered the phone. After a few seconds of listening, she said, "Why, yes, of course." She held out the phone. "It's your mother."

It was 4:30 a.m., I was nineteen years old, alone with the leading object of my dreams, in her apartment, so very close to achieving my only stated (and as usual, shallow) life's goal, and *my mother was calling.* She tracked me down by calling all my friends. They all knew. I was beyond mortified. My evening died with that phone call and so, too, any chance with that lovely creature again. She returned to her standard demeanor of not taking me at all seriously. Why should she, if I did not take my own self seriously? Would I ever? Was I even capable of getting with the life-preparation program? It was beginning to appear even to me that I could not.

I decided to return to college that winter, and they let me back in. I had been having loads of fun just playing, but I knew it was time for me to get my act together and get my education. If I did not get myself off of academic probation during the winter session, then the college would throw me out for a full year. That would be problematic.

Outside class, I started to take serious note of the rapid increase in military activity in Vietnam. Many Americans, previously behind the military effort, were by then speaking out against our involvement under any circumstances. Then the 1968 Tet (Vietnamese New Year) Offensive began—urban fighting was everywhere. The adjustment I sorely needed was easy, and I still could have joined the routine path without serious effort. Yet I still did nothing, except to continue to float through my classes doing too little to make a decent grade.

It was no surprise that I was excluded from college for the next year. One could hear the chorus of laughter from the tragic play that was my life. Soon, I began to hear a solo sound—the siren song of an alternate path; it was a soldier's marching ditty:

Over hill, over dale, we will hit the dusty trail....

Chapter 3

The Remedy Compelled

*N*othing motivated me toward any beneficial action. Nothing, that is, until I took notice of the images of fighting during the Tet holiday of 1968. Prior to that day, I had paid little attention to Vietnam. Of course, I had been horrified at the Buddhists' self-immolations a few years earlier. I could not fathom why someone would do that. What was the purpose? Protest? They *must* be crazy. It was foreign to me, so I did not think about it. I was only fifteen years old, and I made no connection at all.

Just a couple of years later, when American ground forces arrived in Vietnam, I was still barely aware of the world beyond my immediate space. I did not follow any of the fighting; it meant nothing at all to me. Yet, I knew a few guys who were beginning to go, or were already there. I began to watch news footage of the battle in the Saigon area, especially the fighting in the Cholon section. I did not know why I paid attention—I did not ponder—but was completely mesmerized by the armored vehicles and their crews.

The 1968 Tet holiday news coverage was my wake-up call. I realized that I had best become very interested in what was going on in Southeast Asia, because I probably would be impacted by that conflict very soon. (Notice that I came to my discovery rather late.) The military draft loomed larger every day for those of us who were of draft age and not in school or otherwise exempt. The political activists, so-called doves, and the anti-war movement of all stripes came to the media-fore. The U.S. was politically combative and earnestly divided.

My immediate dilemma was that the runaway train that was our involvement in Vietnam came closer to me by the minute, and I could no longer get out of its way. Hell, I could not get out of my own way. No Baby Boomer too stupid to make at least a minimum effort at self-preservation *could* get out of its way. If I did nothing, I would end up a participant. If I grabbed hold of my life, even to make the best of an already bad situation, maybe I could get my life turned around in the process. If I wanted any choice in the matter, it was time to act. I had to take long-term charge of my life—right then. I hoped I might still have some influence.

My high school and college friend, Foots, was in the same situation. We agreed that joining the reserves appeared to be what we needed. We would gladly accept the reserves or National Guard since we were trying to sidestep an undesired trip to Southeast Asia. However, our service to country was not at issue. In the Southeast, it was still an honorable thing, although that was changing. Our concern was for the place and terms of said service. All of the reserve and guard units we approached had from six- to eighteen-month wait-lists. That was far too long for us to be vulnerable to the draft. We were dismayed.

We had a major problem with no resolution in sight. To carry out the next best thing as we then saw it, Foots and I visited recruiters. If we could no longer avoid active duty, then we must *not* be in the infantry, *not* sent to Vietnam, and *not* find ourselves in combat. *Yikes!* Much to our surprise, there were many service programs from which to select. Guys were making the decision every day and performing military service, all while preparing for their future. Most of our friends remained in college and retained their deferment, but we were not that smart. OK, I was not.

We went to see the air force recruiter first. I wanted to fly, but admission to their aviator program required a college degree. Nothing sounded good to either one of us. We went to the navy, and they offered submarines or aircraft carriers. We were intrigued and investigated a few interesting possibilities. We chatted for a while with the navy recruiter and then left. We never considered the marine corps. We knew choosing them would be a ticket straight into the infantry and a quick trip to combat in Vietnam. A few doors away, the army had their own recruitment office.

"Good morning, gentlemen," he said. "I am Sergeant First Class Sweeney. Come on in and take a load off."

He greeted us cheerfully as we entered and pointed for us to take a seat. He engaged us in introductory chat, but then the sergeant got down to business.

"The United States Army wants good men to serve their country. You two look like you'd have a great career path in today's army."

How could we not see right through that? I was tempted to look around for those gentlemen he referred to, in jest, but that guy was too serious, too fit, and too tidy. We had no clue what all the ribbons and decorations he wore indicated, but he might be a real badass, and maybe we should get serious. It was readily apparent even to civilian dumb asses that he had been around. He was old, maybe all of twenty-five, or—eek!—thirty. We were impressed and intimidated. Hang on. Did he say army *career*?

"Looking for adventure?" he asked. "Want to see the world? Go places you've never been to...do things you'd never get to do otherwise?"

We told him candidly we wanted to avoid the draft, avoid going to Vietnam, and avoid the infantry altogether, but we did want something exciting and adventurous, with girls. (Here was yet another instance where I did not view my life past the immediate.) The sergeant told us about numerous army occupational specialties, but very few of them interested either of us. I had always been interested in photography, but becoming an army photographer was not right for me, even though the training would have served me nicely later on in life, given my photography hobby.

The recruiter was not sensing an immediate sale, so gambled—he went all in.

"Then what about a combat arm?"

"Combat?" We were high-pitched and in unison.

Foots explained, "We need to avoid that...for true. And a visit over to Vietnam, too."

"Well, Vietnam *is* your only combat zone. However, there are combat arms stationed all over the U.S. and all around the world."

He did not bother to tell us about the *dangerous* nature of the Korean DMZ (demilitarized zone). A glance at Foots and his total disinterest was apparent. However, I saw what might be a way to accomplish some of my avoidance goal.

"So tell me more." I was trying to be nonchalant.

"Combat arms...infantry...armor...artillery. Infantry is the foot soldier, armor is the tank, and artillery is the cannon. To avoid the infantry, train in armor at Ft. Knox, Kentucky, or artillery at Ft. Sill, Oklahoma. Infantry is just down the road a piece, at Ft. Benning."

"Yes, I know about Harmony Church and Sand Hill," I said. "My dad was an infantry officer during World War II in the Pacific, and his older brother an infantry master sergeant in Europe. Since infantry is out, tell me about artillery and armor in Vietnam."

I was *not* going to be suckered. Nope, not me.

"Fair question," he responded, with the confidence that experience in the army and an understanding of the way the military worked gave him. "Artillery is common in Vietnam. You'd be better off going armor. There are only two brigades of armor in Vietnam. You will no doubt end up in Germany...a very nice tour I must say, or maybe you'll go to Korea. I doubt seriously you'd see Vietnam."

I had no idea what a brigade was.

We continued to talk a while as I probed the armor idea. Foots' interest was all but gone for any enlistment of any type, in any branch of our military. I was intrigued, though. The good sergeant did say only two brigades were in Vietnam. The use of tanks, given the terrain of Vietnam—as I knew it then—just did not make sense. Enlisting in the army's armor branch would ensure that I was not drafted. In addition, it promised to keep me out of the infantry, and should radically reduce the chances I would go to Vietnam. Germany sounded very nice, so that is where I played the odds. The behemoths with their massive guns would be fun, and they must be a blast to drive.

"We'll think it over and get back to you," I said as we grabbed brochures and contracts, and departed. Foots rid himself of his paperwork as soon as he was out of view of the recruiters. I would end up calling the sergeant in the next few weeks. College had thrown me out, and my folks were not pleased with me at all.

"What the hell are you going to do now, son?"

Sheepishly, I responded, "I may enlist."

"Enlist? Well, now…the military *might* just help you grow up."

He was surprised. He was not aware I had a plan, or that I was even capable of planning. Dad knew I was in a pickle, and it was so painfully obvious to each of us that if I did nothing I would have zero options. When I was kicked out of college and lost my 2-S deferment, I expected to be graced with "greetings" from my government any moment, ordering me to report for a medical exam. (Their exam was nothing more than an "alive and kicking" qualification that would yield an induction notice within another few weeks.) In the late sixties, local draft boards had increasing quotas to fill.

Yes, I had a rapidly escalating dilemma. Yes, it was of my own making. The crisis, as I interpreted it back then, was ensuring there was no infantry, marines, or Vietnam in my future. Pick your order. In my view, all the choices were bad. I determined my best course of action would be to enlist in the army for the minimum three years, with a guarantee of armor training. Since there were so few tanks in Vietnam, I would no doubt be in Germany or Korea. I was so confident events would happen that way that I signed up for armor training. When I informed Dad, he showed no surprise or sadness.

"No member of this family has ever been drafted. Your grandmother is a World War I navy veteran, for cryin' out loud. In World War II your grandfather, your Uncle Jimmy, and I were on active duty." Dad added a father's proud smile to his paternal look. "It's good you won't be drafted, no matter what you feel about the draft or this war. It shows character. I think this will make a man of you...I'm sure your mother feels the same."

Dad was right; she was proud. Consider that it was the spring of 1968 and many people in the Southeast were still behind the war, supporting their president. At worst, the local population was not totally against it. There was a little of "My country, right or wrong," and a lot of residual WWII attitude of "We all must get behind the effort." Preventing communist dominoes from falling was the universal mission in those days. Or, were we there to stop some aggressor? Or, were we there to support a country struggling to retain its freedom and sovereignty? Or, was it actually all about feeding the monster that was the military-industrial complex? Perhaps it was all those—perhaps it was none. The surge of negative and radical anti-war sentiment yet to come was still low-keyed around my part of the country, but it would soon envelop the Southeast.

Why did I enlist? It is a very simple concept. I was only floating through life; I knew it better than anyone. I needed a kick-start, a hard reboot, shock therapy, or a cold-turkey suspension of my party-hearty ways. There I was—an almost twenty-year-old, the draft and Vietnam threatening me. I needed to execute my plan, taking the easy way out (yes, yet again) of the catastrophe that had become my life. At some point in the future, I knew I would earn a college degree, for *my* reasons and not because someone else told me it would be best for me.

Sometimes my mother would say to me, "Ya know, not all successful men have a college degree." (A mother's love.) Those people that my parents used as illustrations of how to achieve did have a degree, often advanced. So, too, did those still silent mentors, the examples that were my own personal inspiration, and those to whom I was paying no attention. Should I have been? Would I have been better off? Maybe back then, but not today.

No one was surprised in early May, mere days after I turned twenty years old, that I was invited to present myself to the U.S. Armed Forces Examining Station on May 17, to determine if I was suitable for military service. I drove myself down and checked in. There were many guys from all around Atlanta, most of them imminent draftees. We completed countless forms and questionnaires, every form and activity designed to gather and make a record of personal information and health history.

By the middle of the morning, we were all suffering the indignities of medical exams and testing, and in a very public manner. We stood for hours in our boxers or briefs, cold, in line for some inspection or another, while being prodded, probed, and/or punctured. I am certain that ours was not a unique experience—anyone who was in the service has gone through it.

While standing in line to have blood drawn, one could glance ahead in the line and see the random big guy going to the floor, face first, out cold. Occasionally, some thin guy whose veins could not be located was set aside for a talented hand. Shots and blood drawings were painful, but they did not have to be. The medics were not sympathetic one bit. The yelps and moans emitted by the band of inductees that day only encouraged those medics to be even more brutal.

"Listen up, ladies...turn right toward the wall, drop your drawers and bend over...spread your cheeks," commanded a medic, devoid of compassion or humor. Our line of thirty or so, each cheek-to-cheek, complied.

"It's time for your rectal exam."

The calling medic had made that speech too many times. I would bet the probing physician had even less humor about his duty. Modesty and embarrassment prevented me from looking anywhere except at the wall directly in front of me and that very tiny paint bubble upon which I chose to concentrate. As the good doctor dug deep inside me, I thought I would wet the floor. Well now, *that* was not very much fun. We continued processing all morning—in only our skivvies. I certainly felt fortunate that I was not presenting in the middle of winter. I must have been healthy enough to fight and die for my country because I was ordered to report for induction on May 20, 1968. I would get my clock cleaned.

The day was a beautiful, bright spring day in Atlanta. Beautiful varieties of plants were showing off their springtime finery. Flowers that were still blooming so late in spring were a reminder the hot and humid Atlanta weather was coming. Ft. Benning would be miserable, *very* miserable. I mentally kicked myself for not enlisting when the weather would have been more favorable.

I said good-bye to my family, and Dad drove me to the induction center on his way to work. That was the first time I was aware of an experience shared with him, and I felt just a bit more mature and grown-up. There was little chat between the two of us during our thirty-minute trip, and what talking we did was just light, trivial, and on my part, simply nervous nonsense. Rather than think about what was ahead for me, I enjoyed the beautiful spring morning that was Atlanta. I was aware that I was jumping out of the nest.

"Good luck, son. Keep your head down." Dad let me off at the corner. As I got out of his car, he stuck out his hand.

"Of course, it is *my* head!"

I shook his hand and closed the car door, and then he drove away with my childhood firmly in tow. Dad glanced back and waved, allowing a glimpse of pride in his smile. At that moment, I knew I was alone and on my own. Of course, he was smiling. He had known I would be feeling all alone well before I did. He had already been where I was going. He had survived; I wanted to.

So began my trek into manhood. How would I cope? Would I survive? How would I be afterward if I did survive? All those thoughts ran through my mind in the fifteen seconds I took to reach the front door. I knew once I opened that door that my life for the next three years would no longer be only mine. I was about to be under the complete control of Uncle Sam, and we were to become instant intimates.

When I entered the induction center, I was directed to the assembly classroom. I grabbed the first open seat I saw. An obviously uncomfortable guy was seated to my right. He acknowledged my presence, but we did not speak. The few of us who were in that classroom had arrived several minutes ahead of the appointed time. We watched as each new entry looked around before taking a seat, just as we had done. A few joked nervously, and a few others introduced themselves to those sitting nearby. Most of us were quiet, solemn. A guy took the seat next to me and offered a greeting. We began to commiserate a bit, speculating on what lay ahead for us.

As the room got full, I looked around at the fifty or so who were there. I knew no one. Among the others were a pair of apparent friends, and my temporary friend and I wondered if they enlisted under the buddy plan. I was not surprised that not one of my friends was there; I was the dumbass that would not get serious about my education. Most of those in the room were from rural Georgia and half in the room were black.

We were called in small groups to another room where we swore an oath to the U.S. To me it was overkill, merely a formality; they had us already. Once we were sworn members of the Armed Forces of the United States, we completed our *first* ton of paperwork that day, after which we were subjected to many tests, written and oral. I was beginning to get a sense of the army way: hurry up and wait.

Already I was getting tired, and it was only nine o'clock, mere minutes into what would be a very long and tiring day. Although I went to sleep early the night before, the early hour to rise and the emotional and physical excitement of the day were beginning to exhaust me. After our mid-day meal, a clerk called for the first half of our line to enter a nearby classroom. I thought I heard the word "volunteer," so I paid close attention. I was wise with forewarning from my Uncle Jimmy: "Don't volunteer...for anything." I was *not* going to volunteer for anything else. By enlisting, I had influenced my near-term future quite enough.

"Listen up! I need volunteers to train at Ft. Lewis," a clerk said. He looked over the gaggle of about thirty former civilians. "Raise your hand if you want to volunteer."

Since I lived in Atlanta, I assumed I would be going to Ft. Benning. I had heard many stories from Dad and Uncle Jimmy about Sand Hill and Harmony Church, and I dreaded it. My training would be over the summer, and I knew very well how hot and humid summer in Georgia was. I also knew Ft. Benning is hotter and more humid than Atlanta. When my day had begun, I was expecting some tough training at Ft. Benning and I was not in high spirits.

"Where is Ft. Lewis?" someone asked the clerk.

"Washington," was his terse response.

My interest was piqued, considering that I might find a way to avoid summer in Georgia. Maybe I would get to come home on pass. I was not stupid; Washington, D.C., would not be without summer heat and humidity, but I reasoned it should be less hot and humid than Columbus, Georgia. There might be breezes coming off the Potomac. Besides, with a weekend pass I could be a tourist in our nation's capital. I had been there with my family six years earlier, and I wanted to go back to the Smithsonian. A few of us raised our hands. I volunteered with all the confidence of having thoroughly thought it over, smart guy that I was.

Once selected as Ft. Lewis volunteers, we completed more paperwork, had a few more interviews, and suffered more medical indignities. When the induction tasks were completed, we moved to an outside area in the parking lot to await buses to the airport. Once they arrived, we loaded up and were soon rolling on down I-85 toward the airport. I chuckled to myself at the non-Atlanta guys marveling at the big city. That day was the first time away from home for many of them, and Atlanta might as well have been New York City or Los Angeles. Of course, very few of them had ever seen an airliner up close.

The buses carted us up to the airplane, positioned far away from the passenger terminal. We lounged around on the cool grass, basking in what remained of the sun. We waited for a tire to be changed, usually a thirty-minute task. On that day, it took longer, probably because the low-bidding charter company did not have clout with the local maintenance folks. Maybe we awaited the arrival of a flight crew. Or—was it just another example of the army's way? Primary training: just exhaust and confuse 'em.

My day had begun early, just after dawn, and it was by that time after six p.m. I had only brief chats with other guys throughout the day; we were constantly divided, grouped, separated, and grouped again. Without the distractions and humiliations of the induction center, some real conversations began. I discovered our aircraft, and the guys who came with it, already had a busy day picking up recruits. The plane had flown first into Richmond, then south to Miami, then back north again to Atlanta. The routing made no sense at all, but I thought it, too, was just the army way. We were told we would soon be leaving. I relished the final pleasant moments of clear-blue sky, uncharacteristically low humidity, setting sun and perfect spring temperature.

After an all-too-brief ten minutes, we began to board our chartered Boeing 707. There were six seats across a row split by a single aisle and no class sections. As we filed on board, we were told to take the first available seat. The aircraft was configured for maximum souls on board, and every seat was being filled. Mine ended up being one row behind the left wing, the middle seat. I was not at all comfortable; no place on our aircraft was comfortable; the plane was packed with large, broad-shouldered young men. Our late afternoon wait out on the grass had been so pleasant that I did not mind the crowding very much. Washington should be about an hour and a half from Atlanta, I guessed. (I was not a pilot then, but I was an aviation enthusiast, and I was aware New York and Atlanta were two hours apart by airliner.). Piece of cake! I pondered what we would be doing after our arrival. How close to town was the installation? Within the District? Virginia? Maryland? I had no idea; I would never have.

At cruising altitude, our ride was mostly smooth and comfortable. From my cramped middle seat, I could see the sunset and noticed it should have been behind the wing, but was not. I could see it, though, between the wing and the nose. We were not going northeast; we were heading in a westerly direction. I thought it was perhaps due to traffic routing, so I put it all out of my mind. Thoughts of activities post-arrival were beginning to concern me more. Only after we had been in the air about three hours did I try to make sense of it. Outside, the view was of the blackness of night, sprinkled with varying sized concentrations of bright lights. Where was the almost continuous coverage of lights that is the middle Atlantic Coast? One of the stewardesses (yes, they were called that back then) passed out oranges. When she came to me, I had to know what was going on.

"Has the captain indicated our routing to you? It seems we're taking a round-about way to Washington."

"No. We're proceeding as we usually do." I suspected she gave me her canned answer.

"Where are we? Do you know?" I was puzzled.

She leaned over the guy in the aisle seat, getting all of his attention and certainly making his day, to peer out the window.

"Ah," she said. "Those lights are probably Denver. We should be arriving at SeaTac on time."

"SeaTac?"

"Seattle-Tacoma Airport," she said matter-of-factly.

"Washington!" I slapped my forehead and made a mental note to revisit any future exception to the "no volunteer" rule. Since I was unable to change anything, I had to look for the positive! At least it would not be nearly so hot. Maybe the humidity there, which I was sure would be high, would make the temperature cooler since there is so much water and ocean air movement. Conditions had to be better than Ft. Benning; they just had to. I felt stupid and duped. I gazed out the window at the lights until they were behind us, and then I thought I had better try to rest. As we droned on, I managed to catch a little sleep—a very little.

When we touched down at SeaTac, we taxied past the passenger terminal to an area where OD (Olive Drab) army buses were staged for pick up. When our airplane stopped moving, we stood, stretched, and began a shuffle to the exit door. We had been flying many hours, and we arrived in the middle of the night locally, very early in the new day of our body clocks. None on board was in a hurry; we were all too tired from a very long day. Most of us had not slept very much, anticipating what we were to face. I would bet a few were thinking far ahead to Vietnam, yet there remained a lot of training before we would be qualified members of the U.S. Army. There would be sufficient time for us to contemplate our advanced education in Southeast Asia if we were going to be among the very privileged few.

Chapter 4

Liberating Self with Team

A blast of chilly air hit me as I approached the exit door. On the outside of the airplane, the temperature must have been in the mid-forties, and the cold air was a shock. I was wearing a lightweight, short-sleeve shirt and felt a drizzle on my arms. I considered the weather conditions a portent of uncomfortable things to come.

When we arrived at Ft. Lewis' Replacement Center, we were greeted by drill sergeants in a manner only bestowed upon those civilian pukes who dared to be part of *their* army. They began the intimidation routine while we were still seated on the bus. Nobody moved fast enough nor did they speak authoritatively enough, and we all had long hair and funny clothes. The remainder of that, our never-ending first day (our actual second day by then) is only a blur. I do recall I was disgusted by the mere sight of our breakfast and decided to pass. The lunch they served was not much better—liver and onions—not at all a favorite of mine.

There at the replacement center, we completed yet more paperwork, got our uniforms and supplies, received haircuts, and were subjected to more mental and physical testing. Our stopover there served as the civilian-to-military conversion point; thereafter we would move to Basic Combat Training (BCT). At the replacement center we were no longer civilians, not yet BCT trainees, and certainly not military. Utilizing shock, intimidation, physical punishment, fear, and threats of violence, many vestiges of our previous civilian identity were removed. Only then did we join a BCT company where remaining non-military tendencies were removed—post haste.

In a few days, we were made into a platoon of fifty guys, mostly from my flight. I have no idea where the rest went, but my platoon was assigned to Alpha Company, 1st Battalion,

2nd Training Brigade. It was a standard BCT company comprised of four platoons. Each platoon was assigned a drill sergeant who was responsible for our training. The training after BCT would eventually separate us as soldiers, but there at Ft. Lewis, in *that* unit, we were all going to be the same—trainee pukes—at once the vermin *and* the growth hormone of the military.

"Recruits! My name is Staff Sergeant Rodriguez, your drill sergeant. I will be your mama, your papa, your priest, your rabbi, and your best friend. We *will* be together day and night for the next eight weeks, and we *will* be very familiar. So," he paused for effect, "refer to me by my first name." He inspected us with his steely stare. "Drill Sergeant...you *will* follow my rules. What are my rules?" he asked, looking over his newest group of recruits. "Recruit!" He gestured to the very largest among us. "What *are* my rules, recruit?"

"I-I don't know," came the timid response.

"Speak like you got a pair, recruit. Try again. What are my rules? I need to hear them from you."

"I don't know, sir." He tried to be convincing, but he failed. His voiced cracked, and we all snickered.

"*Sir?*" the sergeant yelled incredulously. "*Sir?* Don't you *dare* call me sir...I work for a living," he bellowed. "Feel free to respond with 'I don't know, Drill Sergeant.'"

"I don't know, Drill Sergeant."

"Fair enough. but since you *don't* know, drop and give me twenty. You did learn how to do pushups over here at the replacement center, didn't you?"

"Yes, Drill Sergeant!"

We all counted silently as the recruit counted aloud.

"I cannot hear you, recruit...I *want to hear you.* Start over at one, and knock 'em out till I get tired."

The recruit started counting his pushups loudly. When the recruit finally exceeded twenty un-military pushups, our drill sergeant was satisfied he made his point and moved on, relaxing the recruit.

"You will get personal with my rules. Rule number one

is," he looked around, "drill sergeants are always right." Our drill sergeant spoke softly, yet firmly, with the assurance of the full weight of the U.S. Army on his side.

"Rule number two is...if a drill sergeant is ever wrong, you will promptly revisit rule number one."

We got his message loud and clear. We needed to please him, so Drill Sergeant would be his name, and a drill sergeant will *never—ever* be wrong. Our drill sergeant formed us up and marched us away from the replacement center, as recruit rabble, to our new home Alpha Company where we became trainees.

Alpha Company included three platoons from Ft. Lewis' typical draw area of the West Coast, and one platoon mostly from the East Coast. A good many in my platoon hailed from rural Georgia, and half of them were black. The other three platoons were probably 95% or more white. The black guys in my platoon were not very happy campers. They had mostly been drafted, and they had no use for Southern white guys and maybe any white guy. The killing of Martin Luther King had happened less than two months earlier, and they seemed to blame us personally.

The drill sergeant kept referring to our barracks as being "permanent." I had no clue what that meant, but the building we were housed in was a three-story concrete block structure large enough to accommodate a company of basic trainees, a mess hall, the administration, et cetera. Except for living in a large room with forty-nine other guys and showering together, it was not an entirely bad deal, for being in the army.

Each trainee at Ft. Lewis wore a white strip above his nametag in order to identify the unit to which he belonged. That was necessary because of a meningitis control program. There was to be no mingling with personnel from another company and very limited and controlled interaction between platoons. We were not allowed to leave our unit area except for training, which always included escorts. Our trips to the PX (Post Exchange) were in platoon size groups, and we were the only shoppers. Weekend passes were never issued—end of story. Our down time was spent within the barracks walls. Every few nights each of us, on a rotating basis, walked an hour or two of fireguard in our barracks bay while everyone else slept.

We were constantly doing army PT (Physical Training), and included our training weapon, the M-14 (automatic 7.62 mm (millimeter) assault rifle, 9.8 pounds empty) most of the time. Everything we did was physical: close order drill, M-14 Manual of Arms training, forced marches with and without full pack, hand-to-hand combat (with knife or hands only), bayonet practice, pugil stick training and daily PT. We were tested at times to measure our fitness and the efficacy of our PT. We double-timed everywhere. Drill sergeants taught us cadence calls to help us learn to march in step. Those ditties were about a fellow named Jody who was back home and safe, having his way with our girlfriend or wife. Very often, the ditties were raunchy. I truly enjoyed it when the drill sergeant launched into "raunch cadence" as we neared office buildings that contained officers and/or women.

When we had classes indoors or when we sat in outside classes and were not physically active, it was difficult to stay awake. Oh, how the drill sergeant loved to discover a trainee who was nodding off. The work was hard physically, but more demanding emotionally because no one could give out first— or ever; there was a high price to pay. Academically, there was little challenge except for those who were the products of rural Georgia's school systems. Sadly, those guys struggled, and many of us tried to help them. Not because it was the right thing to do; no, we did it because it was to our collective benefit. (There is a life lesson there.) Most of the trainees in our company ultimately did fine adjusting to their new life. Some never did.

The morning of 6 June 1968, we got the news Robert F. Kennedy had been killed. I wondered what the aftermath would be. Inner-city riots? What sorts of problems would the country face? Were we not already socially and economically disparate enough? Our daily training went on as usual, and I

Liberating Self with Team | 47

realized that as trainees we were shielded from most of the political and social news that was affecting the rest of the country. We were usually in the dark, unable to keep up with the routine and not-so-routine activities around the world. That information darkness continued throughout my military service.

In our third week of BCT, my platoon was outside the mess hall awaiting our mid-day meal. Our chow line ran along the sidewalk behind our barracks up steps into the building and the mess hall. No drill sergeants were nearby, an unusual circumstance, and a few of us were cutting up while trying to maintain a posture for quick recovery, should one of the drill sergeants begin to pay more attention to us.

Thud! I heard a muffled sound, much like a bale of hay thrown on the ground.

"What's going on?" someone behind me asked.

The chow line about twenty guys in front of me started to break up, and trainees left the sidewalk and moved rapidly toward the grass under our three-story barracks windows. Something happened over there. What? I was not about to move and get my ass chewed. I had an aversion to pushups and the front-leaning-rest position, each a favorite training aid of drill sergeants.

"Get your goddamn asses right back in my chow line," demanded our drill sergeant.

The chow line reformed promptly as guys jockeyed for previous positions.

"What's going on here?" asked another drill sergeant as he approached several trainees milling around, trying their best to get a look at what was going on over on the grass.

"Atten...shun. Left...face!"

Out of nowhere, but with all the authority that only a drill sergeant could muster, we were turned.

"Pa...rade...rest!"

He turned us away from whatever was happening. I still had no idea what occurred. I was curious, but not about to incur the wrath of a drill sergeant. For a few minutes, we heard some mumbling and whispers. Eventually, a voice commanded us back to attention and then "As you were," and our chow line headed on into the mess hall. We were told nothing, but as lowly privates will do, we speculated.

The guys ahead of me who had first moved toward the barracks were actually going to the aid of a trainee who had leaped from the third floor and landed on the grass. We later learned (or was it only a rumor?) that he broke an arm and was recycled (placed in a later training unit). Recycled! I guess he was not fond of basic training. Then again, maybe he was slacking and causing problems, and he had been thrown out.

We rarely got to enjoy quiet time. With fifty guys milling about the barracks bay, it was not the easiest thing to have. On Sunday mornings, I would wait until the bathroom stall rush was over and take occupancy of one, along with the most recent copy of the Army Times. It was an increasingly fascinating read for me, providing insight into what army life was like for a regular soldier. I read about Vietnam, too, just in case. I recall U.S. deaths one week reached four hundred, and that a surprising number of soldiers retired after thirty years as Private, E-1, the lowest rank. How did that happen? Those guys joined before World War II. Did they ever achieve higher rank? I did not want to be either of those kinds of guys. After advanced training, I ran across many soldiers who had found a home in the army for all the wrong reasons, as well as some that got into too much trouble. Rank earned could be rank taken away and regularly was for some people.

Soon after the jumper, our drill sergeant received orders to Vietnam for his second tour. He was not very happy. At an evening formation just prior to his departure from Alpha Company, and after he had spent too much time at the NCO (Non-Commissioned Officer) Club, he became quite emotional about his return, and not in a good way. His standard tough guy demeanor was gone, and he became teary-eyed. He was someone who had the very experience that I wanted to avoid altogether, and he did not want to go back.

The drill sergeant who replaced him was a different sort. He did not challenge us to get us well trained; we believed that he truly did hate us. He was strictly a punisher, not a trainer. He was obviously and openly much harsher to our platoon than other drill sergeants were to theirs. He would castigate us because he could; he was an equal opportunity punisher, too; he spared no one. New to the army, he was to be a soldier for only two years, and he enjoyed telling us that often. He lacked combat and Vietnam experience. I knew that was not good for the platoon, many of whom would be going that way soon. His only army knowledge was his training: BCT, AIT (Advanced Individual Training), and Drill Sergeant School. He was a brand new drill sergeant, a draftee, and we were his very first assignment. Additionally, he was a faux tough guy—faking it until his term ended. He hid behind his sergeant stripes; no one thought that he was anything but a nuisance, an impediment to our best training.

During our M-14 training, Alpha Company was bused to a firing range for a day of live-fire target practice. As usual, some trainees scored higher than others did, but our platoon fared about average when compared to the rest of our unit. When the buses arrived to transport us back to the company area, our favorite new drill sergeant decided, without a known provocation by any of us, that we would march back. We watched buses depart as we fell into a route-step march. We were disheartened.

"Shoot that pipsqueak motherfucker," someone said.

Our drill sergeant, the only supervisor with us on our march, was too far away to hear the complaining.

"So...who's gonna do it...you?" someone asked. "Besides, they took all our ammo."

Other voices chimed in.

"Are we just going to *take* his shit? No other platoon's treated this way?"

"What choice do we have?"

"Tell his mommy. She'll square his ass away."

"He ain't got no mommy."

"Nah...you waste him? *You* go to Leavenworth. He's not worth that. Not to me. I can take anything that little man can dish out."

"We all can...we aren't gonna be here much longer."

"Yeah, we'll soon be in the jungle killing Cong while he's bending over his buddy. What a hero."

The complaining continued until the drill sergeant stopped marching and watched us go by; then he ran back to the head of the column to lead us home.

Why did he choose to make us march all the way back? What had we done wrong? Usually, we suffered his tantrums and his unfair, unpredictable punishment with humor. We knew that it could not last forever. Still, his behavior was not justified and was way beyond routine training abuse. A few of us began to recognize not everyone who has legal authority over others has leadership skill. Our drill sergeant certainly did not, not the new one. I did not want to be anywhere close to him at the next live-fire range.

As happens when a large group is being trained, there are those who are unable to keep up. The reasons may be physical, emotional, desire, intelligence, or social. In training, the whole group suffers from the unfortunate actions of as few as one trainee. The army is excellent at taking a large group of intellectually and physically dissimilar men at the peak of their testosterone drive (their youth), and molding them into a cohesive, competent, order following, physically fit platoon of soldiers. Some trainees fall away in the process, but most thrive in the team-reliant environment.

There exists a time-tested method of encouraging almost any malingerer to get with the program: the blanket party. I was awakened one night by the sounds of yelling from across the platoon bay. One of our platoon mates, with a history of bringing the entire platoon grief, was the guest of honor at just such a party. While he slept, five or six guys held a taut blanket over his bed, and pulled down in unison. They held it in place, pulling downward, preventing defensive movement, and kept his face covered. Two others pounded his face and body with their fists. The party was short, lasting only about thirty seconds. The next day our friend was black and blue, working hard. There was no need for any further counseling.

About halfway through training, a few trainees were called out during evening formations and instructed to report inside. I was among the names called daily, as were guys with a high school education, very uncommon in my platoon. Our test scores qualified us for an MOS (Military Occupational Specialty). We reported to representatives of those specialties: Engineers, Intelligence, MP (Military Police), Medical, Airborne School, Ranger School, Chemical, EOD (Explosive Ordinance Disposal), OCS (Officer Candidate School), U.S.M.A. (West Point) preparatory school, NCOCS (Non-Commissioned Officer Candidate School), WOFT (Warrant Officer Flight Training), and several others I can no longer remember.

OCS was out for me. I had no desire to be a butter bar lieutenant. I shared with Dad a yearning to fly, and I wanted to do more than he did, so WOFT had my interest piqued from the get-go. For that program, I remained behind to get further details. I learned I would have to commit to four years in the army with, no doubt, two tours in Vietnam. WOFT was not going to happen, either. That just did not fit my plan.

Dad grew up wanting to fly. After graduation from Riverside Military Academy, he passed up college to join the air corps with his friends and do his part in WWII. Because he was a stutterer, they washed him out of pilot training, and he trained to become an infantry officer.

I also grew up wanting to fly and had an affinity for the B-17 Flying Fortress (heavy bomber) and P-51 Mustang (pursuit/fighter). As an adult, I joke I must have been a pilot of one or the other and KIA (Killed In Action) during WWII, and reincarnated as a Baby Boomer wannabe pilot.

The Armor Non-Commissioned Officer Candidate School (ANCOCS) was the most interesting (and most modern) of all the MOSs I was offered, especially in light of the comments from the recruiter that armor trained soldiers probably would not be going to Vietnam. I chose that school, reasoning that it would give me rank, a little authority, and a bit more money. Besides, my generation learned from WWII- and Korea-era movies that all officers in combat would always follow their grizzled sergeant's sage advice, right? I was still without a single clue. That would change soon enough.

I qualified Sharpshooter with the M-14. Along with a few others, I was very fortunate to exempt a long, full-pack forced march because my PT testing scores had improved radically. Training policy dictated our exemption and changing that was outside the control of our drill sergeant. We loved that he could not do a single thing about it, although he did his best to include everyone on the march.

Next up: the dreaded Infiltration Course, at night, where trainees low-crawl under *live* machine gunfire with simulated artillery and grenade explosions all around. Live fire was very disconcerting to some, me included. As we filed into the trenches assuming our "over-the-top" ready position, the stench of urine was extreme. I realized that I was not the only guy ever to be nervous about it. I wondered how those Doughboys of World War I had done it, given the accurate live fire from Germans. They were brave young men. At Ft. Lewis, we all went over the top expecting to live when we low-crawled under the live fire. Nobody got hurt—that was no surprise; the guns were elevation-fixed, and no one was so foolish as to stand up.

I survived it all; I understood what the army was doing, if not how they went about it. It took preparation, adapting as necessary, not taking drill sergeants' ravings personally, and knowing the discomfort was finite. That helped me survive the first phase of my training. Others melted down and recycled.

Those of us who succeeded received individual orders to our advanced training unit. When we finally met all of the

BCT requirements, we graduated. Ours was then a happy time. We had survived all that was thrown at us including the "little man" drill sergeant, we were fit, and gaining increasing confidence in ourselves.

We had become soldiers, or so we thought. We went to the PX—finally. I got a six-pack of cold Olympia beer (3.2% alcohol) and sat down in the shade of a large tree to drink it. Life was good again. We saw a new movie that had just been released, *In the Heat of the Night*. The fun I was having lasted only about 24 hours, however, until it was time to leave Ft. Lewis. I was loaded onto an army bus that would take me to catch my charter flight.

Chapter 5

The Sergeant *Is* the Army

I awoke on the morning of 19 July 1968 to an air travel day with a clear blue sky; I was looking forward to the flight. At altitude, the captain pointed out snowcapped mountain peaks down to our south, a beautiful sight. I bade farewell to Washington State, regretting I had not seen more of the area.

My training assignment was to Foxtrot Company, 4th Battalion, 1st Brigade, USATCA (United States Army Training Center Armor). Our barracks were referred to as "temporary," and when I first saw them, I thought back to Ft. Lewis and the "permanent" barracks, and I understood "permanent." Barracks at Ft. Knox were built to accommodate a manpower buildup during World War II and carried the designator "T," indicating provisional status. In July of 1968, there were still buildings across Ft. Knox, and probably many other posts that were temporary. The permanent barracks were built of cinderblock construction, and the temporary buildings were of wood frame construction.

There was no privacy in temporary barracks. The toilets were in one row against the back wall, each side by side. Sinks and toilets were in an open room. In our permanent barracks, there were toilet stalls in the latrine, which afforded a user some privacy. In our temporary barracks, sitting on a toilet was a full-thigh-contact sport, intimately shared with the guys who were seated on either side. That certainly took getting used to, at least for me. I volunteered for overnight fireguard where I could find at least a little privacy.

There were ten of us assigned to the "overflow" barracks, so called because the platoon bay did not have room for our entire platoon. Being a resident of "overflow" meant that fewer trainees were available for turns at fireguard and that we would be cleaning the latrine more frequently. Sometimes we were forgotten when it came to inspections, KP (kitchen police or patrol), police calls (picking up yard trash), and the like. Overall, it really was not that bad. Those of us lucky enough to live over in the "overflow" barracks constantly tried to maintain a low profile.

"All right you turds, roll outta them fart sacks," was how our instructor NCO awakened us. With that nudge, off we would go to an armor trainee's day. For the remainder of that summer, we learned about tanks and armored warfare. We trained on M48a2c Patton tanks, named after the World War II general. We were instructed how to drive, fire and maintain each of its weapons, communicate, and perform maintenance. The phonetic alphabet became second nature to us. We pored over maps and studied tactics. We also spent many classroom hours becoming intimate with the tank's main gun, the M2 .50 caliber heavy machine gun ("Ma Deuce" or "Fifty"), and the M73. The latter is a .30 caliber machine gun coaxially mounted with the main gun, allowing its aiming coincident to the main gun.

We were taught about the types of ammunition available for the main gun: HE (High Explosive), HEAT (High Explosive Anti-Tank), and a Beehive round (anti-personnel flechettes). We practiced with a tank crew's personal weapons: the M3 grease gun that fired a .45 caliber round—its collapsible stock was handy in tight spaces—and the M1911 .45 caliber pistol. The age of those designs caused me a little concern at the time, but they sure were fun to fire. We were assured that although the M3 was not very sexy, it might be our best friend. We were impressed by the knockdown power of a .45 cal round. We disassembled and reassembled all of our tank weapons and personal weapon ad nauseam. We had sessions on how to set headspace and timing of the M2 heavy machine gun correctly. I should have paid more attention in that class, because if it is not set correctly, well, that could make for a very bad day. (It did.) We drove the tanks in traffic and out on the muddy driving ranges. That was a blast, but it was main gun live-fire practice that I enjoyed the most. The feeling of power was awesome, and that gun really cleared my sinuses.

As our training progressed, we spoke of most everything in military terms and increasingly in military jargon. We were becoming tankers, showing the pride of the armor combat arm. In the field and in the classroom, we were preparing for World War III and the Soviet invasion of Europe while using 1950s equipment. We were probably being taught Korean War tactics. We were attending AIT during the third full year of combat troops in Vietnam, yet there was nothing contained in the armor crewman syllabus to train us specifically for that war. That did not escape our notice, nor did it escape our mockery. To our naive minds, the lack of attention to training for Vietnam indicated to us that we would surely be sent to Germany or Korea. Pack the long johns!

It was toward the end of the summer of 1968 and our cadre was comprised of Vietnam veterans. Our instructors often provided extra-syllabus information and direction that served mostly to impress us only with fear and foreboding. Through no fault of theirs, their guidance did not train us sufficiently for Vietnam except for the rudiments of operating and maintaining an M48 tank. The instructor NCOs would preach that we could throw everything out the window "once you arrive in-county." They advised we would be smart to learn by observing those who had been in-country a while. Notice their assumption of where we were headed. Most of us found our training easy and routine, without complications. However, not everyone made the same effort.

Among us in the overflow barracks was a guy whose name I have forgotten, but recall was from Eastern Europe and working toward U.S. citizenship. In the beginning, we thought he was quiet and mostly keeping to himself because he was a foreigner, and not yet comfortable with our ways. It became obvious that our first impressions were entirely wrong. He was knowingly and willingly the reason our platoon was assigned extra pushups and double-timed more than any other platoon. Someone suggested a blanket party.

Yes, I participated. Four of us held a blanket over the sleeping troublemaker. On a nodded command, we pulled it down to ensure he could not defend himself or escape.

"Pull down tight. Don't let go," the fifth participant said.

He began to pummel mercilessly about the man's face and mid-section, at full-strength. Then our guest let out a blood-curdling scream—a victim's wail—of surprise, terror, and pending finality.

"Hit him. Hit him harder."

Our victim became very still, very fast.

"He's just playing possum," someone said.

"Commie bastard's fakin' it."

He was struck in the face again.

We carefully peeled back the blanket, expecting he had been knocked out cold.

"Oh, shit. He's suffocating."

I stared, startled and very concerned. The man was in respiratory distress and gasping for air. I just knew we were going to wind up in Leavenworth making little rocks out of big ones. Someone cupped his hands and covered the guy's nose and mouth, having recognized he was only hyperventilating. The method worked somehow, and he began to whimper. I was not very proud of myself, but I was relieved to know we would not be going to Leavenworth. We returned to our bunks, not as victors, but as men charged with meting out discipline to one for the benefit of many. No one ever spoke a word about the blanket party, or our momentary terror. We were not surprised, however, when our friend ceased being a problem. Remarkably, even his English improved.

On 13 September 1968, our graduation day arrived, and we were a proud lot. Finally, we had become better trained soldiers—tankers—albeit lacking experience. Most of our company had orders that would take them to an armor unit. I have often wondered what became of them; I never did see anyone from my AIT unit again except those guys that went with me to the Armor School. Maybe the other guys did luck out and went to Germany.

I went home on leave for two weeks before reporting to the Armor School and the next class of ANCOCS. Eager for that experience, I had no clue what to expect other than graduation would mean I was a buck sergeant. I reported to the Armor School 8 October and was assigned to class 5-69: Alpha Company, 4th Battalion, School Brigade. As a group, we were promoted to corporal. The class of about one hundred was divided into two distinct MOSs: 11E40 Tank Commander and 11D40 Armor Reconnaissance.

The Armor School, as the name implies, is the army's advanced armor training center. We utilized the very same facilities and many of the same instructors as those attending the Armor Officer Basic Course and Armor Officer Advanced Course. Breaks would find newly minted corporals, with all of four months in the army, mingling with lieutenants, captains, majors, and lieutenant colonels in our army and equivalent ranks from our foreign allies' forces.

Immediately upon settling in, the difference to prior training was apparent. Our quarters were in a permanent building much like a college dorm. The general atmosphere was college campus-like compared to my earlier training. We were still in the army and still subject to training abuse, yet we were otherwise being treated much better. We were no longer derisively referred to as "puke," "trainee," "maggot," or "recruit." We were referred to as "candidate." Platoon bays were subdivided into personal cubicles containing a wardrobe locker, a study desk, and a bunk. We were issued several dozen field manuals and technical manuals to support our study. There was no KP duty, and our meals were served on breakable dining ware, not stamped aluminum trays. The meals were more leisurely; nobody was haranguing us to "eat that shit and get out of *my* mess hall."

Luck was again with me. The platoon was assigned to the third floor of our permanent barracks; I was in a room— yep, a *room*—on the *second* floor. My roommates and I were the only people on that floor. As we trained, one less floor made quite a difference on some days. At the Armor School, I met many guys who were like me: most had attended at least a few college classes, and some had graduated. Most of us did not know what we wanted to do in life. We were not sure about the army, but we wanted to do something different, something exciting, and something that was not routine. The youngest among us was barely seventeen, and the oldest was thirty-two. One had been in the WOFT program for helicopter pilots, and he would be one of our three honor graduates, earning the rank of staff sergeant E-6.

We were greeted by the man who was to be responsible for training us: SFC Kinnard, an experienced armor NCO . He was our TAC–NCO (TACtical–Non-Commissioned Officer). He gave us a brief introduction, informing us of his U.S. Army credentials and qualifications to train us.

Then he gave us quite a shock.

"I don't believe in this program at all...this training of new soldiers to be NCOs."

He looked down and shook his head in wonder.

"NCOs have been the backbone of any army, operational leadership at platoon and company level," he said. "Getting there takes *years* of experience and *hard-earned* wisdom."

He started to pace but then his tone became slightly softer, less hard-edged.

"The army has a shortage of experienced NCOs, because so many have been killed or disabled in Vietnam. In all its wisdom, my army has decided to throw young, rapidly trained, and green soldiers at its leadership need. I think it is just plain wrong."

He took a good hard look at the young, naïve, and very green men standing before him. His eyes met many, lingering briefly. Then he shrugged.

"But you probably won't live long enough to gain that wisdom and truly earn your place in leadership."

SFC Kinnard stopped pacing, looking squarely at us. I thought he was trying to make eye contact with each one of us in turn.

"The sergeant *is* the army," he told us, quoting General

Dwight D. Eisenhower. "And you've got a helluva long way to go before you convince me that you are the army...rank or not."

Then a smile emerged from the harshness.

"My job is to train you," he told us. "The army has given me a home, and I will do the best job I can. I won't take any crap from you, but I'll be fair. You will not like me during training...but when you're done training here, you'll respect me. Why? You will be trained to the best of my ability...and to the best of yours."

He was correct; by the end of training, I had grown to respect him very much. SFC Kinnard performed well the (to him) very unpleasant task of preparing us, and he *did* do it to the best of his ability—and ours.

> "Shake 'n Bake" and "Instant NCO" were derisive terms for the school-trained NCO who had been fast-tracked due to the losses of experienced NCOs in Vietnam. NCOs who earned stripes through their abilities and experience resented the brand-new NCOs who achieved their rank academically and virtually instantly.

As tankers, our education at the Armor School was with a leadership slant and built upon what we learned in AIT, but with better equipment. We trained with our focus on crew leadership within the tank crew and our leadership place within the armor platoon and company. There was more to absorb academically, and more to learn through practice. We were schooled in leadership every waking moment. We rotated being the (student) platoon leader and one of the (student) squad leaders. We learned to call cadence for the platoon; some got the rhythm and some never did. Our voices became increasingly more commanding.

Once, when I was acting platoon leader, I was singled out for a less-than-authoritative command that I had given to the platoon. SFC Kinnard did not like my command voice, so he challenged me to be more authoritative from increasingly greater distances—until I was all the way across the parade field. As can be imagined in that environment, all the guys feigned inability to hear me for quite some time; I was hoarse by the time that lesson was over. I never did well at calling cadence, but I got the command lesson.

Our PT was frequent, at least daily. We mostly ran our own, supervised, of course. When it was our turn to lead, we mounted a raised wooden platform so the entire platoon could see and follow our demonstrator. As candidates using our best command demeanor, we lead PT while performing the exercises according to Army Drill.

"Exercise One, Army Drill One is the High Jumper. It's a four-count exercise performed at moderate cadence," we would begin. "Demonstrator...*post!*"

That was just about all any of us were able to get through before the laughter would begin. Everyone, I mean every single candidate I ever saw attempt to command a PT class, badly screwed it up. Somehow—only because we were periodically corrected and properly reprimanded—we got our PT completed. I contend that it was our abdominal muscles receiving the greatest benefit because we laughed so hard.

We learned to instruct the army way, with syllabi and lesson plans, writing the lessons ourselves. If one truly wants to learn a subject, one should teach it. I taught my class about anti-tank mines, but today I know very little except they go "boom" and can ruin your day. It was for one lesson and only in the classroom.

In preparation for our individual class assignments, we prepared training aids, making illustrations for an overhead projector presentation and handouts. During that session, Steve Sapp and Marc Sievers, my friends from California, nicknamed me "The Southern Stud." Why? I certainly was not one. Perhaps it was merely a dig at the Southern guy or was alliterative. Their appellation survived the Armor School as a source for ribbing at my expense for some time.

We were instructed in the combat science and the art of

calling for and adjusting mortar and artillery fire. We saw several demonstrations of how helpful indirect fire can be. It was challenging and great fun. A recoilless rifle impressed us, except for its lack of armor shielding. The M-72 LAW (Light Anti-tank Weapon) was added to our repertoire. We became increasingly comfortable with our massive fifty-two ton steel steed. The tank's main gun was, well, awesome. I enjoyed the statement it made; few misinterpreted the meaning. Its blast cleared friendly sinuses, and it cleared *out* the enemy. A tank is intimidating, and a sense of power soon sweeps over a new crewman—a new and young tank commander especially.

The newest armored vehicle the U.S. had in the arsenal was presented, but it was not a tank—not in the traditional sense. The Sheridan, an Armored Reconnaissance, Airborne Assault Vehicle, M551, was considered a Light Tank. Our M48 tank was historically a Medium Battle Tank, but by 1968, it was, along with others in its class, being referred to as a Main Battle Tank. The Sheridan was light, weighing in at 17 tons compared to the 52 tons of the M48. The Sheridan's 152 mm main gun fired a Shillelagh missile and conventional tank-type ordinance. The missile required the crew to keep crosshairs on the target for the kill—no fire and forget—limiting the vehicle's mobility. There were other differences: it was air droppable, could swim, had an electric breech, and it used combustible casings for its main gun ammunition. When its main gun fired a conventional round, there was no brass remaining in the turret to be ejected; nothing remained. Accidentally ripping open a combustible casing forced more than one training crew to quickly clear out of their vehicle, so the range safety officer could ensure everything became safe. I knew if I were to go to Vietnam, I did not want a Sheridan. I made a mental addendum to my previously established plan.

At a range during main gun firing one day, a candidate whom I remember but will not name, stood in his cupola with his main gun at maximum elevation, awaiting the range's safety officer to double-check that he had made safe his main gun. He had *not* cleared his main gun. An (inert) training round had been in the breech, the breech was in the loaded position, and, evidently, the safety was not on. When our classmate exited the commander's cupola, his boot hit the commander's override control for the main gun sending an inert round downrange, to every NCO and officer's surprise and consternation. Not good! Rumors that afternoon were the round went into an empty car parked in a community miles away from the range. That was probably not true. I cannot imagine the army could ever allow the possibility, or the town could ever allow the eventuality. There were accidents of every stripe at all levels of training in the military, and we knew not all were comical. We were gaining respect for the risk. Ours was dangerous business, indeed.

Not all of training was dangerous, nor was it fun. Abuse still existed; we were often hassled for no reason other than to mess with us. Misuse us to train us. Maybe it worked. One day after our mid-day meal, we assembled to march to class. Initially, we were in our helmet liner, but an NCO abruptly decided to change headgear.

"Fall in," he commanded. "Get your field caps. Fall out. Hurry...move fast...let's go."

The stairwells were jammed as everyone jockeyed so as not be the last one back into the formation. I would reap the benefit of a second floor room not having to climb that extra set of steps. I was in the back of the formation, so that put me at the front of the pack on the stairwells. I got to my room and grabbed my field cap, returning to the formation as the third or fourth guy. My roomies were right with me. We stood there awaiting the third floor guys; finally, they joined us.

"Fall in." He called us to order and then continued, "Change of plans. Get your cold weather headgear. Fall out."

In a few minutes, we had reformed as a unit wearing our winter headgear, only to be dispatched to recover our helmet liners. There was no punishment for stragglers, nor was there repercussion for our complaints. Instead, we marched off to class with a slightly elevated heart rate. My roomies and I from the second floor fared much better than the third floor guys did. We were happy he had not asked to inspect our wall-lockers. As it turned out, we were fifteen minutes ahead of schedule.

One of my roomies, Gary Patten, had a framed picture of his girlfriend that he would bring out often just to torment us. He was justifiably proud, and he rubbed his good fortune in as much as he could.

"Does she have any friends who look like her? Girls, I mean...who aren't attached."

I asked him this frequently, so often that I was a pest.

"I don't know how I feel about you looking at her that way," he said.

I ignored him, continuing to gaze at her longingly, in an over the top manner, and strictly to aggravate him.

"What way do you mean? I'm just saying that she's very attractive, and you are lucky...How'd you get her, anyway? Damn. She's fine. So mighty fine."

"Cut that out!"

I continued to ogle her picture.

"We started dating back in high school," he said.

"I'm just wondering if maybe she has an attractive friend. One in the market for a lonely soldier...before he goes to Vietnam...and maybe gets messed up."

"Don't even think that," he said.

Did he really think hiding from the possibility would make us any safer?

"Just joking. C'mon, man. Lighten up. Does she have a sister, cousin, girlfriend? What's her mother like?"

"Okay, okay. Calm down. I'll ask her next time I write. No promises beyond that."

"Hey...." I patted his shoulder. "It's all a friend can ask of a friend. Thanks."

About ten days after our conversation, I received a letter from a friend of Gary's girlfriend. She introduced herself as Glinda from Sacramento, and we swapped pictures and began a correspondence. She told me her mother had named her after the Good Witch of the South, from *The Wizard of Oz*. I took that as a good omen. I secretly hoped she would be the Naughty Witch of the West—not truly wicked, just a little naughty. During Christmas leave, I spoke with Glinda a few times on the telephone, at considerable length and expense. We were determined to find a place and time to meet as our friendship was becoming very interesting to each of us. We agreed to a mid-continent location.

After the New Year, all that remained was the capstone FTX (Field Training Exercise), the Military Stakes, some final testing and paperwork. The FTX was designed to provide an experience similar to operations in a line unit. Since we were so close to completing ANCOCS, we viewed the FTX as merely a field trip. Wrong. It was January 1969, and the weather was damn cold the early part of that month in Kentucky. The tank ranges and back roads of Ft. Knox were iced. Homogeneous steel, fifty-two tons worth, does not fare well on sheets of ice even with those small rubber pads in the track. We slipped and slid our way through the days, barely avoiding injuries. Very few of our heaters worked, if any did at all.

The first overnight of our FTX was the coldest. The sleeping bag I was issued was excellent; it cocooned me at a very comfortable sleeping temperature. Just my mouth was in the cold air, my preferred way to sleep. I was so comfortable that I wanted to stay inside it all day. In fact, shortly after bedding down I removed my boots and set them aside—*outside* the sleeping bag. The next morning I was barely able to get those boots on before we began to move. It was quite a while longer before I managed to get them laced and limber. My feet were freezing. A reasonable person would assume a lesson was learned, right? Well, that reasonable person would be wrong. I hated sleeping in footgear, and my habit would pain me once again later in the year.

After our FTX, we ran the Military Stakes. It was cavalry tradition dating back to the horse cavalry days. Back then, it was an annual competition where troopers competed against troopers and unit against unit. The course was navigated on horseback while completing timed military tasks. Accuracy and competence were also scored.

Our more modern version had us on foot along a timed eight-mile course. We ran from station to station stopping at each to perform the task-in-residence. We were required to demonstrate the minimum level of proficiency, at the requisite number of tasks, and within the prescribed time. I have long forgotten many of the tasks, but they included such skills as calculating usable capacity of an existing bridge, destroying a different usable bridge (simulation), armor tactics offensive and defensive, maintenance requirements of weapons, their breakdown, cleaning, and re-assembly, placing and disarming mines, and calling for and adjusting indirect fire. My total time was not fast; I have never been an endurance runner, and I walked when I got tired. So did most guys. Seeing the scores, I was not ashamed of my effort at all.

We graduated on 16 January 1969 with an overcast sky and occasional rain. We were thereafter buck-sergeants.

Chapter 6

The Best Laid Schemes...WTF?

On 21 January 1969, I reported to the very same unit where I had earlier taken armor AIT, F-4-1. In fact, my quarters were in the very same barracks! When in AIT, we called them overflow barracks; in OJT, they were referred to as Shake-'n-Bake barracks. The location was the very same place, but I had a little rank and much greater responsibility. During my AIT, there were no brand new Armor School buck sergeants completing their OJT. The first Shake-'n-Bake class must have arrived for OJT during the AIT cycle after I left. We raw NCOs were to be the instructors, and we would exercise the principle of "if one wants to learn something well, one should teach it." We improved our military and leadership skills teaching armor crewman in AIT. Generally, we had a good time.

Our supervisor was from somewhere in Eastern Europe, had been in the army since after WWII, and he had served as tank commander in Korea and Germany. His mission was to assure we received the benefit of training others and that the current batch of AIT trainees received their armor crewman training to the army's minimum standard. Behind his back, we would make fun of his very long and very protruding ears, by referring to him as SFC Pistolgrips—his ears reminded us of a tank gunner's control handles.

We had fun feeling important and teaching what little we knew. We knew more than our charges did, after all. We did not recognize it at the time, but OJT reinforced our armor training—we learned without trying. We partied after hours when we could get away, and we would chase young women from Louisville and closer. Catch-and-release was demanded by our training reality.

Returning to our barracks after being on a tank range

all day, one of our guys, Scott, was admiring a spent inert Shillelagh missile retrieved from downrange. Our instructors at the Armor School told us the missiles cost three thousand dollars apiece, so we witnessed only one fired. Scott's spent missile was intact, only suffering a few dings and dents.

"Man, wherever did you get that damn thing?" Greg Stumbo (Kentucky) asked.

Scott was busy cleaning mud from the carcass.

"Out on the range today...when we were down setting up targets. It was laying there all lonely and I just couldn't leave it. I had to have it."

"Fool, it could be nuclear!" Stumbo offered.

"Really, now? Do you think there'd be a nuclear missile on a range here at Ft. Knox? The only thing dangerous was the propellant that took it downrange...and that's been all used up." Scott continued cleaning.

"Okay, good point, but what're you gonna do with it?"

"I'm sending it home."

"Herr Commandant!" Stumbo clicked his heels. "I see nuss*ink*...I know nuss*ink*!"

We all speculated what horrible punishment might befall Scott should he be caught with the missile. The Cold War was on and several suggested the Soviets would want it to reverse engineer.

"Get real," said Don Smith (Georgia). "Does anyone think that a brand new, lowly buck sergeant would have any access to this thing if there were any danger the Soviets could get one from us? I'd place real money that they have designed, manufactured, and even fielded an improved version...one that's based on our plans. Hell, they've probably shared it with their allies, and I would bet that even the Red Chinese have it, too."

The discussion had been punctuated with a period. Don made sense. The rest of us went about our business while Scott finished wrapping his missile for shipping and took it to the bus station. We never heard anything else about it.

Don Thrower was one of four black guys in our class at the Armor School and the only one with us at F-4-1. He was a hoot; he had a great sense of humor, topical and irreverent. College educated, his civilian work was teaching school in Chicago. He was drafted.

The U.S. was experiencing civil rights marches (some not so civil), riots, draft evasion, assassinations, protests of all descriptions, and there existed general acrimony between blacks and whites, blacks and "the Man," the hippie culture and "the Establishment," younger and older, and hawks and doves. Many of the young black men coming into the service then were *militantly* against "the Man." To them the army was the ultimate representation of "the Man."

Don Thrower was different. He gave everyone the same treatment he was given. From Shake-'n-Bakes, he received camaraderie, humor, and good-natured abuse. One day Don was not with us in the field. It was no big deal; we hardly took notice since periodically we would be given other company duties. After we finished our day, we sat around relaxing and regaling one another with the usual guy bullshit. Thrower came in.

"What did *you* do at work today, Daddy?" I asked. He was a few years older than the rest of us, and we never let him forget about it.

"No work! I had a medical procedure done."

"Really, what kind?"

"*Major* surgery. I had the end of my dick cut off!" With that, he dropped his pants to show off the bandages.

"Say what?" Grown men wandered over to look.

"I got circumcised...they cut half of my dick off," Don said, grinning. "See my new dick?"

I do not remember who said it, but it certainly *did* need saying. The moment screamed for it.

"Jeez...must not have been that big...it must not be true, guys. Ya know, it sure ain't for Thrower...look at that tiny thing! Is that even usable?"

Everyone had great fun giving Don a hard time, and he,

as he always did, basked in the spotlight.

> *Don Thrower did not go to Vietnam; he received a hardship discharge. His service was a hardship on the school district where he had been teaching, and they sorely needed him there. I believe he served his country greater by staying at home teaching inner-city kids than he ever could have in Vietnam.*

On 3 March 1969, during field exercises, our next duty station orders arrived. Special Orders Number 62: the Armor School's class 5-69 had been assigned to Vietnam en mass. Nope, we would not be going to Germany or even Korea as we had counted on. For us, the destination was Vietnam.

My pre-enlistment plan had unraveled. How could I have not seen it coming? After my initial disappointment and upon reflection, I convinced myself that no one would ever be able to tell me what Vietnam was about. I would be the one to know from my first-hand experience, and I would be able to tell them. I began to view my future exploits as an adventure, albeit with considerable trepidation on my part, and at no small risk. I was twenty, immortal and gave little thought to not surviving. We dutifully trained others, those who might soon be on our own combat crew. Our training efforts took on an importance that had not been considered in previous days.

On 20 March, our overseas orders were punctuated by a requirement to get qualified with the M-16 (5.56 mm assault rifle). We had qualified with the M-14 in basic training, and we concentrated on tank armament during AIT. No one I knew had ever held an M-16, much less fired one. We joked that if we failed to qualify maybe we would not have to go. Our orders were the encouragement to train seriously and to fire as accurately as we could. My records reflect that I scored Expert, the highest level, and better than my M-14 score of Sharpshooter. I would not be a candidate for Sniper School.

Tim Shepherd was another guy I found interesting and was from California, I think. He did as well as anyone at the

Armor School, as a student and as a soldier. Prior to receiving our orders, he had done as well as anyone in OJT. After we received our orders, Tim began to talk about going AWOL (Absent Without Leave) and not going to Vietnam with us.

"Are you going?" he asked me.

"I don't want to go to jail...and Canada's too cold."

"I'm not going," he said. "If I had orders to Korea or Germany, I'd go...I could do that. But I can't do Vietnam. It's immoral."

"What are you thinking of doing about it?" I asked.

"Sweden. I have a friend there already. He left before he was drafted. That's what I should have done...just left the country. Accepting these orders is just plain wrong...the war is obscene and I won't be a part of it."

"Show me one that isn't."

"We are killing people who are just trying to live," Tim said. "Why do we have to force our way on them?"

"I don't think it's all that simple, Tim. I don't want to go either...but I gotta say...once I am home, there won't be a soul who can tell me it's right or wrong. I'll be informed with first-hand knowledge."

"If you survive," he said.

"Yeah, big if, huh?"

Soldiers do tend to carp a great deal, especially when displeased, so no one took him very seriously.

Tim Shepherd was not on our plane to Vietnam. No one from my class with whom I spoke ever heard from him after OJT.

Only a few medical preparations, a little paperwork, and some Vietnam-specific training remained. Along with guys from elsewhere on post who were also headed our way, we had a full day's training in a Vietnamese village mockup. It was full of punji pits, assorted booby-traps, and U.S. soldiers who posed as VC (Viet Cong). That day was really just a lark until we heard that one of the guys playing a VC had died.

While he hid in a simulated tunnel, he accidentally set off a smoke grenade and suffocated, unable to get out and into the fresh air. After hearing that, it was not so much fun anymore. As stated earlier, military training was—and still is—a very dangerous business.

Too soon, our OJT duty was complete.

We departed on thirty-day leave with orders to report for overseas duty at Oakland Army Depot, Oakland, California, on 24 April 1969, by noon, for transportation to the Republic of Vietnam. While I was at home, I tried in vain to keep my focus away from the army and squarely on my pleasure, mostly carnal. I had been working hard at my training for the better part of a year by that time, and I really wanted some irresponsible fun. Actually, I wanted a lot of it. Yes, I certainly did enjoy female company—and intimacy also. I will admit to one young lady whose name I never knew.

My younger brother, Bob, enlisted a few months after I did. While we were away in the army, my Uncle Jimmy came to live with my family for a while. He was divorcing, and things were tough for him. For many years, he had troubles with alcohol, and his personal and professional lives were crashing and burning. My parents took him in and put him in Bob's room, since Bob was stationed in Germany and was not due back home for two years.

Uncle Jimmy was an infantry combat veteran of World War II, rising to the rank of master sergeant while serving in the European Theater. His combat experience included the early Normandy campaign and the Battle of the Bulge. His military service was not a frequent topic in my house, and neither was my father's.

While I was home on leave, Jimmy was out until all hours often returning home after I did. He was a character; we carried the same party-hard gene. The major difference between us was that Jimmy had applied himself all the way through school. While I was still a teenager, I was surprised to learn that Jimmy had a Ph.D. When I asked him what he studied, his response was "old sheep shit." He never gave me a straight answer, but that was Jimmy's style. When I asked Dad about it, he told me that Jimmy had studied ancient Greek agriculture. I do not know if that was even the truth, but I am still impressed he earned a Ph.D.

Author's Uncle Jimmy (l) and father (r). Sixties Mad Men.

I planned to leave home a day early in order to meet Glinda, the girl from Sacramento whom I had written and phoned. The night before I flew to San Francisco, I was lying on my bed in contemplation of meeting Glinda, of the war, and of my life in general. I had been out with friends living what I considered (only in rare reflective moments) could be my last night ever in Atlanta. I had been partying so much I was still lying there, watching late night TV, and I was unable to fall asleep. The effects of alcohol consumption were slowly beginning to wear off.

Jimmy also had a fun night. He was "feeling no pain," as my mother liked to say. We had always been uncle-nephew close with a mutual black-sheep respect. I was the kid, and he was the adult. I had not bridged the age gap with him, yet. He sat on the edge of my bed, and we started to chat.

"Did you have a good time tonight?" he asked, giving me the "I know what you've been up to" grin.

"My last night? You know I did."

He nodded and smiled his amusement. We spent the next few minutes with light-hearted banter and jesting. Then he gave it to me.

"Are you ready for the adventure of your life?"

"I'm not so sure, but I expect that I'll be finding out soon enough, huh?"

I turned away, feeling a little inadequate before a World War II combat veteran. My war was not universally praised, and I had done nothing to *begin* to compare to his service. I never thought I would.

"You'll only be the third in the family to see combat," he said. "Your great-great-grandfather served during the not-so Civil War...that unpleasantness of a century ago...then me in The Big War, and very soon, you. You'll be number three."

He was assuming I would be in combat, but I was not about to make that leap yet. There still was a chance for my plan to work. He knew more than I did about it, though, so I thought I should listen to him carefully. I did.

"The first time you're shot at in anger, you'll be terrified out of your damn mind," he continued, "and you'll have every reason to be. Those people are trying to separate you from your life." Then, as though I did not understand what he was saying, he said, "They're going to try to *kill* you!"

I lay there, dumbfounded. *Why is he scaring me so?* Of course, he was drunk but not sloppy, just loose-tongued. He really loved to say outrageous things just to get a reaction. That is another genetic trait we share, and one that manifests itself with or without alcohol.

"I should tell you, though..." his face became solemn, "the first time...." He hesitated and studied me—he became intense. "The *first* time you are in a firefight...you *will* shit all over your young self."

Jimmy did not smile, nor did I. I was uncomfortable with the subject, but I wondered if that humiliation was really to be expected. Could that really be true?

"You're messing with me...aren't you?"

I was hopeful, and I searched his face for a telltale twitch, indicative of a stifled smile or laugh. I saw nothing, nothing but a somber demeanor.

"Not in the least," he offered. "It's true...happens to us all. It *will* happen to you the first time. Understand that it's very much your initiation into combat...sort of paying your dues."

Jimmy pointed to my uniform, pressed and hanging over my closet door, standing ready for the next morning.

"How many guys do you think have worn that uniform, or one like it?" he asked me rhetorically. "Every swinging dick who has...*and* been shot at...the minority of servicemen...has shit himself. It's the gospel truth. You won't be the first, and certainly, you won't be the last. It's a very long line of good people. Back when a brand new Legionnaire first engaged his enemy, he shit himself. Just steel yourself for the ribbing you'll get. Remember, it's just an initiation! You'll be paying dues. We've all paid 'em."

He stood and walked the few steps to the bedroom door and turned back to me and pointed.

"If you manage to survive the day, well, you'll probably survive your tour," he turned away and then looked back again. "Always follow rule number one," he advised.

"Rule number one?" I asked, "What's that?"

I was familiar with too many rules numbered 'one'.

"Don't panic...panic kills." With that, he was off to bed.

That was the last time Jimmy and I spoke until well after my return a year later. During that time, he got his personal life in much better shape and moved away. I would not get an opportunity to speak to him at any length for a few years.

When I finally did, I had bridged the adult-child gap. My uncle, the combat veteran, was respectful of my service and my efforts. He showed a soldier's keen interest in my tour. That has always meant a great deal to me. We became good friends.

I was up early the next day after a fitful sleep. Both my parents drove me to the airport. They fully understood and had accepted that I was leaving early to meet Glinda. There was no drama when we separated; my parents were never publicly emotional.

The older sister of a high school friend was seated next to me on the plane. She helped me pass the time and kept my mind away from the things we both knew were to come. To be certain, I was apprehensive about Vietnam, but temporarily eclipsing my trepidation was excitement about my new friend, Glinda. Was I wasting valuable leave? What was she like in person? Her letters and telephone chats indicated she was a fun gal. However, I had been fooled before.

As the airplane descended into the San Francisco area, I was struck with the geography. I had never been there before, and the vistas were awe inspiring. The city and bridges were remarkable from the air. We passed over green rolling hills, then down over the water and to our landing. The airport was just another big city airport. We deplaned, and there she was, a cute girl I knew only from one picture, a few letters, and several long phone calls, and she was waiting for me—just me. She was dressed in slacks and blouse, giving an image of a bank teller or secretary. I half-expected a hippie, smoking pot, saying "far out, man" too often, and carrying a huge sign protesting me. We knew each other instantly; she thrust her hand to me.

"Hi, soldier," she said. "Welcome to California."

Her hand was warm and inviting, as was her smile. I was instantly secure my early arrival would not be wasted.

"Hiya, Glinda. I'm Greg, your soldier du jour. It's great to meet you in person, at long last. I lucked out."

"Aw, that's so sweet."

"Nothing sweet, I really think I got lucky."

"We'll see about that," she said. "Only time will tell."

I chuckled. Maybe she did not mean it as I took it, and I reasoned that she probably did not. I was surprised by my feeble retort—an uncharacteristic moment of discretion.

"True," I said.

I noticed that she, too, was just a little nervous; I could see it in her face, and hear it slightly in her voice. That was a welcoming sign, an indication of good times coming. She grew more attractive as we chatted away, becoming acquainted, even though we were already great friends since we had been writing and telephoning for some time. We knew one another well, yet we did not at all. Then she put her arm in mine.

"I brought you a present," she cooed into my ear.

It was getting good, fast. I was already in a fantasy.

"Do tell. What would that be?"

She pulled a paper bag from her oversized, over the shoulder purse. The bag was decorated with an image of a tree that was the store logo. I long ago forgot the name.

"You tell me. Guess."

She held the bag to my nose and let me smell the goods, but she would not let me have a look. She pulled the bag away.

"Some kind of...hmm...bread or baked goods. Let me smell again." I sniffed the opening several times. "Can't tell. Bread, I guess...fruit or nut bread. Smells yummy."

"I stopped at a special place on the way here...this is for later. Well, depending on how later goes."

She was letting me know she would not leave soon—maybe. She was certainly cool; very cool, indeed.

When I first saw her car, I was shocked. The reserved, business-attired gal owned a new Plymouth Valiant, beige, with dozens of bright yellow daisies all over it. Faux-hippie, maybe? Each hubcap had one very large daisy, and there were many more smaller daisies on the doors.

"Are there any landmarks you care to visit?"

"I'd love to see that Ironsides building, the façade, from the TV show...I love that architecture. Anything else is your call. You're the local tour guide."

We drove around the city, and I became a willing tourist. It was a beautiful day. San Francisco was unlike places I had been, and I loved it because it was so different and had such great character in everything. We avoided Haight-Ashbury, thinking it might be unwise since I was in uniform. We went down Lombardy Street, crossed the Golden Gate Bridge, up to Telegraph Hill and into Chinatown. We ended up down at Fisherman's Wharf, touring free spirit boutiques and visiting Ghirardelli's. There was a decided counter-culture aspect to the inventory in many of the high-end specialty stores along the wharf. I was a bit surprised. Glinda was keenly interested in a bejeweled roach clip. She must have been at least a weekend hippie.

The army required that those in the military travel in uniform. The airlines also did if I wished to benefit from their Military Standby pricing, which I did. All day I was keenly aware I *was* in uniform, and I was in San Francisco, the city that my generation saw as Mecca for the counter-culture. My uniform made me conspicuous, yet I suffered no stares or ill words. Just apathy and that was just fine with me.

Just as darkness fell, I suggested we eat.

"Do you have a favorite restaurant?" I asked.

"No. Truth is, I don't get down at all. That's why I was so eager in the shops...can't get it at home."

"Are you hungry? What do you feel like?"

"Don't know...something here at the Wharf maybe," she said. "You decide. I'll be happy with anything."

We checked out the Wharf restaurants. It was not an easy decision for us; everything looked so good (and to me it looked expensive).

"Have you been to that one?" I asked.

"Allioto's? No, I haven't."

"Let's try it...looks interesting," I said.

"I'd be happy with that...let's."

I had lobster; it is one of my favorites. I know I looked silly in Class A's wearing a lobster bib, but I did not care. The food was great, and my dinner companion was unforgettable. We drove to a park later and spent time lying out under the stars. What a glorious night it was. We talked for several hours, moving into her daisy-mobile as the temperature turned cooler. We kept each other warm.

As dawn broke, we drove over to Oakland to be closer to the Army Depot and found a motel room. I resolved to return to her that evening if we were not shipped out right away. She telephoned her boss and claimed illness—the girl seemed to have some spunk. We had not slept all night, so I was certain she would still be there later in the day if I could get away. My reporting time was approaching, so I left Glinda at the motel and reported for duty. In very short order, I received a Hong Kong flu shot (ouch!) among several other inoculations, and did a large amount of paperwork processing for my overseas assignment.

Mike Mitchell, a local California boy, had grown up somewhere nearby. Many of the other Armor School guys hailed from close by, too. Mike was constantly singing the brand new Beatles song "Get Back," and he was surprised I had not heard it yet. I complained we backward folks from the South never got any new music until New York and California were tired of it.

We were assigned quarters, and then received a steak dinner. I had never been impressed with the army's version of steak, but I enjoyed it anyway. To my surprise, the one I ate that night was actually a very good steak and cooked just right. We joked that it was our last meal, so they were feeding us officer rations—the good stuff.

Our instructions were to remain in the area since we were to continue processing the next day. I just had to see Glinda again, and I hoped she stayed. I found a phone and received the good news; she was waiting for me. I tried to find a way out to be with her that night, but could not. We were kept too busy. I asked her to stay one more day in hopes that the next day it would be easier for me to find an escape. She agreed—she truly did have spunk.

The next day we moved to another building. It had one large room that had been partitioned into bunk areas, and they offered a bit of sleeping privacy. The common areas had several comfortable lounge chairs and a few other homey items to make our stay more pleasant while we passed the time. It was all contained in a warehouse in an industrial park. We were not anticipating a long stay, only a few days before we would move to Travis Air Force Base and catch our flight.

The officers had better quarters and, of course, they were allowed to come and go as they saw fit. Officially, we were not. We were warehoused, but we discovered no one was paying close attention. I wanted to get to Glinda, and Mike Mitchell wanted to be with his girlfriend. The two of us walked out and made our way to a nearby street where we hailed a cab. Technically, we *were* AWOL and out of uniform, yet we decided to take the chance. We thought that our leaving was a small risk given the rewards possible, and we were not very concerned. What could they do—draft us and send us to "The Nam?"

At the motel, Glinda answered the door wearing a huge smile and smelling wonderful. Fresh. Clean. Simply put, *very* nice. We began right where we left off earlier, becoming even better, and more intimate friends. Our time together passed swiftly and too soon; it was time for me to leave. I had a new friend, but how would that friendship fare over the next year?

We sat on the side of the bed, trying to say good-bye. Glinda was slightly angled toward me, and I was squared to the front. She held my hand in my lap. I wanted to get closer, to be emotionally intimate with her, but I did not think that was the right time. I was about to head into the unknown that was ensconced within a well-known iffy situation. How would it be for me? Would I come home? In what shape would I be? I knew I had no business making anything out of our time together other than what it was—pure joy. (Later I would reflect, wondering if my joy were indeed pure, or if it were borne of my predicament and Glinda was my final rendezvous before I died.) At that moment, though, all that truly mattered was the bond we had formed so quickly, and the separation that was coming. There grew a silence, a beast of a silence, and it stood large between us, encumbering any emotional advance. After several minutes, Glinda perked up. She felt the weight of the moment, too, yet did not let it spoil what little time was left.

"Whatcha thinkin'?" she asked.

"Many things. You...me. My trip. I hope to get to see you again. I think we hit it off damn well. I like you a lot." I looked into her eyes and smiled. "I think you found me tolerable. Not a danger and fair-to-middlin' to spend time with."

"You kidder!" She punched my arm. "It's been a great time. It never has to be anything special...just fun. It *was* special, though, and I hope you will think about us often."

"Oh, yes...it was special to me, too."

I stood, pointing to my watch.

"It's time. Time for the condemned man to take that long and fearful walk...the dreaded one." I joked.

"Don't be so damn dramatic. You'll be fine. You have a good head on those shoulders. I think you're a survivor."

"I hope I am. I'll certainly try to be one."

"You really *will* be coming back, won't you?" She placed her head on my shoulder as we stood at the door.

"I sure as hell hope so."

Why would she ask me such a thing?

"I mean to see me, here in California."

It was difficult to be honest with her. She was certainly fun; I liked her; but would I make an effort—all that way from my home and after whatever I might encounter? I did what any red-blooded American guy would do in that situation.

"You may rest assured," I promised.

My cab arrived and I left Glinda standing at the door, waving. I returned to my temporary home.

I never saw or spoke to Glinda again, although we carried on written correspondence for about half of my tour. Our friendship was lost due to the lack of proximity and the war. (Or her new boyfriend?)

Early the next morning, we boarded buses to Travis Air Force Base; they dropped us off at a gymnasium. Travis was very active, and the sounds of jets taking off and taxiing was loud. Hurry up and wait. It must be the air force way, too.

We had been waiting a few hours when a large door cracked open and allowed a streak of the midday sun inside. Through the door, we could see the tarmac where a Boeing 707 was refueling. Men came streaming through the door of the plane and down the airstairs. Some kissed the tarmac, others grinned, and others remained pensive.

To those returnees we must have appeared as choirboys. We saw them as master warriors, anointed with the wisdom combat survival brings. Some were golden-dirty and without any sort of military bearing or demeanor. They were distant, introspective, and not celebrating openly. Those guys were intimidating. They knew, and we did not. Those men were the obvious *combat* veterans. They had begun their adventure as death's enemy, and they became intimate with that enemy. How would their experience shape their futures? How would it shape ours when we came home? Few of those returnees made eye contact with us. They wanted nothing to do with us, the freshest of the fresh meat. Those who did look our way only viewed us with misgiving, doubt, and pity. I did not get it then; I would eventually. Many of those returnees seemed to be Saigon warriors who never left the relative safety of the rear. They were too neat, too clean, too starched, and too pressed. It was they, the apparent office dwellers, who were the tarmac kissers and grinners.

After the 707 had been serviced, we embarked. We sat six abreast, separated by a single aisle, the aircraft configured for carrying maximum souls—it was packed. It was typical military air transport; function, no frills.

Our first stop was Anchorage, Alaska, where we refueled and remained for a few hours, alone in an empty terminal. The bar was closed, and we were displeased and thirsty. There was a groundswell of grumbling. At least one army chaplain was with us, and he was a guardian angel. He must not have been Baptist or Methodist because he demanded that airport personnel get the bar open—and immediately. They did so, and we enjoyed our all-too-brief stay. Thank you, chaplain; thank you Anchorage airport.

The day was clear and visibility amazing. I was in awe of the scenery and aware that I was only being offered a taste. I vowed to return one day and really look around. As of this writing, I have not, but it remains on my short list.

The next fuel stop was in Japan, at Yakota Air Force Base. They had the best snack bar I have ever seen. Maybe I should have joined the air force instead of the army. The tiny bit of Japan I saw at the base was beautiful and so very, very clean. I vowed to see as much of off-base Japan as I could someday as my father had done right after World War II. He was enamored with the beauty of the country and loved its people. As with Anchorage, I have not, but it, too, remains on my short list.

> *Family lore holds that when Dad arrived on the mainland of Japan, not long after the war ended, he sent a telegram home. The entire message read, "It's not true." My grandfather laughed hysterically, while my grandmother stared at him wondering what was so damn funny, and what was not true. My family humor, again.*

Once our bird was refueled, we winged our way toward Vietnam, trying to entertain ourselves and get some sleep. I recalled reading a few weeks earlier about a Vietnam-bound flight of U.S. soldiers who wandered into Soviet airspace. The Soviets launched fighters to escort them to a landing, and passengers and crew were kept for several days. That was just nine months before our own flight; another thing for us to worry over. Those troublesome Ruskies might not be as forgiving a second time.

There was time for reflection, and reflect I did. Since I had joined the army, each time I was about to go home I would hear Simon and Garfunkel's song, "Homeward Bound." Coincidence? No doubt, or else I was not paying attention other times when it played. In any event, I decided I did *not* want to hear it again until I was ready to go home.

Sometime in the middle of the night, we left our cruising altitude. We had spent about twenty-two hours in the air in those very small seats. I had lost all sense of time: hour, day, even date. (The day and date would remain mostly irrelevant for me during the next year.) As we descended, the cabin got increasingly quiet as everyone drew within himself. Not one soul was joking, and not one I could see was still asleep; each of us was alone with his thoughts. I looked out the window and saw only darkness; we must still have been over the ocean. Where were the lights indicating a twentieth-century population? On our final approach, the airplane began to roll briskly in both directions, and then it was wings level for a few seconds. Then we began a rapid descent. After several anxious moments for us, the aircraft captain spoke.

"Gentlemen...sorry 'bout that. We're dodging artillery fire up here," he announced, "but it shouldn't take us very far off the approach. In fact, we currently have the runway in sight and are cleared number one to land."

As we descended, some distinguishable ground lights made our faster than usual approach speed evident. After touchdown and stopping in what was an unusually short rollout, we taxied at high speed all the way to the terminal and to a full stop. I dared not look outside. No, hit me with it all at once.

Those of us on a first tour were unsure what awaited us outside the airplane and, like me, were not very keen to find out. There were just a few steps left to the exit when warm and humid air embraced me. It carried an unfamiliar aroma, like nothing I had ever smelled before. Later, I came to know that as the smell of Vietnam: a wood and earth note up front, a quick finish of charcoal and back-ended with a mixture of primitive, civilized and war smells that were Southeast Asia, both good and bad.

The warmth initially enveloping me was blast-furnace heat when I stepped from the airplane. The temperature felt like ninety-five degrees, and the humidity must have been ninety-five percent. Yikes. We were arriving in the middle of the night. I knew then the weather in Vietnam was going to take getting used to, even for a Southern boy.

We had arrived in Bien Hoa, South Vietnam, a large U.S. airbase a few miles northeast of Saigon. We were in a war zone, as evidenced by the explosions and small arms fire we heard off in the distance. How far is that fighting? Who among us is comfortable, and where is that fool? Certainly, that guy had been to Vietnam before. Those of us visiting for the first time were making each move tentatively, not in any hurry to make mistakes.

Upon exiting the airplane and briskly walking through the terminal, we reassembled to board buses for a nearby base, Long Binh. The buses were not at all like the ones back in "the World" (which was considered anywhere other than Vietnam, but almost exclusively meant the States). The bus windows had heavy screens to protect riders from grenades. That got my attention. As apprehensive as I was, the few miles to Long Binh were like any paved American road: traffic signals, fast moving vehicles of all descriptions, and so-called, secure.

We arrived at the 90th Replacement Detachment for our in-country processing and assignment to our units. Our body clocks were at zero-dark-thirty with little sleep. Any sleep, in any place, would be a most-welcomed respite, even if it were less than five-star accommodations. There was to be no deep sleep for us for a while, though. We endured several briefings, completed the requisite paperwork, exchanged U.S. money for MPC (Military Payment Certificates), and grabbed naps that were too brief. Then we waited more and napped more.

Finally, after being given temporary resting quarters, we explored the area while we awaited assignment to our new units, to be posted on a bulletin board twice daily. Weapons had not been issued to us, but I was not too concerned. The base had plenty of guards posted; surely, *they* carried live ammo. Other than checking the postings twice daily, we were free to avail ourselves of whatever benefits the area might have to offer. Despite the proximity to the perceived danger on the outside of the wire, replacements were always in motion trying to find something to do. Aside from the bar hooch less than two hundred feet away from our sleeping quarters, one favorite activity was the steam bath, followed by a massage.

After first taking a steam, we enjoyed the hot and cold baths, going from one to the other and then back again until we were nearly exhausted. Then we practically crawled to the adjacent massage room, crowded with tables attended to by young Vietnamese women—girls, actually. They were the masseuses and did decent enough jobs, despite giggling and pointing to erections that frequently presented for their amusement. All along the outer walls were curtained rooms where one hired a special-talent masseuse with inclination to manage said erections. The women of those rooms were not giggly young girls. They charged more than a masseuse, too—something like three dollars MPC. Many replacements found temporary comfort there.

Part II

Rude, Crude and Socially Unacceptable

I'm not afraid of death; I just don't want to be there when it happens.

—Woody Allen

Chapter 7

Surviving Danger's Dragoons

Those of us coming from the Armor School were openly concerned about being relegated to an infantry unit located in the middle of *the* most dangerous place in South Vietnam. We had no clue where that might be, but we were convinced we were headed there. The first assignments were posted, and my friend, Steve Sapp, saw that he had been assigned to the 9th Infantry Division, the Old Reliables. Since the rest of our names were not on that list, we—OK, mostly just me—gave him a lot of grief for being sent to the infantry.

"Steverino's a grunt," I teased. "A ground-pounding, gravel-agitating, dog-face, walking grunt."

"Not so fast, my Southern friend," he said. "Maybe, maybe not. Just 'cause I'm going to an infantry *division*, does *not* mean I'll be a grunt. There's still some hope."

"Nah, ya gots no hope, my flower-child friend. None at all...zilch. You're infantry."

"C'mon now...you know I'm no hippie. I'm a farmer."

"Yeah. A farmer hippie."

"No way," he said. "Never."

"No matter, you are still a grunt."

"Let's see where *you* end up."

As my luck would have it, the very next posting had the orders for Jon Laird, Sal Miccio, Joe Chiacchio, Bob Leighty, and me to report to none other than 1st Infantry Division—*the* Big Red One. My heart sank; I was not at all happy. Sapp was still around to console me.

"If'n you're gonna be one, then be a Big *Red* One." He repeated it often and with great glee.

I know, I know. I deserved it. It was all in fun, after all.

I was not going to just *any* infantry unit. No, not me. I

was going to *the* foremost infantry division of the U.S. Army. The irony of my past choices was not lost on me.

Soon, those of us who were to go to 1st Infantry were transported by truck the few miles to Di An, the division's rearmost basecamp. The AO (Area of Operations) for the 1st Infantry Division began just north of Saigon. In time, we would learn that our AO ran northward all the way to the Cambodian border. There was no question where 1st Infantry Division units were located; the area was announced by a large sign having a gigantic replica of the division patch (a red numeral one against a green background) painted on it. On the sign was also inscribed the division motto: "No Mission Too Difficult, No Sacrifice Too Great—Duty First!" Uh-oh. What in the world did I do? What in hell happened to my foolproof plan? I learned the division call sign was "Danger," and that turn of events did not bode well at all.

After checking in at division, we were transported to Jungle School. Sometimes referred to as Snake School, it was the division's six day in processing, acclimatization, and training center. It was also the distribution point to our units. We had classes on the Geneva Convention and learned how un-cool it was to mutilate a deceased enemy (We did not know already?), sweated profusely, tried to adjust our sleep and bowel habits, and visited a range to fire several types of weapons, most of them new to us.

It was right there at Danger's Snake School that I turned twenty-one; I could legally drink. What could I do about it? Not a damn thing, it is just another of those little ironies I find amusing. I know; they were of my making.

On 6 May 1969, Miccio, Chiacchio, Laird, and I were further assigned to the division's cavalry unit: 1st Squadron, 4th Cavalry, commonly known as "Quarter Cav." Things were looking up; I had indeed avoided a ground-pounding unit, yet, I was in *the* infantry division. Until I saw my orders, I was not certain that I would not be a full-blown "leg" (infantryman).

Laird, Miccio, and I were assigned to Alpha Troop, and Joe Chiacchio was assigned to Bravo Troop. Joe left us at the end of Jungle School, and I would not see him again until early July. We had a chance to chat for a few minutes and compare notes of experiences, our fears, and our hopes. By then, we were no longer FNGs (Fucked-up New Guys or Fuckin' New Guys), and we began to find our own (relative) in-country comfort zone.

> About a week after seeing Joe in Lai Khe, the ACAV (Armored Cavalry Assault Vehicle) he commanded detonated a large anti-tank mine. Joe was KIA. Two months after seeing him, I saw his ACAV—rather, what remained. The damage was astounding; I do not know how or even if anyone survived.

Jungle School: author, Sal Miccio and Jon Laird.

Leaving Jungle School behind, we were transported to our squadron's rearmost HQ (headquarters) complex at Di An. Upon arrival, we took notice of our new unit's welcoming sign, in cavalry colors of red and white, with its simple motto: "Paratus et Fidelis." Translated from Latin it stated that my new unit was "Prepared and Loyal." My life began to look a bit brighter. Danger I was surely not seeking, preparation I could handle, and loyalty was natural to me.

The radio call sign for Quarter Cav was almost quaint; it was "Dragoon." I liked that since I was familiar with the term. It made sense for a cavalry squadron, and ours was the lucky unit in our army to have it. "Danger" is equally proper and historically descriptive for the division, as I was to learn soon enough. I was not aware of the role in American history that the 4th Cavalry Regiment *or* the 1st Infantry Division played. I would be soon enough, and I would embrace it.

Miccio was left behind somewhere for some reason, so Jon Laird and I were taken to Alpha Troop's Di An HQ. The troop's welcome sign, also in red and white, read simply, "Hardcore." I was in a unit whose motto was "Hardcore." Oh, shit, again—my spirit came crashing down. I suspected I was in for a very bumpy ride.

A clerk advised us we would be in the field the next day. Alpha Troop was conducting operations near a town called Song Be. When the next morning came, we were given what may have been the second best advice we would ever receive. (The first had been from the NCOs at Ft. Knox warning us to listen to those who had the experience.) We were told to "Lose the white boxers...in fact, lose underwear. Lose those socks, too. They'll only bring you grief." Those words were from someone on his way home, someone who had spent "quality" time in the field. I took his advice, and for my entire year in-country my uniform was boots and pants twenty-four hours a day, seven days a week—*only* boots and pants—unless I was wearing a flak vest and helmet, and on rare occasion a shirt.

Cavalry as it was defined by Quarter Cav in Vietnam was made up of Headquarters Troop, three troops of armored cavalry (tanks and ACAVs), and one troop of air cavalry—scout helicopters, gunships and an aero-rifle platoon. The air troop (Delta), like its armored siblings (Alpha, Bravo, Charlie), worked in smaller elements wherever and whenever Quarter Cav assets were summoned within 1st Infantry Division's AO, or were otherwise assigned.

Our AO covered the areas of major conflict from north of Saigon to Cambodia. Some place names were Iron Triangle, Trapezoid, Catcher's Mitt, the Michelin Rubber Plantation, and War Zones C and D. The latter included An Loc, Quan Loi, Loc Ninh, and Song Be, towns and villages along the Cambodian border. Their names became part of my everyday life—then and now.

Each cavalry troop was made up of a HQ platoon and three line platoons. Each line platoon had three M48A3 tanks and seven ACAVs (commonly referred to as "tracks"). Every vehicle had one M2 heavy machine gun. The tanks had a 90 mm main gun, and each ACAV had a pair of M-60s (7.62 mm machine gun), one per side. Each vehicle had a standard crew of four; each crewman had a personal weapon, mostly M-16s, but there were also M-79s (40 mm grenade launchers), and .45 caliber pistols (M-1911) in the mix. All vehicles carried hand-launched flares, hand grenades, smoke grenades and, hopefully, enough ammunition. One vehicle carried a chest full of C-4 (plastic explosives), blasting caps, detonation cord, and fuse. The platoon also had two or three Starlight scopes (night vision devices, early generation), and the tanks had a Xenon gas searchlight with a CS (riot control gas) launcher on top. The HQ ACAVs and the VTR (Vehicle Tracked Recovery) were similarly outfitted. HQ had several specialty vehicles as well as communication and medical tracks.

I met Quarter Cav field troops the first time just outside a village whose name I never knew, along the road to Song Be. There were concerns more prominent in my mind than what that village's name was, but its charcoal production smell remains with me. I was going up country for the first time, to the field to join my unit. I knew we were joining Alpha Troop and that they were working somewhere in the Song Be area. That is all I knew. Where in hell was I? At that early date in my tour, referencing a map would have been no help; I did not have a clue where we were or what we were doing. Someone could have pointed to our location on a map, and it would have made no difference at all to me. I was trying to absorb everything I encountered and get my feet planted, without six feet of fresh earth covering them. I had a sense of wonder at all things that were Vietnam. It resembled nothing I knew and smelled radically different from anything in my experience.

A pair of ACAVs arrived to retrieve Jon Laird and me, Quarter Cav's newest ghostly pale FNGs, dressed in brand new green jungle fatigues. We knew we had many lessons to learn, and that we needed to learn them unerringly and promptly. We hoped we would live long enough to do so. I do not know today, if I ever knew, which platoon the ACAVs were from or who the guys were. Later in my tour, they may have been great friends. Not at that time, though, I had not yet paid any dues. They looked upon the two of us with disdain and revulsion; we were FNGs, the lowest life form, dangerous to others and expendable—worse, we were Shake-'n-Bake NCOs.

I remembered the stare of many returnees at Travis Air Force Base. We were not at all like those guys, not yet. The ACAV crews barely noticed us, or simply ignored us, being more interested in securing a couple of blocks of ice. First lesson learned: we were too new to matter. Another lesson was apparent: ice was indeed a *serious* luxury.

One of the TCs (Track Commanders) instructed us to mount up while he saw to his purchase of ice. I felt we would be left behind if we did not move fast enough to suit him. We figured out how to climb aboard with no help, and secured our top space where we would hold on for our dear lives. The two gunners/observers riding behind the Track Commander sat on reclaimed (or midnight-requisitioned) jeep seats. There were but two such seats, so we FNGs lost out. We were not part of the crew, and they treated us as intruders. Underway, we must have appeared as insecure as we were, even though we did our best to look the part of a confident and competent NCO. We fooled nobody.

The ride seemed to take forever—mostly because of my concern that we would be attacked at any moment by what remained of the Viet Cong along with the entire NVA (North Vietnamese Army), including Soviet and Chinese advisors. Jon, from Arizona, was probably used to the heat and not so used to the humidity. I, on the other hand, had experienced very high humidity and triple digit temperatures routinely in the summer. It was much hotter and with a higher humidity in that part of Vietnam than I had ever experienced at home. The breeze generated by the speed of the ACAV felt wonderful on my moist skin. Given our response to the overloading of so many and varied sensory inputs and our trepidation, we must have been a sight. We were very much typical FNGs, indeed.

Twenty minutes into the trip, I began to feel the sudden and immediate necessity to evacuate my bowels. Getting used to the high heat was one thing, getting my internals back in order was quite another. My problem was diarrhea, and I needed relief right then or there would be a mess. That would not endear me at all to the crew. What could I do? I asked the TC to pull over and let me have at it by the roadside.

"I've got the serious shits. Pull over...I'll be quick."

I got a look I had never seen before. How could I *dare* to ask something so stupid? (I questioned myself.) His response was, "How stupid are you, FNG?"

Very stupid to be sure. It seemed we agreed—I was without question a dumb ass.

"Well, new guy, you are just going to have to hold it. We don't pull over. The area may be crawling with Gooks."

I did not know it then, but we were in a quiet area—an area in which seasoned troopers felt safe. I surely did not and I am sure Jon did not, either.

"Can't help it. My bowels aren't working right yet, and I really need relief. I'm in serious pain."

"Aw...poor baby. Can't stop...won't stop. We gotta keep moving. Hang your ass out the door."

Someone suggested using an empty C-Rats (C-Rations) box, and it seemed smart. I was too occupied with cramping to investigate alternatives. I used a box to relieve myself while holding on to the open hatch release cable as we swayed and bounced along with the road. I was not very secure over my target, but somehow managed to find rhythm long enough so as not to soil the ACAV or myself. I knew I would never hear the end of it if I had.

With my mission accomplished, I squared myself away and it became hazardous waste disposal time. I rose through the hatch thinking I would throw my package over the back of the ACAV. Those guys moved *very* fast (think warp-speed) to stop me, as if I were about to toss that loaded box straight up and into the wind—and all over them. They made disparaging comments laced with never-ending expletives, some new to me, regarding my ancestry and intelligence. They strongly recommended I open the back door and *drop* it out ASAP. The two observers had M-16s—I assumed they were loaded. I took their hint without any argument, doing precisely as they had instructed. Another lesson learned: do not piss off the guys you need to help get you back home.

When we arrived at the NDP (Night Defensive Position), Jon was assigned to Lima Platoon (first), and I was assigned to Mike (second). Both platoons were out on missions, so Jon and I waited for them to return, and tried to enjoy the limited shade. When second platoon arrived, I was relieved there were no Sheridans. (Recall those light tanks with combustible casings.) *Good news*, I thought.

I met the second platoon leader, LT (lieutenant) Mike Armstrong (referred to as Mike Six), and I was assigned to an ACAV. I wanted a tank, but I would have to wait for one. I would replace a fellow named Hoagie finishing his tour. I took command of the track the next week when he left the field to return home. Already assigned to the track was Wayne Witwicki, the platoon medic. Most guys called him Doc or Boc Si (Vietnamese for medic or doctor), so I did, too, and I still do. Ronnie Singleton was the driver, but I do not remember who the fourth crewman was on that day.

> *I did not know that LT Armstrong was on his second tour or that he was a mustang officer, having first*

been an enlisted soldier. I only learned of it recently, when several Quarter Cav guys stopped over for a short visit on their way to a 1st Division Reunion.

That first night on guard, a trooper that was not an FNG and certainly should have known much better, went outside the perimeter to move his bowels. He failed to let anyone know. A guard spotted him as unidentified and then alerted all vehicle guards to the movement at the wire. The guy was nearly killed by friendly fire. Others on guard in our sector of the perimeter were more cautious than I was; I almost fired several rounds in that direction. He would probably have been safe from my inadequate FNG efforts, though. Another lesson learned.

"Mike-1, Mike-1, this is Mike-6. Sit rep, over." The calls always began in order according to vehicle number. They were hourly and were to ensure vehicle guards were awake, alert, and that everything was OK.

"Echo-five," we all answered in turn. Things were all right at that moment.

The next few days were uneventful for the platoon, save responding to a Special Forces camp a few times and driving off attackers. I could have been told that we were marching on Hanoi, and it would not have made much of a difference to me. I do not remember seeing any serious action, mines, or booby-traps during that first visit to Song Be. It was in those early days, though, when I heard an AK-47 (NVA/VC assault rifle) fire for the first time. It has a very distinctive report and is clearly recognizable. It sounded to me like a slap or crack, and I have never forgotten it.

My thoughts often drifted to being on the opposite side of the world from the comfort of my family and friends. Back at home, there was no one who wanted to kill me, I think; the NVA/VC wanted to drive us away, never to return. Even when I considered the notion of being such a large target, I was having a visceral reaction to the part I played in the power of an armored cavalry platoon. I was a very young man, a kid still, and wielding great firepower. I slowly gained comfort, feeling stronger with each new experience.

My crew educated me about what to expect. Booby-traps and mines were our constant menace, as were RPGs (Rocket Propelled Grenades). I learned a single man with an RPG could easily ambush us from our rear whenever we were in areas where it was difficult to turn around and respond. The jungle (rain forest, sometimes multiple canopies) is just such a place. Others told me that when VC hit; they struck fast and departed faster, often vanishing before we could target them. When the NVA hit us, they tended to stay and visit a while. All of the above proved true on many occasions during my tour.

My enlightenment had gotten me thinking a lot about wounding, dying and death. I was constantly concerned about detonating a mine or being wiped off my ACAV by a tree-mounted claymore. When I concentrate or am nervous, I tend to bite my lip or chew my tongue. Why? I do not know. I first noticed I was doing it in Vietnam, and I worried about permanent disfigurement. My hope was that if I *had* to lose a limb that it would be a leg and not an arm. I also feared being seriously burned.

> *I went to a party while I was home on leave before going to Vietnam. At that party was a guy who graduated from my high school two classes ahead of me, had been to Vietnam and had lost a leg. At that party, I saw him gleefully toying with two very attractive young women who were guessing which of his legs was real. I watched from afar, as he commanded their full attention; they did not pity him. His strength of personality and the way he handled his loss made him attractive to them. I greatly admired him for that.*

At dusk, the cacophony produced by jungle critters was a signal that either their day was done or they were awake and ready for their nocturnal activities. The jungle would buzz from all the insects, and as it grew darker, all but a few would cease their signals. When the jungle became quiet, we heard from the fuck-you lizard. That is right—a lizard (gecko, actually) whose call breaks the silence of a dark night and says, "Fuck you." I had first guard one night, and my crew was still awake. I barely heard the first call but noticed it was something unusual. Suspecting Ho Chi Minh had a bead on me, I tensed. After a few minutes, I heard the sound again.

"Fuck you." It was louder, closer. I was at maximum pucker factor when I heard it again, "Fuck you."

I turned to someone and asked, "Did you hear that?"

"Sure did, Sarge...don't sweat it. Not just yet, anyhow. It's how the NVA communicate. If they say 'fuck yo momma,' then they're coming at us. Wake us up then."

I was the butt of their joke and expected more.

"Okay, really now, what is it?"

"It's just a lizard...he'll pipe down after a while."

"A lizard?" To me it sounded human. "Not human?"

"Nope...lizard. Nothing at all to worry about. Just keep your eyes open." Sage advice, I thought.

Just about midnight, long after the lizard had gotten quiet, and as I was about to wake my replacement, the tank next to me broke a torsion bar. It startled the hell out of me since it was so close and so loud. Whoever was in the tank cupola on guard started cussing a blue streak. He did not want the extra work. Broken torsion bars were common after busting jungle (driving through jungle knocking over anything in our way), but they took physical effort to replace. There was another serious noise problem. At the least expected moment, usually while on guard duty in the very dark middle of the night, the hydraulic system motor on a tank would start whining very loudly. When that would happen, which it frequently did, the bad guys thereafter knew a tank was nearby. The truth is probably that they already knew we were there, how many of us there were, and who was constipated. It was all very disconcerting.

We drove through a picturesque little village adjacent to an improved, but unpaved road. On the opposite side of the road was a large creek or small river next to a large hill. We halted and shut down our engines for further instructions. I was enjoying the picture-perfect vista when from behind me I heard whooping and hollering. Over the radio I heard, "Eyes left!" I turned to see a young Montagnard woman, topless, with a gorgeous body and very attractive face. She was not paying us one bit of attention. She walked on down our line of vehicles then stepped off the raised roadway to where she could access the water. Using a bowl, she began to bathe. Very nice—indeed! That was so much better than a *National Geographic* magazine, and we saw her in person. Weeks later, on guard duty, I wondered if she was a deliberate distraction. I hoped that someone that day was aware of that possibility. I had certainly not been.

It was there in the Song Be area that I realized every place we had been through since arriving in-country was, in fact, a much safer place than being out in the field. For the remainder of my tour, I would only feel safe when I was in a basecamp, FSB (Fire Support Base), or on my way home. Those first weeks helped me become acclimated to the heat and to settle my gut; finally, my sleep cycle began improving. One might think that feeling unsafe practically every moment would ensure alertness. No, not when you are bone-tired. Still, I just could not get the sleep rhythm right. I was not alone, though; it was a serious FNG problem—always. I caught myself nodding off on guard several times.

One night after I had been in the field for two weeks, the platoon sergeant, SFC Saunders, and the platoon leader, LT Armstrong, were checking on all of the guards. They came to my track and there I was, zonked out cold. I am sure my mouth was wide open, and I was probably dreaming and drooling. They awoke me, and I was sorely embarrassed; I was *supposed* to be a leader. That night I stayed awake on guard without any trouble, and thereafter I found my sleeping rhythm a little better each day. Try as I might, I remained lost and useless. I *was* an FNG, after all.

On one dark night, we were in an NDP in a bamboo thicket on a small rise that looked over the top of the jungle. During daylight hours, I could clearly see the jungle canopy and into Cambodia, not too distant. In the darkness, though, I could not distinguish jungle top from sky. The nighttime horizon melted into a single dark vision, beginning a few feet to the front of my track. The only distinguishing features that night were the stars directly overhead in the clear Vietnam sky. Once again, I was faithful to my FNG status. While my crew slept, my thoughts drifted a long way away, and I was thinking of everything except what I should have been.

A little after midnight, I saw an unfamiliar light to my front and off in the distance. It did not seem to be a threat to us in our NDP. The yellow light hovered silently, and then it darted about. I could not quite get a handle on it. It glowed vividly with a halo, and it had a variable trailing light of much lesser intensity. The light disappeared only to become visible and much higher seconds later. They were the weirdest things I had ever seen, and I was unable to determine what they were. *Top Secret aircraft?* I wondered. I considered waking someone up and asking, but being an FNG, I considered that unwise. I was beginning to make progress—I was not *entirely* stupid anymore—but I was still a very dumb-ass FNG. The lights in the distance abruptly stopped.

The Orient is a mysterious place, I thought, *and spooky, too.* I noticed a solid and wavy red line, and the yellow lights returned. Just as the first line disappeared, another curved red one appeared elsewhere. The lines moved independently of the lights, but they did appear to be in proximity to one another. They were varying length, thin, wavy, red lines just appearing in the darkness of the midnight sky. Adding to the mystery, I heard a sound like I had never imagined. I thought about fire dragons and mythological creatures. What the hell was it? The sound was far away and was a short, guttural, deep buzzing, increasingly gaining depth, lasting only a few seconds. Those glowing yellow lights, the buzzing sound, and the red lines were surely in concert. What were they? I said nothing to my crew; they were asleep. I knew there must be a rational explanation; there had to be. I was in a mysterious place whose people had daily lives that were foreign to me, and I was scared.

The power of suggestion, my own of course, had won out. When I experienced the very same conditions at a much closer range, I realized that I had witnessed aerial assaults by helicopter gunships, complete with flares and mini-guns. The mini-gun was a Gatling-style machine gun that fired 7.62 mm rounds at an absurd rate of up to four-thousand rounds per minute. It was extremely effective at placing a very dense shot group over a wide area. I became very used to them, and quickly. Thankfully, only our side had that awesome tool fielded; it was a great friend to have.

With all that was new to me—people, sights, sounds, smells—and with our being in almost constant motion—the long days flew by. My daily and very lonely solo night guard remained an interminable, fearful, critical duty, and I no longer had trouble staying awake. I continued to have strange sleep patterns. (I still do.) I could fall asleep at any time, day or night, anywhere, under any condition, and I was frequently called out for it by one of the platoon's other Shake 'n Bake NCOs. He had arrived a few months before me, and was more experienced; everyone accepted him completely. He had paid his dues. I seriously disliked the guy. He was relentless, yet he was unable to get through my thick skull. In my disdain for him and his inconsiderate methods, I was rejecting both him and his valid and valuable message.

For the next few weeks I gained composure and settled into my new life. I was more comfortable and growing more confident each day. There still existed non-sleep problems, and too many of them, but even they began to improve. After being in the heat and humidity for a few days, I had forsaken my shirt during the daylight hours since it was so unbearably hot. Someone on another track noticed my exposed arms were beginning to burn and he let me know all about it.

"Hey, new guy! You're going to burn the shit out of your arms. You might wanna put on a shirt," he advised.

"Nah...I brown quickly. I'm always hanging out by the pool...I'll be darker pretty soon," I said.

"You're acting a fool," he advised.

He just shook his head at the newest FNG, that foolish young NCO who refused to take advice from a lower ranking, in-country-wise soldier.

My bravado was sheer idiocy. Within a few days, huge blisters appeared. Someone warned me, and I had ignored the advice, typical FNG behavior. My blisters soon burst and crusted, leaving me with large scabs of three by four inches on each arm. (Today I am constantly watching those sites for skin cancer.) After I recovered from *that* stupidity, and my arms browned, I had no further problems with the sun.

I frequently wrote Glinda, my brother, Bob—who was still in Germany in the army—and my friends back at home. I endeavored to inform them what was happening in-country, and a few details of the things I experienced every day. I wanted to help them understand the difference between the media portrayal of the war and the war I knew. It was a tough sale; I do not think that they cared or understood what I was trying to accomplish. My friends *never* got it. (Once I was back at home, I realized the problem was "You had to be there.") Remaining true to my earlier form, I only flirted with the girls I wrote to; I needed their gentle way. My routine was violence, and girls I knew provided a very good distraction. They provided soft words of encouragement and concern. The women would not have been interested in our harsh goings on, unlike the guys. A few in-country friends received all manner of ornery correspondence from their friends back at home, and a few guys excitedly opened mail only to discover "Dear Johns." None of the people I corresponded with were disparaging of my service or me personally, and I was lucky I had no one that could write me a "Dear John."

When I wrote to my parents, I softened all my news. I wrote to them as often as I could (or was inclined), which was not very often—maybe once every two or three weeks, and I was extremely careful what I said to them. Here is an early—19 May 1969—and typical letter home:

Dear Folks,

Sorry I haven't written in so long but lately we have been very busy. I am with the troop now. It's really a great bunch of guys. I'm not on a tank yet, but ACAV (Armored Cavalry Assault Vehicle) and I am the commander. Since I have come here, I've only been in basecamp one night. The rest of the time we are out in the boonies—busting jungle.

At night we see fire-fights in the distance. It's a beautiful sight, until I think about what's actually going on out there. The most effective weapon seems to be the helicopter.

The people are what amaze me. I don't think I ever imagined such poverty. The Montagnards are primitive and the women go topless.

So far I've been to Bien Hoa, Long Binh, Di An, Lai Khe, Phouc Vinh, Quan Loi, and several small villages and hamlets. I am waiting to go to Saigon. They say it's nice.

Please excuse the dirt, but I'm sure you understand.

Love and miss ya,

Greg

It was rare that I knew exactly where we were. Alpha Troop traveled all over the map; we were always in motion. There were missions we had during that time that we would be repeating ad nauseam during my tour. Foremost among them was our role as ready reaction force, the fire brigade for the 1st Infantry Division. We would respond anywhere to other units who got into trouble, or those wanting to improve their odds dramatically. Often when Quarter Cav arrived on the scene the bad guys were already gone, probably because they heard us coming and were thereby convinced to withdraw from the battlefield. On occasion, however, we were had to force them out when they were not yet convinced to withdraw of their own accord.

When we were not responding to a call for help, we were providing security for Rome plows, road clearing teams, FSBs, or escorting the daily convoy from Lai Khe north to Quan Loi along QL13 (highway number 13, which we called Thunder Road). We might also troll for bad guys at times, in RIF mode (Reconnaissance-In-Force). When we had a target we began a search-and-destroy or a search-and-secure mission. When we had no specified target we would RIF, employing recon-by-fire in hopes the enemy would shoot back. If they did, we always tried to engage and eliminate them. We worked with mech (mechanized) infantry and straight-leg infantry frequently; we provided rides for the latter, and together we searched out our enemy.

A Rome plow, so called since it was made in Rome, Georgia, was a heavy bulldozer with protective cage for the driver and sharp dozer blade used to cut down trees. Their work enhanced road security by cutting the jungle back one hundred yards, reducing the ambush opportunity. In addition, Rome plows cleared vegetation in areas of likely enemy activity, such as known or suspected basecamps.

Chapter 8

Fake It till You Make It

I settled into a daily routine, trying mightily to overcome my inexperience and fear. I gained a little confidence with each new experience, and I began to comprehend what my role in-country was. I learned new things I had not previously even considered, but the respect I so craved had still to be earned.

Veterans at every level of stateside training warned us of our enemy the Viet Cong. They referred to him as Charlie, Sir Charles, Chuck, Victor Charles, or Vic. Those sobriquets were usually used to demonstrate otherwise unspoken respect, but it was the pejorative terms we used the most in-country. Those included Gooks, Dinks, Slants, Slopes, Zipperheads, and nonsensical mutterings on the occasion those standard offensive terms were not enough.

There was little mention during our training of the NVA. When I arrived in-country, we were fighting almost exclusively the NVA. VC were from the local area and were insurgents; the NVA were from North Vietnam and were a regularly trained and a much better equipped invading army. The Tet Offensive of 1968 had decimated the local VC units working within our AO. When I arrived in the spring of 1969, the NVA were carrying the weight of the battle against South Vietnam and their allied forces. Previously, the NVA had supported the VC by filling the holes in their ranks, or helping to launch an offensive. The few VC that we encountered used hit-and-run tactics against us, but the NVA stood and fought—at least for a while. We used the terms Charlie or Gook mostly, indicating either VC or NVA, with equal respect or loathing. I truly did not care what those people were called. Whoever they were, whatever their allegiance, they were all trying to kill us—and we, them. Sometimes when we stopped for our nightly NDP, a

Mad Minute would be called. For one minute all the guns fired madly into whatever woods, grass or brush was around us, hoping to "kill 'em all and let their god sort it out." At such times, moniker did not matter.

Whenever I felt clean (a relative thing), that would be the very moment a helicopter would select a location close to me as its landing spot. Anything unsecured or not heavy enough would be thrust into the air. As bad as a Huey was, it was better than a Chinook, a twin-rotor helicopter. Helicopters of many descriptions often landed nearby. They brought us fuel, ammo, food, mail, sodas and beer, and often infantry to join us on a mission. They also served as an ambulance for wounded men and a hearse for the dead.

We were working in some very tall grass once when we linked up with a Huey that had been dispatched to bring us the mail, sodas, and beer. The pilot refused to settle into the ACAV-high grass for landing. My ACAV was located in the best position to receive the delivery—what a trip that was. The door-gunner offloaded by passing several cases of drinks and the mailbag to my crew, who stood tall atop our ACAV. That pilot held his Huey in a near-perfect hover; excellent work. His load shifted as they offloaded the goods and as the door-gunner moved about, yet he held that bird firm as its centers of gravity and balance constantly changed. He had a gentle touch; the chopper barely swayed. It is amazing what the army does with kids.

The rainy season began in the middle of May; rain poured down for days, and the temperature turned cold. Normally, our daytime temperature would be on the high side of 100°F, but with the constant rain, temperatures remained in the sixties and seventies. We were freezing. After days of extreme cold (to us) and a perpetual overcast, the clearer weather returned. We were in a cycle of scattered showers, rather than the never-ending rain. The oppressive high heat and rainy season humidity increased our misery index. The one benefit we realized from the rain showers was to catch a sky-shower by standing naked in the rainfall. Some used soap, but I feared the rain would cease mid-rinse, and I would be left itching for days.

The volume of rain caused the previously dry, dusty soil to liquefy into a viscous mud. Left alone the mud was not a major problem, but when churned up by tanks and ACAVs repeatedly, we were left with a full-blown quagmire. FSB Mons III was like that when we secured it for a few nights. Walking was just about impossible where tracked vehicles had frequented. My ACAV was parked between a tank and a bunker that an infantry unit had built earlier. The structure would have been a fine bunker in the dry season (except for the rats), but not so much during the rainy season when it was flooded. I chose to stay on our dry ACAV where we could close or cover hatches to stay dry. We were more comfortable and much healthier for it.

Just before dark, I heard the tank beside us yell for Doc. The driver slid off their turret and hurt his back. We carried him on a stretcher into the center of our perimeter and the CP (Command Post). Several times along the way, we became stuck in the knee-high mud and dropped our patient. He screamed in pain. After dark, a Dustoff (medevac helicopter) arrived to transport him to the rear. The pilot was reluctant to land because of the quagmire, our antenna-laden CP, and the low overcast. Dustoff pilots often attempted what no other chopper pilots would; this one did and he landed safely. His approach and landing was one of the rare times I ever saw a chopper use its white light in the field. With the patient on board, takeoff was a non-event for both the pilot and for us, except for our being in the spotlight again while in the middle of enemy territory. One of our guys began a simulated tap dance, acting as if he were in the spotlight on stage. Only his arms moved, though, his lower half was locked in the mud up to his knees. He relieved my tension; the others had never been bothered at all by the event.

The tank driver recovered and became a jeep driver in Quarter Cav's rearmost basecamp at Di An.

We worked out of FSB Mons III for the next several days, RIFing the area, searching for bad guys during the daylight hours, and at night we secured the Mons III perimeter. Intel said enemy was all around us, and by our second night in residence our perimeter was probed. The probe was followed later by an attack. My very first—I lost my cherry. That night I swore I saw a few bad guys thirty meters away. Later, when I was more experienced, I determined it had merely been the darkness and vegetation playing tricks on me. My routine fear and my fear of shitting myself had added to my confusion. The bottom line, though, is I had fired in anger for the first time, and I was shot at for the first time (that I knew of). I had survived my baptism of fire, and my pants were clean(ish).

During the attack, we had aerial support from Spooky, a C-47 outfitted with mini-guns and flares. Spooky circled at low altitude, under cloud cover, and was invisible from the ground that night except when firing its mini-gun. What a show! I gained more respect for our aviation assets, given their skill at providing suppressing fire so close-in. Spooky's fire had been *very* close-in.

> *Uncle Jimmy was brilliant. That night, my very first close exposure to enemy fire, I was so worried about shitting myself I did not panic, and training came to the fore. I learned a basic lesson, and I understood the rule #1: "don't panic." That old master sergeant had given me the greatest lesson I could learn: the panic rule has universal application.*

I was still green and a little unsettled from the firefight as we busted jungle the next morning. We were moving to link up with an infantry unit that was to be inserted by Huey. Their LZ (Landing Zone) was deemed cold (no enemy activity was expected), but we RIF'd the area to be sure. A Cobra team normally circled overhead during an infantry unit's insertion. They could usually spot movement and deal with it while the grunts (infantrymen) were assembling to advance. When the transport choppers arrived, I marveled at the infantry's air delivery system. Of course I did—I was an aviation freak. The choppers lined up for the LZ at staggered altitudes and made their approaches. Once near ground, the infantry on board stood on the Huey's skids, ready to jump to the surface. The Hueys leveled off from a few inches to a few feet high; the grunts jumped, and then the choppers pitched nose down and climbed to rejoin the other empty birds. Quite a sight, and colorful, too, from the smoke used to mark the landing location.

Sometimes a Huey would appear to be crashing as its center of balance shifted when the grunts were jumping off. That was interesting and very entertaining to watch. As an aviator, I know that a chopper pilot was always on the edge of losing control of his aircraft. It was not due to poor flying skills, but due to the inherent instability of helicopters and a shifting load. Chopper pilots are to be shown respect if only for their ability to manage multiple tasks using each of their limbs in concert.

We often worked with Hunter-Killer teams: an OH-6 Cayuse scout helicopter (Hunter), and an AH-1 Cobra attack helicopter (Killer). I loved watching those guys work. Others did not like it so much for what it meant—bad things were about to come our way. Sometimes when we had grunts on board our tracks, we stood back while the Hunter-Killer team worked over an area. Other times we RIF'd by busting jungle, while the Hunter reconned the area ahead of us. The Killer circled overhead as a raptor seeking prey, watching out for the Hunter, his little bird, ready for the kill. As the Hunter flew among the treetops, all eyes on board were in search of enemy movement or signs of recent activity.

Those Hunter pilots were insane. They would drop down into a mid-jungle clearing to get an eye-level view into the wood line. Occasionally, a Hunter would descend into the jungle and then, within seconds, he was in a nearly vertical ascent escaping ground fire. When the Killer saw or heard the Hunter receiving fire, or knew he had a target, he was already rolling in on that target with rocket and/or gunfire. Cool stuff when watched from a safe distance. We were often very close to the Hunter in action, but he was often eyeball-to-eyeball with the enemy we all sought.

Mail was something that most of us awaited like kids on Christmas morning. It was always good to hear from home and friends, but it was not easy for us to write every day. When we had down time, we could catch up on our outgoing letters. Keeping the mail flowing was extremely critical to our emotional well-being, and sometimes there were problems with delivery. The rain had fallen hard most of one day, and we anticipated getting a hot evening meal in the field and some fresh mail. (We reread letters frequently.) One platoon established an NDP while the others continued to RIF nearby. A Huey dropped off his load and departed, leaving it in a wet, marshy area in the center of the NDP. Our mailbag had been dropped into a puddle. It was common in 1969 to use felt-tip pens for writing informally; they made attractive and colorful letters. Writers did not consider that felt-tip ink was not water fast. That day, some of the mail was illegible after getting wet. I recovered enough of two of my letters to know who had sent them. Others were not so fortunate. Later, I remember seeing plastic inside the canvas. I do not recall seeing it there before, but maybe it was only left out of the bag on that day. How many of us lost touch with friends because letters were never answered?

The last day of May found second platoon securing FSB Thunder I overnight. My daytime mission was to take my ACAV to OP 25 (Observation Post 25)—an observation tower located between Thunder I and Thunder II—and observe, searching for bad guys. After ensuring the tower had not been booby-trapped, we all climbed up to check out the area. Our canvas of the immediate area found no enemy and no signs of recent activity, so we relaxed and wrote letters home. After initial trouble with my mail finding me, it was finally flowing properly, and I needed to catch up on return-letter writing. I adapted the approach of trying to write letters home whenever we halted and were to remain in place for a while. As with most guys having a circle of friends back in "the World," I was constantly bombarded with questions. During that time in May, a 101st Airborne Division battle was all over the news at home. That prompted the question, "Are you on Hamburger Hill?" I discovered no one back home had a clue about the war in Vietnam, except those who had come before us.

As June began, we worked the area along QL13 from Ben Cat north to Quan Loi again. We made thunder runs, a non-ordinance H&I (Harassment and Interdiction) effort, by traveling fast and making our presence known up and down the road; we wanted to draw an attack if there were enemy nearby. Sometimes we would RIF along the jungle's edge, and often we went jungle busting. For the remainder of my tour, as we passed through, by, or near any area that afforded any protection to enemy forces, we were hyper-alert to ambush. Occasionally, a lone NVA/VC might launch an RPG round at us from behind. It usually missed, I think. I cannot remember a hit. They caused us much consternation. As quickly as they fired, they disappeared into thick jungle. Tanks were too cumbersome to pivot quickly and counter-attack. We always responded with heavy fire, after which a dismounted patrol was dispatched to search for wounded or dead. It was normal to find no evidence of their presence, but we knew they were there and probably still watching us.

We routinely formed two columns when busting jungle, a tank leading each column. We drove through the jungle trees toward our intended target. When a tank was unable to continue because of a large tree or thick vegetation, it backed up a few feet, fired a couple of canister rounds to clear the area of the problem, or just drove around it. Tank canister rounds were like large shotgun rounds, and anything in their way would yield, except for the largest trees and termite mounds. Most trees could be knocked down and driven over, but when a tree was too large, we would go around it. Some hefty trees were felled that way, and the wood was left to rot. The NVA probably made use of some of it, but the Vietnamese loggers would not come into some of the areas we busted. I would be willing to bet they recovered much of it after the Americans left and the locals made a fortune. I have often wondered what exotic woods we cavalierly trashed. Teak? Mahogany? Certainly those, and we probably ruined many more types, as well.

On occasion, a village seal was required. The idea was to surround a suspect village, preventing the enemy's departure overland and to insert ground teams to search for weapons and enemy personnel. Our role was that of armored perimeter fence. Late one afternoon we sealed a suspect village for the night. Although there was not activity overnight affecting my sector of the perimeter, there was activity in and around the village.

Still very much an FNG, my imagination continued to run wild. My track was parked next to a large mound, one that initially seemed to be merely old dirt. What was it? It was much bigger than the huge termite mounds I had seen. Someone told me that my mound was some sort of ancestral burial mound. Apart from it just being creepy, I worried that one or more NVA/VC could assault me from the cover the mound afforded them. I was freaked-out by the whole thing and failed to realize for a while that there was another track just on the other side of that mound. Surely, he would see and dispatch any assailant. Right?

When the time came for my guard that night, I took my place in the cupola, ensuring all weapons were combat ready. The last one I checked was our thump-gun, the M-79 grenade launcher. We used two types of rounds: our standard, an HE (High Explosive) round, and an anti-personnel round that contained shot. I noticed the breech was open and a round loaded. In my FNG wisdom, I closed the breech.

Thoomp!

An HE round left the gun.

"Day-yum motherfucker! Are you trying to kill me, new guy?"

Joe, whom I replaced on guard, was standing on the

front end of the track taking a leak when the round bounced off the deck and flew past his head.

"Keep that thing open until you need to use it. It ain't shit for safe while it's closed," he chided.

He was startled, as was I, but he did not seem overly bothered. Similar events were too common.

"Sorry, Joe. Really, I am."

I was embarrassed, and I assured him I had learned my lesson and would not be repeating my mistake. I silently longed for a day when I no longer felt like a total FNG. Surely, someday I would gain the requisite experience to allow myself some in-country confidence. Most of the time, though, I felt as if I wore a large red ball on my nose.

During my guard that night, I contemplated what might have been—I could have killed or very seriously injured Joe. What would have happened if an anti-personnel round had been loaded instead? Joe would have been toast. What if I had placed that HE round squarely into a hooch, killing the family inside? Luckily, an HE round needed to travel a set distance while rotating to arm itself. When the one I let go hit the deck of our ACAV, it stopped the rotation and prevented its arming. Joe was lucky—I was an idiot. I have no memory what we did with that unexploded HE round at daybreak, if we did anything. I hope some kid did not play with it, and/or that it was not used against us.

My ACAV's tracks had shown signs of wear for some time and needed to be replaced. A pair of brand new ACAV tracks arrived by our resupply helicopter late one day, after we began to set up our NDP. I viewed the tracks as a present to the entire crew. New tracks would make our lives much easier; we had spent too much time manhandling tracks back onto the drive sprocket. Not only was it not so much fun and physically taxing, but it could be life threatening, too. By the time we got the new tracks off-loaded and dragged into the security of our perimeter, it was just about dark. I was ready to get the job done at first light the next morning, but First Sergeant Poncerella convinced me otherwise. (First sergeants are traditionally referred to as "Top," short for "top sergeant," since they are the highest-ranking NCO at company level.)

"You need to go ahead now and get them changed out ASAP," Top advised. "It's important."

I did not want to do them ASAP; I wanted to be safe. My concern was the noise we would surely make and the light we needed to do the work.

"But what about noise and light discipline? Wouldn't it be safer at dawn? It wouldn't take us very long," I said.

"Nope. Do it now. It's gotta get done ASAP. We have an early date."

Immediately, I got a sense it *was* important. Besides, Top had spoken and he was the boss.

"Wilco, Top." (Wilco indicates, "I will comply.")

I was not totally convinced, but I planned to do the best I could. I returned to my track and instructed the crew to move our ACAV to NDP center where the tracks were, and we would get to work. They complained, but I informed them of what I knew, and that there must be a good reason. We tried to hold the noise to a minimum, but it was impossible given that we were banging steel with steel and that we started up, idled, and revved the engine a few times. When we absolutely had to use a light, we tried to shield our work and ourselves as much as possible. We used it sparingly. There *were* side benefits; the Southeast Asian sun was not pounding down on us, and it did not take us as long as it would have in daylight under safer conditions. Still, I would have preferred to change them in daylight.

At first light, we promptly cranked up and moved out of our NDP, scarfing down C-Rats on the fly. We did not go far until we halted. That action was typical: often we would wait for another unit for a combined operation, or we might await coordination with Higher (our next higher authority) before moving out to an objective. Lounging around, we enjoyed the fresh start to a new day, with a guard for security. We did not stray too far from our vehicle in case of a movement order or, horrors, an attack. Before long, all track commanders were summoned to the platoon leader's track.

"Guys, we are in for some fun this morning," Mike Six said. "In about fifteen minutes there'll be an Arc Light (B-52 bombing mission) strike just a few meters from where we NDP'd last night. As soon as the last bomb falls, we'll return for a BDA (Bomb Damage Assessment), capture any dazed or wounded enemy, and get a body count. If there are surviving bunkers or tunnels, we'll check them out and blow them. Each track will dismount one crewman." Then, almost as an afterthought, he exclaimed, "Button up when told. We are at the *minimum* safe distance from the target." (Button up means to close hatches.)

We returned to our vehicles and informed our crews to prepare for the festivities. Curiously, the attitude of my crew was, "No shit? Far out!" As for me, I was hoping those air *farce* guys aimed correctly. Soon the platoon net crackled with a call.

"All Mike vehicles, Mike Six, mount up ASAP. Button up. I say again, button up."

The platoon leader alerted us, and we all responded our compliance. We waited; it seemed like forever. There was the usual gallows humor from all.

"Hurry up! If I'm a-gonna die make it quick, but please, you high-flying motherfuckers comfortable up there in the air-conditioning—aim good. Ya hear me? I'm not ready to go."

We laughed nervously. None of my crew had experienced being so close to a bombing strike before, and we hoped our trust was not misplaced. Then all hell broke loose. It started with a long rumble in the distance, growing in intensity, and getting ever closer to us. The sound was loud and powerful—very frightening. They were long rolling rumbles. The bombing *did* sound like thunder rolling. (The Rolling Thunder bombing campaign had ended a few months prior.) The bombs shook my ACAV fiercely, lifting it. We were bounced in our seats for what seemed like forever, until the rumbling ceased. We did not dare open our hatches. All I could think was, "Wow! *That really was interesting.*" I hoped no NVA was on my ACAV just waiting to drop in a grenade. An Arc Light mission was very destructive, but I wondered if that one was thorough enough. When the order came to unbutton, we did so very carefully. I checked out my track and saw that the deck was OK. It was dirty but OK. I continued my visual search, finding no enemy. The two ACAVs on either side of me were clear of any enemy. There were no NVA or VC on any track. Whew!

We moved out to accomplish the BDA, and were on-site within a few minutes. The earth and its vegetation that was so violently churned up had not fully settled; some of the lighter debris still casually floated down. We drove around craters that were fifteen to twenty feet across and ten or so feet deep. Our tank drivers had to be very cautious, lest they fall into a crater and roll over. Their job was challenging given their size, their weight, and the instability of the surface in the target area. ACAVs traveled much easier. We searched for survivors and bodies, and I counted zero. I could not identify any bunker, and captured no prisoners. Others in the unit did. The condition of the area convinced me that I never wanted to be on the business end of an Arc Light mission. This was the point when I made an about-face. I thereafter became a much better, and eventually a good soldier.

When we stopped within walking distance of a village or hamlet, or in some cases within driving distance, several young women would appear out of nowhere. I learned quickly, mostly because I was paying very close attention, that they were short-time girls—an apt handle. With the requisite two dollars MPC, a short-time girl could be yours for a short time.

"GI want short-time? Baby-san, numba one. You like?"

Each woman would market her specialty. Up and down the entire line of vehicles they went, if allowed, introducing themselves to every guy they found until one accepted. More than one usually did. If no one was interested, we heard calls of, "GI numba ten!" When a girl finished one soldier, she would clean up a little and then go for another. Enterprising girls they were, but hardly hygienic. The rumor was that we could catch "black syph."

"I don't mess with them gals," one trooper said.

"Pussy," was the response from the other. "You don't like girls? We could get you a short-time *boy* if you like."

"Yeah, I like girls. Have you seen my girlfriend?" the first one asked.

"No. Is she round-eye?"

The first trooper pulled out a black and white Polaroid picture: female, about twenty, very attractive, and very naked. Then he produced another; the second was gyno-graphic.

"Wow. Hot. Yes...I certainly would," the second one said.

"No, you won't. She's why I won't get with them gals. I don't want the black syph." He pointed to the pictures. "I want to go home and get on her a lot more than I want a few minutes with them whores. They're nasty."

"What's the black syph?" I asked.

They told me it was a strain of syphilis so devastating that if we got it we would be relegated to life on an island off the coast of South Vietnam, never seeing our country or loved ones again. (It was a lie; we were young, remember.)

"Heard of a rubber, doofus? Solves that problem."

These two, in their extremes, were the exception. The clap (gonorrhea) was not rare, and a few of the guys would suffer the disease repeatedly. One fellow, whom I will not name, not long after purchasing two dollars MPC-worth, screamed as he urinated. He would go to Doc for medication to clear up his clap. Once cured, he again indulged and began his screaming cycle anew.

One of our senior NCOs, who had been in the army since Korea, was very amusing to watch. He was often the first to claim a short-time girl. (It is true that rank has its privileges.) After making a verbal contract, he would grab a stretcher and head for some sort of cover, usually a shrub. A few minutes later, he would emerge from the cover, the stretcher folded and thrown over his shoulder, and he would climb back on his tank, refreshed. The woman immediately went back to work soliciting another customer. I found the stretcher curious, since most guys were not so particular.

They did not care whether it was on dirt, an ACAV floor, standing up or just receiving oral sex. The younger ones were not concerned about the audience, whether appreciative or harassing. Those younger guys had no trouble focusing. Why did I? Since arriving in-country, I had been force-focused, and the ability to focus was starting to stick with me.

Since we were a unit needed throughout the division AO, it did not make any sense for us to return to basecamp often. We had need for ammunition and fuel almost every day, so our mess hall would hitch a ride with resupply when they could. Almost daily, when it was time to set up our NDP, a Chinook helicopter arrived with a sling load of ammo, fuel bladders and—we always hoped—hot food onboard. I always enjoyed those hot meals when they came out to us. The real treat for me was the fresh, cold Foremost brand milk, a brand I knew from "the World." I would take a quart and savor the whole thing. Delivery sometimes included chocolate milk, as well. We really appreciated the small pleasures.

When we were not enjoying a hot meal, we ate C-rats. We opened the cans with a P-38 opener (supplied with each meal), which some guys wore around their necks. Another opener, the B-52, was the standard bottle and can opener routinely referred to in "the World" as a "church key." Built-in opening devices had not yet found their way onto cans in those days, so both P-38 and a B-52 were critical items to a field trooper.

I learned to appreciate only some of the C-Rations, or more correctly, components of those meals. The only meal I never opened a second time was ham and lima beans. We mostly ate C-Rats right out of the can, but we appreciated them more when we heated them. They were even better when we added hot sauce or mixed them with other foods. Two tank track end-connectors made an excellent platform over which to warm a C-Rat can; C-4 provided the heat. C-4 was an ideal fire source as it burned continuously and at a constant temperature, and with a flame that was short and broad. It was readily available. C-Rats were mostly for snacks and other meals, but not always. Some nights, due to mission constraints, we consumed C-Rats instead of a mess hall hot meal.

Occasionally, there were replacement personnel, R&R returnees (rest and relaxation), recovered wounded, parts, or other goodies coming to us, as well. A few times, I unhooked the sling from underneath a hovering Chinook, hoping the huge aircraft would not get shot down or experience some sort of malfunction. I stopped doing that after the novelty was gone, but my shoot-down concerns did not abate.

I learned just what the derisive term REMF meant (Rear Echelon Mother Fucker). There were uncooperative and not sympathetic rear-echelon soldiers who enjoyed screwing over field troops—they were REMFs. Not every rear-echelon soldier was a REMF. Not by a long shot. For instance, if a guy served time in the field and then landed a rear job, or if he had been wounded, recovered in-country and stayed in the rear, he would not necessarily be a REMF. When anyone stationed in the rear gave any field soldier grief just because he was able to, or was simply not cooperative when he otherwise could have been, then he was a REMF. Most guys in the rear were helpful and thankful of their rear-echelon status; a few were idiots. Fewer still were REMFs and deliberately or carelessly added to field troopers' misery. REMFs magnified a trooper's discomfort—because they could. Yes, the entire spear should be held in high regard, but is the fighting tip that should be held in the highest.

Only twice while I was there did second platoon receive SPs (Sundries Packs). They contained items like bootlaces, shaving cream and razors, toothpaste, cartons of cigarettes, paperback books—things we never had enough of in the field or did not get in our C-Rat meals. I am sure the spirit of an SP was for the field troops first, but since I saw only two in the field, my guess is the REMFs enjoyed them, too. Perhaps someone was making a profit on the black market.

I recall one of our Kit Carson Scouts (a former enemy working for our side) taking cartons of L&M cigarettes from an SP home on three-day leave. Nobody smoked L&Ms except my grandmother, and she was not in-country. When he came back, each pack of those L&Ms had been opened, the tobacco taken out, and marijuana put in. The Vietnamese had a taste for our American tobacco, and GIs had a taste for Vietnam's cannabis. Yes, I did—off-duty and only when we were in very secure *rear* areas.

The opposite of a REMF were the troopers who felt more at home in the field in spite of the danger. A career NCO we had, Pappy Guy, was such an example. I do not know his real story, but I believe he had been a combat soldier in WWII and Korea. He seemed to revel in the work, virtually *never* going to rear. I was told he arrived with the division four years earlier and only left Vietnam to visit his wife in Hawaii once a year. The field was at times *extremely* dangerous, miserable, never comfortable, and we were out there twenty-four hours a day, seven days a week. There was no one I knew of as dedicated to the field as Pappy Guy, but most I knew preferred the field to the bullshit a soldier experienced in the rear, especially when it emanated from REMFs.

In Vietnam, I realized the distinction between a lifer and a career soldier. There were soldiers who found a home in the army. As long as they had "three hots and a cot" they were happy and only wanted to feed at the easy trough. They were lifers. However, many more believed in military work and were professional in their actions, whether theirs was a support role or one of closing with and destroying the enemy. Whether their work was for career, country, employer, mission, or the guys whom they were supporting, they were career soldiers.

Each of Alpha Troop's platoons worked independently usually, but on occasion with another platoon. Rarely would the entire troop be together. We teamed up with first platoon, led by LT Jack Tinsley, so often that we really got to know those guys well. A few of them became good friends, just as my Armor School classmate Jon Laird had become. We rarely worked with third platoon, but I got to know and respected them, too. We were all Quarter Cav and took great pride in that, so, naturally, we all were the best of the best. We had high unit esprit de corps.

Our third platoon's leader was a Hungarian, LT Zoltan Szabo, who left Hungary after the 1956 uprising against the Soviet-backed government, came to the U.S., and joined the army. By the time I met him in May of 1969, he was a First Lieutenant serving as the platoon leader for third platoon. (He later was promoted to captain prior to going home.) From my perspective at the time, LT Szabo was a competent combat leader with the respect of all the men in his troop.

I wondered what his real story was. What had he done to leave Hungary? Did he leave his family? Was it dangerous to escape? I never asked.

Chapter 9

The Ominous Reality

On 9 June 1969, the first mission we were assigned was to provide security for Rome plows while they cut away jungle. The plows worked a staggered line, the first plow making his cut, and the remaining plows each following just inboard of the first, at safe but close intervals. We were offset just a few meters beside the plows and on the new cut, moving in a racetrack pattern and shifting in their direction as they cut down each new swath.

Although my sleeping on guard duty problem had begun to abate, I continued to sleep at inappropriate times. One such time was that morning while we monotonously rode alongside Rome plows as their security. I really should have been paying attention and actually providing security, yet I nodded off in my cupola. I was awakened by one of my crew. When I turned to see what he wanted, he pointed to an ACAV passing us in the opposite direction. The TC on that track was Sergeant Donald Smith, one of second platoon's other Shake 'n Bakes, and the one who was very much on my case about pretty much everything. He shook his head showing his disdain, and as they passed, he shouted to me, "Stay alert, you damn fool." He did not care much for me, and I did not think very highly of him at that moment. Nope, not at all. He may have been—OK, he *was*—correct, but I sure as hell did not like his methods. I flipped him off, only after he passed of course, but I did remain awake as we continued to drone on.

LT Armstrong called with a mission change. A road clearing team was ambushed, and we were minutes away. Upon arrival, we found that two APCs (Armored Personnel Carriers) were struck by RPGs. They suffered one KIA and two WIA (Wounded In Action).

We assembled to follow the designated lead tank in one

of two columns. Upon our arrival, one of our ACAVs moved to aid the wounded, and the remainder of us went hunting for the ambushers along both sides of the road. We reconned by fire, shooting into the grass and wood line at no particular target, but hoping to score a kill. I was firing my Fifty—Ma Deuce. She was a wonderful friend in battle and suitable for a myriad of targets, but she was terribly persnickety about her headspace and timing. If they were not set properly, then the machine gun was useless. Such was my luck that morning. Unfortunately, that was not an opportune time to remove the back plate and adjust the headspace and timing. My Fifty was dead, and I was not sending rounds downrange, so I pulled up my M-16 and rejoined the fray. I pressed back against the cupola hatch cover in an effort to steady myself, and I began to fire on full automatic (Rock-'n-Roll).

We were placing heavy fire into the wood line as we moved rapidly, parallel to it. Every fifth round was a tracer, chemically treated to glow at its base to aid in aiming, and they ignited the dry, tall grass. The ride was very rough. I was tossed about my cupola; more than one bump was so bad that I came completely off my seat. We hit one bump as I was firing my M-16 on automatic, and a burst went wildly into the air. When I fell back onto my seat, I shot a single round right through my own gun shield. Imagine my surprise. That shield was there to deflect small arms fire—it did not. A tiny piece of metal lodged in my left leg above the knee, but it did not bleed. We continued to recon-by-fire for a while longer, with no results. There were calls of "Gooks on the loose," but I never saw any enemy that morning.

BOOM!

We all immediately turned in the direction of the blast and knew what happened without being told. The sound and the image were very familiar—one of our vehicles had hit a mine. It was a relatively small mine, and no one was hurt. The ACAV involved suffered only lost road wheels and broken track. Mines, tree mounted claymores, and booby-traps were an all too common occurrence for us. Sometimes they were deadly, sometimes they were seriously injurious, other times they were benign. They always caused at least a little damage to our vehicles and property, and they always induced fear—if only an apprehension of encountering one.

"All vehicles...Mike-6. Maintain a perimeter around the disabled track, facing out. Keep your eyes open. We may get some company."

Guys from several vehicles dismounted immediately and walked to the disabled track about one hundred feet or so behind my track. I do not know either why or how it came to be, but several guys were milling around the blast area. John Holland, one of my track's gunners, was dismounted and one of them.

"Look at this," I said to the remaining gunner, as I turned to him and pointed to a hole in my gun shield. He pulled his eyelid as though he had something in his eye.

"Hell, that must be why I am almost blind," he said.

"Is it okay? Your eye?" I asked.

"I can see, but it feels like something's in there."

I checked and saw nothing except irritation, but I was still concerned. I sure as hell did not want to have blinded him.

"I don't see anything. Flush it out and let's get Doc to check it." I did not want to take a chance. "Don't rub it!"

BOOM!

The second blast was louder than the first, indicating a much larger charge. We turned to face the disabled track and saw a grey-black cloud rising from the center of activity. We felt its pressure wave, even though it was mostly dissipated by the distance. Without question, we knew it was a second mine. Even with my lack of experience, my FNG proclivities, and my lack of a sight line to the detonation, I knew the mine had been devastating; it was too big a blast and at the center of activity. Out of the smoke and debris, I saw SFC Saunders stagger away from the blast area. LT Armstrong grabbed him around his shoulders and helped him to the rear of a track. His wounds looked very serious, and he was having trouble breathing. LT Armstrong and others dressed his wounds and comforted him until he was treated and evacuated.

"Stay alert! Watch for movement. These may have been command-det mines." (Detonated on command, such as when the enemy saw an opportunity.)

We could not see the blast site from my track because the command track was directly in our line of sight. I could see there was frenetic activity in the immediate area where the smoke had just risen. There were guys up and moving around uninjured, so my crew stayed put and guarded our front, hoping that we would hear good news. Our radio net was mostly silent; it was eerie. We were apprehensive, scared, awaiting information on casualties. There were sure to be many and some had to be severe. Our close proximity without any information only made our discomfort worse.

Within minutes, multiple Dustoffs came to carry away our wounded. I recall there being over a dozen WIA who were evacuated, and some wounds must have been grave. There was such a serious medical need that our squadron surgeon flew out to the site to help our medic, and I am sure he brought other help. Our medic—Doc Witwicki, the squadron surgeon and others provided aid as best they could. Doc had been very close to the blast and had some minor shrapnel wounds himself. (In the following days, his non-serious wounds looked like blackheads or boils covering his entire chest, stomach, and arms.) After that morning, Doc was quiet and reflective for a few days. We missed his irreverent humor.

John Holland had also been very close to the blast, right behind someone who died, yet he suffered no visible wounds. He remained to help the wounded and the dead, suffering the carnage up close. When he returned to our track after the WIA had been flown out, he was at first agitated and shook uncontrollably. I was told a week before about an operation in the Michelin Rubber Plantation three months earlier when John had narrowly escaped death, and his friends right next to him had not. I requested he be sent to the rear. John stayed with us that day, but thereafter his duties were in Lai Khe. He never came back to the field.

Four second platoon men were KIA that morning:

> PFC Johnnie J. Carraway
> PFC Larry R. Jenkins
> SP5 William R. Gregory
> SGT Donald R. Smith

The four KIA were placed inside the disabled ACAV, and it was prepared for retrieval. Our VTR joined us and towed the track to our motor pool at Lai Khe. I have often wondered how the ambient heat of the day and the heat from the 1000 hp engine exhaust of the VTR affected the remains inside that buttoned up ACAV. I was thankful I did not find out. That day's event instantly reduced our manpower by fifty percent. We reshuffled our crews, and in the days to come we received replacements to restore our platoon as a fighting element.

Sergeant Smith was the Shake 'n Bake who had been on my case ever since I joined Quarter Cav. I regret that we never reconciled, given his problems with me were fair and of my making. I was a better soldier because of his uncompromising insistence that I measure up. The morning of 9 June ensured that I received his message posthumously, loud and clear. It was a vivid reality check. Thereafter, I was wide-awake with a new perspective: it really was for keeps.

For the next few weeks we escorted convoys, secured FSBs, RIF'd, and occasionally busted jungle. On 22 June, we withdrew from the field to Lai Khe to perform our quarterly maintenance program. Any standdown was a vacation—we were in a secure basecamp, received three hot meals daily, took showers, enjoyed outhouses, saw movies, visited the dispensary for medical complaints, and shopped at the Lai Khe PX. Sighting a "round-eye" (non-Asian) woman was its own very special reward, since we only ever saw indigenous women out in the field.

One evening there were a few of us fully absorbed in general BS when Top joined in the conversation. Naturally, the BS ceased immediately. He engaged me, in particular, in a chat that surprised me.

"I'm an old army NCO," he began. "I started in the brown boot army, and I do things mostly the old army way. I was taught when a superior says jump...you ask 'How high?' on the way up, and then smartly carry out the command. I recognize your generation doesn't work that way...younger troopers want to know the reasons why."

"We do...and *when* we do we're better motivated," I said. "Sometimes the dumb, ignorant view is the clearest view."

Top seemed to agree, nodding in acceptance.

"But men must show respect to superiors and carry out their instructions. No way around that," he said, "You have an ability to communicate very effectively along the chain of command and get missions accomplished."

"Doc" Witwicki at Lai Khe during Quarterlies.

I shrugged, very surprised, and a little embarrassed.

"I've never noticed, Top. I respect others and lead with

nice...they get back what they give. I know I have the weight of regulations behind me if I need them, and so do they. I'd rather not need it. I hope they'll respect me...if not, it's a case of respect the rank. But I'd really prefer they respect me."

We continued to make small talk until he left for bed. I had no clue why Top had singled me out, and why we were discussing my communication abilities. Maybe it was the way I handled the track change the night before the Arc Light strike. For whatever reason, an "atta boy" was nice, especially after feeling so incompetent for so long. I was beginning to find a new me, and my confidence soared. I was starting to feel competent and trusted.

A 2-holer, shit burning and a pisser on right.

There were urinals (pissers) and outhouses (shitters) that were strategically placed around our troop area. Urinals were a fifty-five gallon drum filled with gravel and buried. My first sighting of an American woman occurred while I relieved myself just outside our troop orderly room. She was an army nurse and wandered by within just a few feet of me. I recall wondering if I should salute or not. We did not usually salute troop level officers, but seeing her made a difference. I chose not to. We exchanged pleasantries while I was exposed and urinating!

The outhouses were multi-holers, and below each hole was a cut-down fifty-five gallon drum on a slab. When we were fortunate, the receptacle had just been cleaned. If not, we enjoyed one of the perfumes of Vietnam. We were lucky at least one local Mama-San had been hired to "burn shit." Yep, she would remove the drum when full, add kerosene, alight, and stir. The smell was terrible. When I first witnessed shit burning, I thought back to high school and *Macbeth*—"Double, double toil and trouble; Fire burn and cauldron bubble." I was warned that sometimes Mama San might begin her task by pulling out the container, chattering away, no doubt a warning for the occupant to cease all operations.

At the end of June and well into July, we continued the same operations we were performing before Quarterlies. We worked the area along QL13 (on and off-road) from Ben Cat to Quan Loi, RIFing, making thunder runs frequently, busting jungle, securing vulnerable sections of roadway and escorting convoys.

While we were off-road RIFing, we carefully maneuvered around bomb craters in a heavily bombed area. It was still the rainy season, and the craters were full of muddy water. One crater became our swimming hole. We had halted for a while and immediately took advantage. We moved a tank closer to the crater, traversed and elevated the main gun, and positioned it center-crater. A few of us climbed the barrel and jumped in. One fool dove in. What fun it was! What leeches? There must have been, but I do not recall any.

I found convoy duty to be very easy duty as long as our equipment continued to work, and we were not stuck in an ambush kill zone. High speeds did keep us cooler, but the dirt we churned up made us orange, including the backs of our teeth. At the turnaround point, Quan Loi, we usually had a refreshing break because our parking was among the rubber trees, and that afforded us shade. Sometimes we rested for a few hours while waiting for the trucks to offload. Those naps were briefly restorative, but we needed more sleep.

Road convoys hauled fuel for ground and air vehicles, ammunition, food, personnel—anything. They were always a high-value target, and it was not very difficult for NVA/VC ambushers to score a truck kill or two, but they could not stop the constant flow of materiél. Small-scale ambushes were frequent, and every once in a while the enemy made a significant effort to destroy an entire convoy. Earlier, on 6 June, there was a monster ambush of a Lai Khe-Quan Loi convoy where Quarter Cav was providing security. My platoon was not involved, and from the stories I have heard, I am happy to have missed it.

B-52 bomb crater providing field recreation.

On a few occasions when my ACAV was on the tail end of a huge convoy, we would pass through the kill zone of an ambush that had been sprung earlier. Sometimes a fuel truck or two had been hit, and they would still be burning as we passed. Other times I was at or near the front of the convoy and parked in the rubber to cool off, awaiting our return trip, when elements arriving later said they had been ambushed at a place we had driven through unscathed. I was happy I was not an ammunition or fuel truck driver on convoy duty. That could not have been good duty. I was nervous just being near them when we passed through one of several ambush alleys on Thunder Road.

We liked providing security for an FSB, as it usually meant hot food, showers, and, not least of all, shitters. The downside was the rats, *giant* rats. Every FSB older than a day had them. The rats knew precisely when a new FSB was built, the location and the layout. They were merely waiting for a U.S. unit to occupy it. Some guys liked the safety of an FSB bunker to sleep in, but I had heard too many stories of rat bites from those who slept in one. I much preferred a stretcher, a camping cot or when I finally got on a tank, the back deck or bustle rack. I found medical litters comfortable until I sampled an aluminum camping cot—a must have. I know it was a relative thing, but I had some splendid sleeps on a camping cot wearing only my pants and covered in a poncho liner. For rain protection, we slept under lean-tos fashioned out of a poncho. I took off my boots at night, since I was no longer in any danger of them freezing. My feet thanked me for it and so did my boots—they had time to dry out from my sweaty feet.

We arrived late one night at Thunder I FSB. Usually there was a hot meal for the unit providing security for the artillery in residence. We were not happy that they did not provide us one; we were hungry for real food. Things usually have a way of working themselves out, especially in the army. In the early morning hours, a single-man requisition party made entrance to the artillery's field mess and liberated a single canned ham. Imagine my surprise the next day after we pulled out of the FSB, and I was informed such a delicacy was on board. We enjoyed that ham a great deal, and I asked no questions. I did not want to know anything about it—I might be forced to discipline someone.

It may have been on that day that a news crew was with us. There were two males: one a cameraman and the other a reporter. The reporter was not a then-current household name; he may have become one later, and I do not remember what his name was. (Many older and now-retired TV news guys made their newsman bones in Vietnam.) We joked their only use to us was to report our ham liberation of the prior night, such that it might result in our receiving a higher level of field catering.

Our creature comforts were few in the field. We got along with what we carried on and inside our tracks, or that which we could liberate from another unit, like a ham. Our ACAVs made good use of jeep seats for the gunners to ride on top—most units outside Quarter Cav used full C-Ration boxes as seats. Ice was always in very short supply, and when it was not supplied to us, we would buy from the locals when we could find it. I once paid ten dollars MPC for a case of bottled Pepsi—I guess I needed the sugar. I must have needed it so much that I ignored the admonition not to drink the locally bottled beverages. The rumor was the VC put ground glass in the bottle. That must not have been true—at least for my purchase—as I suffered no gastric complaints.

The field also provided plenty of entertainment. The aforementioned fuck-you lizard and an assortment of very strange insects were interesting. So were mosquitoes that could have been used as an armed escort for an Arc Light mission. They were the largest, most aggressive skeeters I have ever seen. And the ants. Ants? No big deal, right? Wrong. The little red critters would clamp onto your skin and double back on themselves at their mid-body joint. They hurt. Busting jungle was especially fun when ants were knocked off the foliage and onto the vehicle. It was hilarious to watch as a vehicle crew stripped completely naked, all the while brushing ants away and smacking at them with whatever they could find. (It was funny as long as it was not happening to my crew or to me.) The insect repellent that was issued to us was worthless against red ants.

Civilian buses, ancient cars, Lambrettas (three-wheel utility vehicles), and motorcycles provided us endless hours of entertainment. The Vietnamese civilians managed to pack everything on their vehicles: chickens, ducks, or bicycles. Just about anything they wanted to. Periodically a crowded bus would pull over to the roadway shoulder and passengers would get out and walk a few steps to relieve themselves—very publicly, both men *and* women. Today I still see a young woman with her baby slung across her back and her straw hat cocked rearward, as she squatted, pulling her pants leg aside and urinating. I certainly was in a different place.

We traveled the countryside both off-road and on using unimproved roads, improved but unpaved roads, and very rarely a paved road. Our environment was rural—Vietnam rural. We passed through primitive villages and hamlets, some friendly, some not so pleasant, and some apathetic. Kids were always lining the roadway waving and begging in hopes of scoring a C-Ration item, usually one that none of us would ever eat. When we halted nearby, they would steal anything they could. It was sad to see them begging, stealing, and fighting for our trash and other discards.

It was not unusual to pass through a town, village, or hamlet and see a few VC bodies lying in the street near the activity center. We suspected that the bodies were awaiting family pickup. Out in the remote areas where a firefight or battle had recently taken place, it was routine to see body parts—legs, arms, feet—just a few steps away from the village hooches. Children often were at play nearby just as if nothing was unusual.

Our vehicles were constantly in motion, but our bladder relief was not to be denied. If we were cruising along at road speed, such as when on convoy duty, an ACAV crewman could open the ramp door at the rear, fight the dust, and go. A tanker would have to step down off the turret, holding onto the turret's grab rail or bustle rack, hang over a bit his back to the wind, and let fly. It was fun to watch, but not so much fun to do—it was usually only tried once. Drivers had to hold it until we halted and shut down. All bowel movements waited for when the mission would allow. Some took opportunities, but I waited for our overnight preparations.

At the end of each day when we set up our NDP, each vehicle put claymore mines about fifty or so meters to their front. Before dark on most days, I grabbed my M-16, our track's claymores, sections of detonation cord with blasting caps affixed, a low-voltage electric wire with a blasting cap attached and a handful of C-Rat toilet paper. I placed the claymores to provide a good coverage area for our track and ensured it was coordinated with the coverage of the tracks on either side of us. Every crew did the same. We daisy-chained claymores using detonation cord.

When my claymores were setup, but prior to arming, I would move a few steps away and evacuate my bowels. I did not dilly-dally. Afterwards, I placed the blasting cap attached to the clacker wire into the receptacle of the end claymore. Everything thus prepared, I walked the electrical wire back to our track and attached it to a clacker, ready for detonation. Whenever there was enemy activity to our front, the clacker was used to send a one- and one-half volt electrical charge down the wire to the blasting cap located in the end claymore, thus detonating the whole line of claymores.

After a few months of my end-of-day field routine, I was struck with the thought of some poor NVA private enjoying the relative comfort of a well-concealed bunker and watching me squat, zeroing in on a testicle and pretending to blow it away. I am sure that he had a hearty laugh with his cohorts. I am certain I was safe (most evenings) because he must have known that he could never fire—doing so would have made my day very unpleasant, yes, but he would have incurred the full and competent wrath of an armored cavalry platoon. Modern mounted cavalry can inflict unbelievable horrors on a small infantry unit. My friend the NVA private's day would have been unpleasant—or ceased altogether.

Can you say, "Duck on a June bug?"

Chapter 10

Hardcore Dragoon

Claymore mines were a helpful addition to our feeling of well-being, but I earned an extra-added pleasure. Every couple of days we found bunkers or tunnels. We could not just leave them as they existed since they might be used again, so we rendered them uninhabitable by blowing them to smithereens.

One morning I eagerly inserted myself into the middle of such an effort—mostly out of curiosity or maybe boredom—after we discovered a bunker complex. It was not a new one and it looked as though it had been occupied in the not too distant past. A C-4 charge was placed in all the bunkers, and then detonation cord was used to daisy chain them together. Once every charge was installed and ready, it was time to set the fuse, typically a burning fuse attached to a blasting cap in the C-4. The fuse had a predictable burn rate, when it was measured correctly, that allowed sufficient time to get to a safe distance. The electrical method employed either our claymore clacker with its fixed-distance wire for the electrical charge or our plunger style detonator (think Wiley Coyote) when a much longer wire was necessary for our safety. We preferred the burning fuse—less muss, less fuss.

"Who remembers the rate of burn per inch?"

We each offered our thoughts and recollections, and somehow memories were jarred. As it turned out, I was the only one to remember correctly and admit it. Therefore, I was the lucky fool awarded custody of the platoon's demolition chest containing a roll of burning fuse, a roll of detonation cord, two dozen blocks of C-4, blasting caps, a roll of wire, and Wiley's plunger. In that instant, I had become second platoon's so-called expert, and thereafter got to blow stuff up. That was indeed fun, but I had concerns for my crew's safety.

The energy produced by a planted mine's interaction with our onboard demo chest would be monstrous. I did not worry so much about hitting a small mine that would not harm us or seriously damage the vehicle; my concern was for hitting a mine that was just large enough to set off the demo chest and blow us apart, cell by cell. That was no fun to think about, so I did not—not very often.

Hughes OH-6. White spot is the hole in my gun shield.

We joined other units in an assault on a known enemy basecamp. I do not know what our mission was or with whom we were working. That is just the way it was for us—the mushroom style of command: keep 'em in the dark and feed 'em bullshit, unless and until they need to know. We were usually told only that which we must know to succeed in the mission, but we always wanted to know more. Our fuller knowledge probably would not have changed the outcome, but I do not think it would have hurt it, either.

That morning's assault was into old growth jungle with small openings of grass and swaths of defoliation, allowing us to move faster. The area was not like typical jungle busting:

most of the vegetation was light, and there were few large trees. We were working with Hunter-Killers, who provided scouting and quick-response air cover. It was not long before we found a bunker complex, and we halted to investigate. It was in use. Ahead about fifty meters, a Hunter darted about very near tree level checking for signs of enemy. He appeared to be in a very casual mode until he yanked his bird skyward, as his on board observer sprayed M-60 fire on targets we could not see yet.

"Keep moving. There are hundreds of them on the run," he radioed us. "Go...go."

The Killer rolled in on fleeing targets. Other units kept up the assault and killed many of those who fled, while my platoon remained in the basecamp to clear it, check it out, and destroy it. A few guys from our platoon went into tunnels that began inside some of the bunkers. I never found out for sure, but we thought at the time that we had found an aid station or hospital. In one of the tunnels we found a wounded patient, unconscious on the operating table, a head wound. The operation was interrupted, and his attendants had fled. I do not remember what we did with him—if he was even alive—or if there were other wounded.

One bunker we checked out contained some personal items, and I passed them all on up the chain of command. Included were the apparent journal of an NVA soldier and a picture of him, a woman, and a child. That picture truly put the war on a personal level for me; our enemy was more like us than not. I do not know if the owner of that journal even survived that day or the war. He may have been the one with the head wound. I regret I did not keep the picture.

Within a week, we sealed another village. The next morning we rode up the hill just outside the village to pick up an infantry unit that would be joining us for a day of jungle busting. We spent hours RIFing and reconning by fire. We were frequently halting, the reasons unknown to me. Perhaps it was to plan or coordinate among units, but as usual, we had no clue what or where our objective was. Other than to kill the enemy, that is.

We got to know our passengers fairly well, learning where they were from back in "the World," the missions they had been getting, and most important to all of us, how long they had until their DEROS (Date Eligible to Return from OverSeas). On my track that day was about a squad, which included the platoon's medic. My crew and I took quickly to those guys, as we were all about the same age and temporary soldiers.

We drove cross-country for about thirty minutes. Our passengers hated the bumpy ride, and we teased them about it. They reminded me of my discomfort the day Jon Laird and I were brought out to Song Be. Once our cross-country trek was accomplished, we assembled our vehicles for entry into the jungle in two columns, tanks in the lead. Prior to moving out, we were told there might be an occupied basecamp in the area, and we should expect resistance from an unknown size enemy force.

Just inside the jungle cover, we determined it certainly *was* occupied, and they did not want to leave. All hell broke out around us. Our passengers jumped from the vehicles faster than we could yell, "Get the hell off." They grabbed any cover they could find, all of it behind us. Carefully, we backed up just enough to regroup and assault on line. During the initial phase of our assault, and after some well-placed .50 caliber rounds into a bunker to my front—the only bunker I could see—my sector was quiet. There was no obvious activity in other bunkers, nor was there any firing coming from those bunkers. There was activity elsewhere on our assault line. I heard explosions and automatic small arms fire coming from my right and my left.

The infantry slowly advanced from behind our vehicles to beside them, and we all began to move forward. They moved cautiously and very deliberately to clear the bunkers. A few advanced in a low-crawl to a point twenty feet in front of the bunker located directly ahead of me. There were the distinctive reports of AK-47 fire, and dirt kicked up all around the lead man. He was hit and out of the fight; he was not moving. We placed suppressive fire on and into the bunker, then their medic, one of the guys whom we had become quick friends with, crawled up to give aid. He was immediately cut down; he was not moving, either. We placed more suppressive fire into the bunker. We had to cease-fire when a third man advanced and managed to drag their medic and then the first man to safety. They never moved, except for the death-flop of useless arms and legs bouncing off downed logs. I knew that the two men were KIA.

F-100 after bomb release and before detonation.

We laid waste to that bunker with concentrated Fifty fire from several ACAVs. The infantry, along with their wounded and dead, were loaded onto our tracks, and we withdrew to a safe distance to regroup. In fact, we left the jungle and called for air support. A Dustoff arrived and evacuated all the WIA (including Quarter Cav men) and KIA from the battlefield.

Within minutes of our jungle exit, a pair of F-100 Super

Sabres was into their bomb run on the complex. There must have been a FAC (Forward Air Controller) somewhere in the local area for target acquisition, but I never saw him. I only saw the fast-movers when they were close to the target on their bomb run, just before they released their load.

Moments after detonation–right on target.

    Their targeting was excellent. Once they expended their bombs, they dropped napalm, and then finished up with 20 mm cannon fire. They placed their entire ordinance load on the target. It was a close-in show for us.

    We escorted the infantry back in to mop up. There were many NVA dead, but no wounded were found. They probably took their wounded, all the weapons they could carry and dragged away their dead. That was their custom.

    A few days later, we received a three-day in-country R&R at the division's standdown center at Di An. To us, who were used to the privations natural to a combat mission in the field, that was country club living. We enjoyed excellent food, beer, steaks, ice and sodas, a Philippine rock-and-roll band, and a swimming pool. The ice was unlimited. It is an interesting afternoon to sit with a bunch of clean, yet still smelly guys, and listen to a half-attractive Filipino woman belting out, "Lolling on the Liver." She looked all of twelve years old in her mini-skirt and white plastic go-go boots. She may have been.

While we were there on standdown, one of the guys from Lai Khe advised me that Top said some nice things about me. I did not understand why, but I appreciated it; atta-boys were few and always welcome. Hearing what Top said made me feel stronger and more confident—he was the ranking NCO in the troop, after all; if it was good with Top, the soldier was good. That R&R, even though we were still in-country, served me very well.

We went back out to the field on yet another mission to investigate an old basecamp. The complex was in a defoliated area, so we did not have much trouble getting there. We found bunkers and other evidence of occupation, but it was obvious no one had used them in a long time, and probably not since there had been a jungle covering. We did not find tunnels, only a few bunkers and exactly one shitter, NVA type.

We had a new guy, an FNG named Freddie, who looked like a combination of Wally Cox and Woody Allen. I was no longer feeling like an FNG myself and relished allowing the entire good-natured abuse and distrust roll smartly away from me and squarely onto someone else. Toward that end, I instructed Freddie to blow up the shitter we found with a frag (fragmentation grenade). It was an unnecessary endeavor, but good for a few laughs. I wanted Freddie to feel like an FNG as I had. I did not grasp that strength begets strength, nor that I had the experience and skills to mentor FNGs.

"Freddie. Come over here," I beckoned. "We need to blow this thing, whatever it is. Drop a frag in there, yell 'fire in the hole' three times, and promptly beat feet to a safe distance."

"Sarge, I don't have a frag," he responded.

"Damn...*get* one, new guy. They're some hanging in the

track...you know, that green exploding thingy."

Freddie ran to our track and back, almost tripping. Those within earshot saw what was going on and distanced themselves from an FNG with a frag. As did I. Freddie never bothered to look around at any of us, he just pulled the pin, releasing the spoon as he dropped the frag into the shitter. He turned and ran for safety.

"Fire in the hole. Fire in th...."

Boom!

Bamboo and old shit went flying. Freddie was only ten feet away. The hole was not very deep—my miscalculation. Someone might have gotten hurt, and I was lucky. Freddie felt he had screwed up.

"Sarge, I'm sorry I didn't get all three out."

"No sweat. Nobody's hurt. Hopefully, you learned from it. You know that was a shitter, don't you?"

"A shitter? Really?" He was not amused.

"Yes, private, someone had to do it." I patted him on his shoulder. "Today that someone was you."

I was a hard-ass taking advantage of Freddie for my own amusement. We all considered that he was performing a rite of passage. Not just harassment, but an initiation complete with life-saving lessons. Freddie learned about grenades—the fuse time was not always accurate. In later months, my boy Freddie did the same thing to pale and scared FNGs.

We received word that man had landed on the moon; we were proud. The landing was 20 July, and we got the news a day later. We did not know yet the names that would become synonymous with that venture: Michael Collins in the orbiter, and Neil Armstrong and Buzz Aldrin on the moon's surface. For many nights after that day, when I was on guard at night and the moon was visible, I would look up and wonder what it must be like to travel there. Forget about landing on it.

At the end of July, Alpha Troop was placed op-con to (under the operational control of) the 1st Cavalry Division, Airmobile (1st Cav or 1st Air Cav). The entire troop moved north to work out of Quan Loi, the basecamp for the 1st Air

Cav's third brigade. One squadron of the 11th Cavalry, a few long-range artillery units, and special forces who worked clandestinely in Cambodia were also there. The Cambodian border was a just a few klicks away (one klick = 1000 meters), and Quan Loi (LZ Andy) was to be our temporary base. We considered it good duty, much like constant convoy breaks in the rubber trees. The temperature was a little cooler at that higher elevation, and we RIF'd in the rubber trees where it was always cooler due to the foliage overhead. The trees were lined up like soldiers, equidistant from one another to assure healthy growth and maximum yield. There were a couple of ACAV hulks, stripped of anything useful, which remained from earlier battles. Certainly, after our forces had recovered the weapons and ammunition, the locals retrieved anything and everything they could repurpose.

    I first read about the rubber industry while preparing a junior high school project, and I have been fascinated by the harvesting of latex ever since. I saw cliché pictures and films of the indigenous population scoring the trees and collecting its milky substance. Rubber plantations always seemed to me to be, no matter where in the world, a splendid place to live, at least for the manager and the owner. The image I had was enhanced by movies released during the fifties and sixties romanticizing French Colonial Vietnam. The plantation was often a major character in those films, and all the women were drop-dead gorgeous. They always had my attention. I still think Catherine Deneuve is hot!

    The French Colonial homes and the plantation buildings I saw nestled among the rubber trees were often abandoned, yet they were still picture-postcard images. I liked buildings located amidst the rubber trees, cocooned within a clearing, the sun highlighting their features while surrounded by the darkness of rubber tree shade. Viewing them from within that relative darkness, the contrast of the off-white stucco and the red tile—tropical French Colonial style—was very inviting. I retain that mental image today. I wondered if those buildings had been a casualty of the Japanese, French, or Americans, or merely a downturn in the rubber business. There was no noticeable battle damage.

During a RIF within the rubber trees, we came upon a group of buildings appearing unoccupied. A plantation road led us to the formal entrance to those buildings, its entrance gate long since repurposed by the locals. We moved through the rubber in a two-column formation, tanks in the lead, when we stopped with one column's tank poised just across the roadway from the entrance. From a distance, the quaint little village appeared to be empty and long unused, but our experiences had taught us that mines or booby-traps could be anywhere. When we worked among the rubber trees, we bent antennas to avoid setting off a tree-borne claymore mine, but our enemy planted mines also. There was a discussion about mine-sweeping for in-ground mines before proceeding, but someone determined the best approach was to fire two canister rounds into the ground to set off any possible mines or booby-traps. There were no secondary explosions, but we were still unsure how safe we were. The sweep team was called forward to do their thing. How was anyone confident we were safe to proceed? There was too much metal in and on the ground. Without incident, however, we continued our march, bypassing an inspection of the buildings in favor of a distant cursory check.

Intelligence indicated there were multiple divisions of NVA that would soon be crossing over from their sanctuary in Cambodia. At first, we heard there were two headed toward us. That warning morphed into five regiments that would be arriving any day. The novelty of expectations began to wane and with it our keen edge. There was an ever-present sense of increased infiltration to come, but we were in business as usual mode. We RIF'd endlessly, trying to find just one of those supposed attackers, with no success that I knew.

We were then placed op-con to our Big Red One sister unit, the 1st Battalion, 16th Mechanized Infantry, and they were in turn op-conned to the third brigade of the 1st Air Cav. We secured FSBs Eagle I and Eagle II for a couple of nights each, but we spent most of our nights out in the wild, as usual. A firebase was very comfortable to us, but the Eagle FSBs were new and without standard FSB conveniences like well-built bunkers, showers, shitters, and a mess hall. There, even the red-legs (artillery) were roughing it. A few days later we were informed each FSB had been probed after we left, and one had a full-on attack. The word was that attacking NVA overran friendly forces and inflicted 95% casualties. (Note that casualties refer to dead *and* wounded.) I have never known the true story, but what we heard was consistent with what we learned during the following month: the area was full of enemy—North Vietnamese regular troops.

Outside Eagle II a day prior to their attack.

We moved closer to the Cambodian border along with ARVN (Army Republic of Viet Nam—our allies) infantry. We rested on a hilltop that afforded a long distance view into Cambodia. The skies were clear, and we watched a sortie of B-52s make a bombing run inside Cambodia—part of Nixon's "Secret Bombing." It was a sortie of three aircraft that dropped their load on their target, located only a few klicks away and at a lower elevation than we were. Once the bombs began to impact, their pressure waves were visible against the clear blue sky and were quickly followed by huge, roiling, soil and debris clouds. We had the experience of riding out a B-52 strike close in, and the resulting damage to the jungle was very impressive. Indeed, we did not envy anyone's job out there in the target area.

As the B-52s flew away, Hueys arrived to shuttle the ARVN unit out to the target. Despite the obvious beat-down given by the B-52s, the LZ must have been *very* hot. The Hueys returned to pick up a second load of ARVN as soldiers from the previous insertion clung to the aircraft. The ARVN were not dedicated to the fight that day—or any fight on any day that I ever witnessed. We were amused, but not at all surprised. The strike must have laid waste to the area, but the reality was the NVA were only pissed-off. They were well entrenched in their Cambodian sanctuary, as U.S. forces were to discover later during the Cambodian Incursion.

It was on the same high overlook into Cambodia that we set up an NDP. In fact, it may have been that very night. After dark, with one guard up on each vehicle, we did our usual thing: eating C-Rats, reading mail, writing mail, listening to cassette players, and generally playing grab-ass. Short-time girls were not there plying their services, either day or night, and that was a sign of worse things coming. Someone noticed a light in the rubber trees, and we all speculated as to its origin. Did we see a daytime fire still burning? Perhaps a dumb-fuck NVA scout with a flashlight? (Really?) Maybe an NVA cooking fire? (Again, really?) We could not tell. So what do enterprising combat troops do when confronted with such a conundrum? Blast it into oblivion, of course.

We requested artillery and received none, but Cobras did answer the call and were guided to the target. Excepting those men who were assigned as a vehicle's guard, most of us were congregated around the platoon leader's track watching the show. The Cobras made several runs, first missing the target over, then under, and then left, with each explosion safely away from us. The Cobras were called in closer to us; we thought there was sufficient safety margin. I do not recall whether the next volley was on target, but I still hear the sound of shrapnel from the Cobra's rockets pinging off the aluminum and steel all around us. Our platoon leader, Mike Armstrong, was standing atop his command track adjusting fire when he received a piece of shrapnel in his leg and was dusted-off. He was the only injury from the rockets, I believe. If there were others, they would not have been serious.

With our platoon leader out of action for a while, our platoon sergeant assumed command as our acting platoon leader. We continued searching for NVA infiltrators, and we wondered how they could hide so damn many people and do it so well. We set up our NDPs at locations where we hoped an ambush might yield good results. One evening, after we set up our defenses and secured the vehicles for the night, I sat down in someone's folding aluminum lawn chair inside our perimeter. I was quite comfortable and relaxed. I chatted with a few guys, enjoying the shade and a peaceful sunset. The peace was broken by the clear report of an AK, not too distant. We all sprang to our feet to charge to our vehicles for the attack that may be coming.

"Relax, boys! It's only Charlie zeroing his AK," Top said. "The real battle will begin with a helluva lot more than one shot from an AK. Standdown...we're ready."

"I sure wish I knew where all those Gooks are," I said. "The only thing I know for sure is they're not right here, not right now."

"They *will* be here soon, young sergeant...soon enough." Top knew more than I did, for sure. "Someone above our pay grade knows where they are and that information hasn't come down the chain-of-command yet. We must not need to know."

We, Alpha Troop, were a small, very mobile, and very high-powered part of the protective forces for the Quan Loi basecamp. That night, 11 August 1969, second platoon was assigned to NDP astride route 303 along the main approach to the Quan Loi basecamp. We were to be an ambush force.

As usual, we set out our claymores, put up our RPG screens, and settled in for the night, comfortable in our routine. At dusk, we were instructed to strike our NDP and reestablish farther east along route 303, where it intersected and formed a "Y" with 345. Late repositioning, while not a daily activity, was not unusual. Uninformed as we were, we just followed instructions and made the best of the situation. We thought it was a tactic to confuse the enemy; it usually confused us.

Our platoon was fielding (for ambush purposes) only two tanks and six ACAVs. The remainder of the platoon was in the troop's temporary motor pool at Quan Loi for repairs. When we arrived at the intersection, a tank was deployed at each branch of the fork covering the northeast and southeast approaches. We were not expecting bad guys to be marching right down the center of the road, but we did expect them to be inside the rubber coming down both forks.

Our tanks would be a formidable obstacle to them. SFC Nolan placed his command track between the tanks facing east, and the other ACAVs occupied the remaining perimeter to cover the north and south flanks. The roadway to the west, away from expected approaches, was lightly covered by the adjacent ACAVs. Our perimeter was tighter than we preferred because the rubber trees were mere feet from the roadway. Usually, we were spread out much more. We were prevented from doing to the rubber trees what we did to the jungle, which is to roll right over anything to clear fields of fire. To do so would have created an international incident.

SFC Nolan called all track commanders to his track.

"Is everyone all settled in?" After our assurances, he continued, "I've got some intel you might have interest in."

"What ya got?" It came from behind me—Miccio, easy to distinguish with his Long Island accent.

"Heavy activity one klick east...on the move. Coming this way. They tell me there's activity all over the area. Quan Loi is expecting a major attack tonight, and so are An Loc and Loc Ninh. The force coming at us is expected to take part in the attack on Quan Loi." He smiled and said, "I don't know for sure, but we may have company soon. Everyone...stay alert. Get your folks rested...and get your weapons ready for a fight. Maintain your noise and light discipline... stay alert!"

I took second guard hoping my guys could get some sleep. While we accepted the intel and acted accordingly, we were skeptical. Routinely we chased intel reports only to find nothing, or worse, find only ancient and/or useless signs of enemy activity. Since we had been chasing a "large force" of multiple regiments for over two weeks by then, we operated at a business as usual level—until we saw them, we would not believe they existed. We set up our defenses routinely. The sky was overcast with a light mist, so we set up ponchos in a tent-like fashion over vehicle cupolas to stay dry while on guard. We actually expected nothing to happen, so we settled in for the night.

Chapter 11

Dustup in the Rubber

I lay down on a pad stretched across our ammo cans to catch a few winks. I was relaxed listening to a favorite song, "White Rabbit," by Jefferson Airplane. I covered myself with my poncho liner; it was getting chilly. I was dry where I lay, but I had concern that it might rain harder, and I would get wet. Then, too soon, it was my turn on guard.

I had not been on guard for long when activity began at Quan Loi basecamp. We could see the ricocheted tracers and heard several distant booms, enhanced by the low overcast. Our motor pool guys there told us they were being probed. They had a good view of the action, uphill from the perimeter defenses. They suspected they might soon join the fight if the enemy contact was determined to be a full-on attack.

A probe could mean a few RPGs and/or AK rounds fired to test reaction and strength, or it could be just harassment. If the activity lasted a while or had concentrated fire, it might be an attack. That usually indicated that sappers were on their way in. They would attempt a breach of the concertina wire by crawling through, heavily laden with satchel charges (portable explosive devices) intent on destroying targets inside the perimeter defenses or to clear a path through the wire. If they could create a path, then their main-force infantry could charge right through, attacking targets on the inside. The volume of tracer fire visible from our distance, and number of booms we heard suggested to us they were being attacked, not probed.

I began to believe the intel. We were alerted to watch for enemy near our intersection as well, to our northeast along the northern branch of the fork. The tank that covered that route launched a flare and reconned-by-fire. There was no return fire, and no enemy movement was detected anywhere around the perimeter, and things quickly settled back down. Each guard kept watch over his track's fields of fire while his crewmates slept. We spent most of our lives in "free-fire" zones (we were clear to fire at anything). Often, we used recon-by-fire to determine if there was any enemy activity, and on occasion, we would receive return fire.

Bill Schull was a gunner on Lynn Claybaugh's track, and on that night, their track was immediately to my right. Sergeant Rebas's track was just to my left. Our three tracks were each covering the south. Bill was the guard on his track while I was the guard on mine. He had a Starlight scope for our side of the perimeter. Bill was a stutterer and since my father was, I was always patient when he spoke; others were not usually. Because I was, he was speech-relaxed around me. We enjoyed the fireworks around Quan Loi from our safe venue for maybe an hour, and we were making conversation about it over the radio. Then I heard what I thought was a muffled metal sound to our front.

"Did you hear that?" Bill asked.

"A-firm, it's probably only water buffalo. You've got the Starlight, check it out."

In my peripheral vision, as I was straining to see into the blackness along the lanes of rubber trees, I saw Bill raise the Starlight scope—then immediately drop it.

"Mike-5, Mike-5, I-I-I...."

An RPG round flew past at cupola height. It found Sal Miccio's track, located directly behind us. They were put out of the fight by the first shot. Our world erupted violently in a cacophony of battle: assault weapons, machine guns—light and heavy, tank main guns, grenades, RPGs, and yelling. At least one man behind us was screaming. It continued for a long time.

I wasted no time returning fire—with absolutely no fire discipline. The first belt of ammunition expended may have been one long burst. (Standard ammo belts for the Fifty were 100-rounds in length.) As I expended one belt and discarded the empty ammo can, I ducked inside the track to retrieve a full can, opened it, placed the can in its cradle, opened the Fifty cover, placed in the new ammo belt, closed the cover, and pulled back the charging handle to seat a round. Only then did I begin to fire again. Anyone who operated a Fifty was exposed to enemy fire while reloading. That night we were reloading often.

> *Miccio's crew was wounded to varying degrees. I would find out later the screamer was Miccio; he had received a head wound and was dusted-off. The doctors sent him to Japan for treatment and then home, where he received a medical discharge. We got a letter from him a few months later and learned he suffered only a slight loss of peripheral vision. He had been planning to buy a bar on Long Island—I never found out if he did. I do not recall any of his crew returning after being dusted-off.*

Lynn Claybaugh made it to his cupola right away, and we began having a fun time, laughing and cutting up. That is true—but our levity was borne of fear and not of confidence. Our experience and our training came quickly to the fore, and it interrupted what might otherwise be panic. We were too busy to be consciously afraid. That said, there has never been a question in my mind that our fears fed our humor.

Incoming green AK tracers crisscrossed in front of us as the NVA tried to stop our machine guns. With the addition of outgoing red rounds, the show was colorful and spectacular. There was a lot of hot lead in the air; my Fifty was virtually non-stop—all of them were. Standard procedure is to fire five to seven rounds, pause, fire five to seven rounds, pause, and repeat. Everyone from our side seemed to be doing the same as I was, firing and loading as fast as we could.

Night among the rubber trees was dark ordinarily, and because it was overcast, we had nearly zero visibility into the rubber without artificial illumination. Too few hand flares were being launched, and when they were, the NVA were not visible. Those guys gave away no movement, freezing in place. They were excellent at hiding in plain sight. We could only guess where they were by their tracer source, and when we targeted them, they were gone. The NVA were everywhere—and danger close.

Hand flares were usually fired into the air to pop open up high and drift slowly downward, hanging on parachutes illuminating the area as they fell to earth. Placement of a hand flare was difficult within the rubber trees. One of the few flares that helped me landed about fifty meters down the lane to my left. I did not know where it came from, but its light silhouetted a single NVA as the flare lay burning on the ground behind him. I sent a few rounds at him and was aghast when I saw a tracer just miss him, and then, to my horror—and brief celebration—his shoulder and arm were gone. The next (non-tracer) round had struck home. The force knocked him backward, spinning, and he was down. He was out of the fight and probably out of life. I took pride at that moment, asking Claybaugh if he could do so well. Lynn was firing as fast as I was and not about to miss an opportunity. Over the din of battle, I swear I heard him yelling at the NVA; I do not know what he yelled, but he *was* yelling. I silently spoke encouragement to myself.

> *Today I am grateful I could not see that NVA's face. In my experience, and I think it was true for most of us who served in combat in Vietnam, we did not very often see our enemy, especially his face. We normally only saw a little evidence of their presence, or maybe some fleeting glimpse. Rarely did we get a good look and have the time to target him. During my entire tour, I saw only three or four enemy that I may have been able to take a shot in the direction of, much less actually hit. They usually just melted away. Of course, after most of our actions we would find bodies and parts of bodies, proving they were there, even if we could not see them.*

When another flare provided overhead illumination, I saw two distinct lines of holes in the overhead poncho-tent we had fashioned for protection from the rain. Two AK rounds had passed within two or three inches of scoring a head shot—my head. They each left multiple holes as they passed through the ripples of the taut poncho material. Indeed, that was a case of known-close, but close did not score. When a burst of energy increased NVA fire, either shrapnel from an RPG or an AK round severed a line securing the poncho. Our field-expedient rain-roof came crashing down on me, and I was blind. It certainly *could* have been problematic, but it was not. If the battle at that point had not been so frightening, the great comedy of my recovery might have been fun to watch.

I noticed that Rebas' track had not been firing their Fifty very much. I looked over and saw a rubber tree lying across his cupola. He was frantically trying to field repair his Fifty *and* get out from under the fallen tree—all while AK rounds zipped by and RPGs exploded around all of us.

Two of Rebas' crew had been wounded by a sniper. The driver took shrapnel to his nose when an AK round hit his gun shield, sending metal shards in all directions. Steve Shamey, who was also known as "Yosemite Sam," and who would later be on my tank crew, received a wound to his leg very near his crotch. He was dusted-off that morning and he came back to duty with us within a few weeks.

My Fifty continued to work hard, and got hot, very hot. The bad guys were moving closer to us, and I was concerned we might not be able to hold them off for much longer. Our hand-to-hand combat classes during training—all twenty-four hours of them—came to mind. Was I trained well enough to engage an enemy soldier in hand-to-hand? It would be a fight to the death or to the point of incapacitating injury. My Fifty needed to keep working so I would not have to find out if I had that in me.

I was alarmed that other Fifties around our perimeter were quiet. My Fifty's headspace and timing—a lesson I learned well back on 9 June when I shot a hole in my own gun shield—were just right that night. However, I was firing bursts that were excessively long. Every RPG or hand grenade that landed nearby threw up earth, but I did not notice it so much. I did see the minerals in the dirt glow for an instant, sparking as the dirt hit the glowing hot barrel. The rifling in the barrel was gone, absolutely shot. Nothing I fired arrived anywhere near where I was aiming. As rounds left the barrel, they began to arc. Lynn and I had fun with that, making a game of it. I reached the point that I could almost target again, aiming by estimating the arc and the distance.

The NVA were surrounding us. I first realized it when the tracks covering the north side increased their rate of fire dramatically. We were too close within our small defensive perimeter—dangerously close—and we presented the NVA good targets. Some of the RPGs landing between Rebas and me, and between Claybaugh and me, probably came from the north side.

Generally, when an RPG managed to strike a vehicle it was considered to be an accurate shot. That night RPG rounds were all over the place, as if they had been area-fired and were not meant for a specific target. If they were trying to hit a vehicle, they were lousy shots. They may have tried to overwhelm us with RPG fire. Had they scored many hits, they sure as hell would have been right in the middle with us—and quickly. We could not let that occur.

After a while, I felt pain in my thumbs and saw that I had been burned by the butterfly triggers—I had one large blister on each thumb; that gun was *very* hot. Adding to my misery I was barefoot, my usual nighttime custom, and I was standing on a pile of hot, greasy fifty-caliber brass. During a brief lull in enemy fire, I collected my wits. It was past time to put on my boots. Duh?

Luckily, no grenades landed inside any of our vehicles. Although their RPG fire was extremely heavy, few rounds scored vehicle hits. Many of those fired were caught by RPG screens (chain-link fence) placed in front of our tracks. Still, we were not at all in good shape. The outcome of our fight had not been decided. Second platoon was alone, very close to being surrounded if we were not already, and without artillery or air support.

We had only two tanks, and six ACAVs—some thirty men (including wounded who were not able to participate) too many inoperable weapons, and were getting alarmingly low on ammunition. Alpha Troop's second platoon, my platoon, was fifteen minutes from being overrun and the enemy mixing in with us, fighting hand-to-hand for survival. Claybaugh joked we had them right where we wanted them. *Like hell!*

It was not until an hour or so after the fighting began that cavalry came to our rescue—in the literal sense—in the form of our third platoon. Two of their tanks moved to join ours: one moved toward the north fork; the other the south fork. Third platoon's ACAVs helped to secure the rest of our perimeter. The intensity of the fight again increased. Third platoon's tank working its way to the northern fork received an RPG hit to their turret. I turned to see the tank roll down the road about twenty-five meters, turn into the rubber trees, and stop against a tree.

Alpha Troop's first platoon was instructed to join us. As they approached our perimeter, they came under intense fire. An NVA machine gunner located just to the front of Lynn's track opened up on the lead tank in the advancing column. He tried in vain to silence it.

"Street! Machine gun...see it? I can't get him and he'll pick off Lima," he said.

I turned my Fifty in that direction, fired a few rounds and watched them arc, missing the spot where I thought the gunner was. A new burst of fire came out of the darkness—a line of red dots a few feet apart arced over the head of the commander of the second tank in line. The NVA gunner was beginning to find his target. I let loose another burst at what I hoped was the gunner. I missed. He opened up again, missing his target, but just behind the tank's commander. The enemy soldier had found his elevation and his range—his next burst would be a problem. I fired at him again. I saw two of my tracers go into darkness to the left of where tracers left his machine gun. Considering our belted ammunition standard of every fifth round a tracer, and given that I saw two tracers disappear into my targeted area, I guessed at least one Fifty round found the machine gunner's prone body. No more rounds came from that machine gun for the remainder of the night.

The lead tank from our first platoon advanced to join our platoon's tank on the north fork. Reaching our perimeter on the northeast side, it was struck by multiple RPGs igniting a fire in the turret. The increase in radio chatter caused me to turn and see what the commotion was. I saw the fire and its growing intensity for just seconds before I observed the tank commander and one crewman egress to the rear of the tank; each appeared uninjured.

Over the next few minutes, the fire grew much larger. Another tank moved up and pushed the burning Big Boy (tank) down the north fork, safely outside our perimeter. The pushing tank joined the battle at the north fork's defenses. Soon, the burning tank's main gun rounds started to cook off, with the explosions mostly contained within the turret. Fire would shoot straight up and out of the hatches each time a round exploded. As they began to subside, it was the diesel fuel that continued to burn. Fire and explosions were routine for a few more hours as the tank burned.

> *Three crewmen from the first tank hit (third platoon) got to safety. Their driver was found with a severe head wound. He was evacuated and later died.*

> *Three crewmen from the second tank (first platoon) also got themselves to safety. Their driver, Stanley Mensing, was found in his driving compartment. He had not survived.*

There were two disabled ACAVs that still had most of their ammunition load, so when there was a lull in activity, I put someone else in my cupola and ventured out to find and redistribute ammo. On my way out, I noticed a few lightly wounded men seated in my track. None of the wounds was serious, so I had them rejoin what remained of the fight.

When I took some ammo to the command track, I saw Chum, our Kit Carson Scout, behind the command track. He was trying to clear his M-16—but the charging handle would not budge. I could see what was wrong, as could anyone else. Chum could not, not at *that* moment.

"Chum, what *are* you doing?"

He did not look up but kept trying to clear his weapon.

"M-16 numba ten."

He berated his weapon. Knowing the barrel would be hot, I grabbed his M-16 by the stock. I felt the heat.

"Here's your problem, Chum."

An AK round or shrapnel had struck his weapon right at the bolt, bending it about 10°. It was never going to fire again—except around corners.

"It shit," he said, as he threw it to the ground. "VC numba ten. I kill more VC. I get AK."

He ducked into the command track to rearm himself and rejoin the fray. I redistributed more ammo, giving a little extra to Lynn and me since our Fifties were doing so well. I know someone else helped me with the distribution, but I do not remember who it was. We remained without any air or artillery support; Quarter Cav was on its own. We no longer believed that we were in imminent danger of being overrun, but the NVA were keeping up a good effort. Prior to that night, we were confident we could handle a platoon or company of enemy. The consensus was that is exactly what we faced—a company of NVA, hardcore NVA. They came at us, pulsating in the ebb and flow of battle. As dark as it was in the rubber that night, we knew we were hurting them.

After three hours of very intense fighting interspersed with brief lulls, we finally received illumination. Once their fire mission was over, Cobra gunships were cleared into the area. They circled fifty meters out assaulting the attackers—they beat hell out of the NVA. Rockets, mini-guns and 40 mm grenade rounds rained down on them. The momentum of the battle had begun a slow turn in our favor when first and third platoons arrived, but the Cobras broke the back of the attack. Once the gunships expended all ammunition and departed, the violence subsided.

During the lull, Dustoff arrived to collect our wounded. To accommodate pickup, our perimeter needed to be widened to allow for the Huey's blades. The pilot was still very close to striking the rubber trees, and I watched in awe. He made a rapid vertical descent, landing firmly. The wounded were quickly loaded, and the pilot made a nearly vertical ascent, disappearing into the darkness. It was on the ground all of about ten seconds and retrieved all of our wounded. By then, the battle was less intense, and we did not yet realize the gunships had repulsed the attack. We were still receiving seemingly indiscriminate AK and RPG fire, but the lulls were increasing in duration. We believed they were regrouping for another assault, but we soon realized, given the proximity to daylight, that they were breaking contact and clearing the battlefield of their weapons, wounded, and dead. We needed to stay keenly alert until we knew the battle was finished. Our weapons, the ones in working order, had fired nonstop. My M-60 gunners had displayed good fire discipline; I had not. Second platoon was once again critically low on all types of ammunition.

Contact was completely broken as daylight arrived. We had been in a violent battle with a regular NVA unit for five hours, maybe longer. When I knew the fight was finally over, I noticed that my hands were shaking. My fear was subdued in favor of training, adrenaline, and my fight or flight reflex. My trembling hands were the only visible manifestation that my adrenaline was receding—but my whole body was confused, and my head hurt terribly.

In the clearing light of dawn, we saw that we had done

considerable damage. Carnage was before us: bodies, body parts, blood trails, and abandoned weapons. How many wounded were taken away? How many dead were dragged off to be buried elsewhere in an attempt to confuse and confound our body count exercise? Many of the rubber trees were halved and many more denuded. I was glad that third platoon was given the task of clearing the battlefield of weapons and dead. It would not have been much fun. The truth is: I did not really want to know just how close we were to being overrun. For a few hours, the rest of Alpha Troop went hunting for survivors, to no avail. Once again, our enemy melted away—he just disappeared.

We returned to the intersection, and I dismounted my ACAV to view our booty. Captured weapons were placed on poncho liners on the ground all lined up in perfect symmetry, organized according to weapon types: hand grenades, RPG launchers, RPG rounds, AK-47 assault rifles and one enemy machine gun. Beyond the captured weapons, and just off the road at the edge of the rubber trees, was a disturbing scene—a pile of NVA bodies thrown into one big heap. There was no organization and no symmetry. They were just thrown there like yesterday's stinking garbage.

Several guys took pictures of weapons and dead. They were joyous, almost gleeful. I considered that disrespectful behavior shown the remains of our enemy, but I said nothing to them. My celebration was not about the killing, but about our victory and survival. Staring at that pile of dead men, I contemplated that just a short while earlier they too had been living breathing human beings. I was again struck with the fragility of life and how quickly—and violently—it can depart.

I muttered, "Do you wonder what they were thinking in those moments just before death?" No one responded. Did they truly hate us? At the very moment of their death were they satisfied to die for their cause, or were they compelled by other factors? I was glad as hell to be alive and not wounded. My few moments of self-pity concluded, I abandoned my brief venture into the philosophical—I recovered an inner hardcore.

The bodies presented great physical trauma. Some were barely recognizable as ever being human. They were dirty, nasty, stinky—the fresh meat was already beginning to rot. Those with larger wounds were a strange color of gray; they were bloodless. One had no visible wounds. Some wag joked it was due to his heart attack when he realized he had picked a fight with Quarter Cav.

> *I regret I did not take photographs of those weapons and bodies that day. They would have served as a gratitude check. When feeling as though my world were crumbling all around me, those pictures would have clearly stated—"Hey, dude, whatever your perceived problem, ain't no big thing."*

At day's end, I was exhausted—we all were—and much more so than usual. I pulled an early guard and then settled in ready for sweet sleep to take me; I started to think about the fight. Then the realization hit me—I had not panicked, nor had I shit myself, thanks to Uncle Jimmy and my training coming to the fore with humor.

As I felt a comfortable embrace of rest, I considered what might have been. During the battle, we suffered two KIA and twelve WIA, some of whom would never return to the troop. We lost one tank and one ACAV destroyed, and one tank damaged (maybe destroyed), and one ACAV damaged.

There were twenty-three NVA bodies locally. I was not of a mood to be nice to them, but I do recall that I continued to respect that little guy. Yes, he was trying to kill me, but he was up against formidable odds with a very low chance of his long-term survival, yet he soldiered on, living in holes and tunnels, ducking powerful daily assaults by infantry, cavalry, artillery and air support. Their dedication, loyalty, and love of country, or their belief in their cause—whatever it was that motivated them—was to be respected.

In the opening minutes of the clash, the main antenna on second platoon's command track had been shot away (it was not discovered until daylight). SFC Nolan wondered why no one was responding to his calls for support. Well after the initial assault, a Huey heard the distress call and relayed messages to Alpha Troop HQ. Only then were the other Alpha elements alerted to come to our aid.

Author's fighting position as seen the evening of 12 August.

That night there had been major operations by the NVA all over the region—Quan Loi, Loc Ninh, and An Loc were all targeted. The NVA were determined to take and hold at least one location even if only for a short time, but their plan failed everywhere. Artillery and air support were very busy that night. That is another reason Quarter Cav got so little help, and what we did get was so late. In the following days, second platoon, as well as other units, found numerous multiple graves—many containing three bodies. The "official" body count credited to Alpha Troop was sixty-six. I believe there were many, many more.

> *SFC Nolan said he submitted awards for twenty men of second platoon; only two were awarded.*

Forty-four years after the battle, I learned that a DSC (Distinguished Service Cross, second only to the Medal of Honor) was awarded to SP4 Alfred L. Porter, the tank commander of the first tank (third platoon) that arrived in support of second platoon.

Chapter 12

Continued Survival Not Assured

The next day we relaxed and enjoyed some rare casual time. Not down time, but casual—we were on minimal guard and catching our breath. A Huey arrived in the center of our perimeter, but most took little notice except for red dust being blown around. Its occupants appeared to have come for an officer conference, a common event. I was doing something much more interesting when I heard my name shouted. I was summoned by either SFC Nolan or one of the platoon leaders to join the group at the helicopter.

"Jump in," I was told.

"Say what?" I had no clue what was going on, but since I am always interested in flight, I was encouraged. "What for?"

"Don't sweat it, just get aboard," said CPT Newell, Alpha Troop CO.

He told us we were going into Quan Loi to get a shower. A shower? Hell, yeah, I will go! The limited seating onboard the bird was occupied by higher rank leaving me sitting on the floor with my feet on the skids and holding onto the seat frame. The Huey powered up, rising to a low hover, did a quick pirouette, dipped its nose and climbed to altitude. I loved it. Maybe I should have gone to flight school after all; it was so cool! The scenery was gorgeous—jungle some distance away and just below us, the lush, deep green of the rubber trees contrasted with the orange-red soil. The whole area looked colonial to me, very French colonial. Too soon, we banked toward my side of the aircraft to make our approach to landing. I had seen many infantry units many times being inserted by Huey, with the guys sitting in the doorway, their feet on the skids. However, I never saw a Huey in so steep a bank with them sitting like that. This pilot banked steeply—steeply enough that I wanted a stronger grip on the seat frame. Some clown laughed and tried to loosen my death grip. I can report that I did not fall out, but I was briefly concerned.

It was true! We showered with water warmed by the sun. We were given a clean uniform, as well. Someone informed me—I may have been the only one out of the loop—that we were to receive impact awards. I had not even considered the possibility, but I was curious. I felt I was privileged hanging out with officers, a senior NCO, and two others, more like me in age and reasoning.

As quickly as we cleaned up, we were unceremoniously relegated to a truck for our return to the troop. That truck trip back began our grunge process anew. When the truck stopped, so did our breeze, and the red dust caught up with us. I began to sweat uncomfortably. When we were dirty, we did not care if we sweated, but when we felt relatively clean, it was quite bothersome. Again on the ground with the dirty and common folk, I was getting grief from others about being clean. I was called a few nasty names, all in fun.

We, the clean ones, were assembled into a line as the Huey returned. It brought the 1st Air Cav's CG (commanding general) out to present the awards. I was next to last in line. When the general came to me, his references were incorrect with respect to name, rank, and award, and I did not correct him. He pinned a Bronze Star Medal with "V" device on me, and we had a brief conversation that I could not recall five minutes later. We exchanged salutes and he moved on to the last guy in line. The general referred to him using my name and rank, and he pinned an Army Commendation Medal with "V" device on his chest. When the general turned and walked away, we chuckled. Later we could exchange them, but at that moment, we stood at attention, the good soldiers that we were. SFC Nolan and I were the only second platoon members to receive an award for action in that battle.

The general credited Alpha Troop with saving Quan Loi basecamp. The NVA attack on their perimeter was designed to breach the base defenses; the unit we battled was expecting to walk right through those defenses or the main gate, with no opposition. The general told us we were engaged with a battalion (reinforced) of the 272nd NVA Regiment, and they were meant to be the occupying force for the basecamp. I was stunned: we battled a unit that was well over 500 strong, and we held them off despite shortages of men, malfunctioning weapons, and a lack of timely air support and artillery. We were indeed fortunate—or hard fighters.

The next day the troop entered Quan Loi basecamp to get hot food and showers. I gladly took another. As we drove in, we saw many soldiers were still busy cleaning up. Along the perimeter was a freshly dug hole, very large, with a dozen or so enemy dead in it. A deuce-and-a-half (two and a half ton truck) arrived, backed to the edge of the hole, and dumped in a fresh load of bodies. A few meters farther down the road, a bulldozer was loading more bodies into another truck for transport to the mass grave. The NVA had paid dearly in and around Quan Loi. I wondered what the NVA body count was when their whole offensive was totaled and if they considered their losses worthwhile.

I went to the mess hall with Jon Laird and Doc Witwicki for lunch. As we passed by Cobras revetments, we saw the remains of two Cobras that were destroyed by sappers. Two of the four crewmen were KIA. There was not a lot remaining of those two aircraft. Several days later we heard a sniper had been ferreted out from beneath the PX after killing a few 1st Air Cav soldiers. I never knew the truth and I have always wondered. Doc was unusually quiet during lunch, not giving of his usual irreverent humor. From previous experience, Jon and I knew he would be back to full-on-Doc soon. The troop needed his humor; I needed his humor.

That particular August of 1969 is strong in my memory for more than just the early morning hours of 12 August. The Tate and LaBianca murders by the Manson family occurred just a few days before, and the Woodstock music festival was held just a few days after. Those events sandwiched the most physically violent and emotionally traumatic event that I have ever experienced. The violence perpetrated by the Manson family, the battlefield violence of 12 August, and the touted peace and harmony of Woodstock have caused me to examine details of each repeatedly over the years. I was "eat up with it" for some time after returning home.

Perhaps a factor in my fascination for Woodstock (aside from the music) was my family vacationing during the festival at my grandparents' cabin in Smallwood—only five miles east. My sister had just turned sixteen and could not understand why our parents would not let her go. That area of Upstate New York was special to me. When we were children in the fifties, Bob and I spent most of our summers at the cabin with our grandmother, her friends, and our grandfather when he would come up from New York City.

For several days after the battle, we would pass through the intersection where it was fought. By the second day, we could not pass by the bloated bodies fast enough to avoid the horrible smell of rotting human flesh. That stench cannot be washed out, nor can it be blown out of your nose—it remains with you for a long time. Each day the locals would take a few bodies from the pile. Then one day we drove by, and they were all gone. Still, a bad smell lingered.

Easy duty found us every so often. We spent a few days securing the garbage dump at Quan Loi. I do not mean as an on-post garbage dump guard—we guarded the approaches to it from outside the perimeter fence of the basecamp. We were securing a section of plantation road adjacent to the camp dump, and we were nestled comfortably among the rubber trees. The area was cool, comfortable, and allowed excellent daytime sleeping. The mission did not require *all* of us to stop and search the locals as they tried to cart away whatever they could dig up from the dump. One man on a motorbike had a large box of spoiled pork chops, U.S. issue. He was not at all happy with us for taking them away. They had probably been destined to fatten up his pigs.

Just off that road, which had been one of the escape routes for the unit attacking Quan Loi, we found several graves, many containing multiple bodies. The battle had been almost one week earlier, and most of the soft tissue was gone from the remains. One guy's face was still attached; it had dried and shrunken leaving him with a leather mask. A few of us wanted to be hard-asses, or maybe we were just bored, so we relieved the body of its skull. That was a nasty process. Our plan was to clean it and then display it on our track, in hopes of spooking the enemy and demonstrating our hardcore attitude. We filled an empty ammo can with water and lots of C-Rat salt. We placed the can over a C-4 fire. We figured the boiling should clean all the tissue away, and we would not have to worry about a biological hazard. What we did not consider was the stink a week-old skull makes as it boils. Our bad idea was abandoned. The smell was just one more of the perfumes particular to Vietnam in those days, but one that lingered with me for too long.

Near the village of Quan Loi (not the basecamp proper), a member of my crew bought a monkey. We had a blast with the little guy for most of the four or five days we had it. He often leaped from our vehicle while we were moving, and someone would jump off and give chase through the rubber trees to recapture him. We were lucky no booby-traps or mines were found that way. One day we awoke to discover our monkey was foaming at the mouth. We wondered if he had some rare disease peculiar to monkeys, but thought he had rabies. After discussion, we arrived at the consensus that our monkey should immediately be dispatched. There must have been temporary restriction on firing weapons, because shooting him was not an option. We decided to run over him with a tank, so we tied him to the track. Our plan went awry when he did not cooperate. As the tank began to move, the monkey panicked and jumped up onto the drive sprocket where he became entangled in its teeth and the track end connectors. He was done for in half a second. To add to our cruelty, we did not inform the driver (my boy Freddie) of our plan, and we accused him of killing our pet. We were just guys giving other guys good-natured (and so immature) grief.

Later that day I went to the demo chest to retrieve some

C-4 to blow up a bunker or tunnel, and I noticed strange marks on a couple of C-4 blocks. It hit me! The monkey did not have some mysterious Asian monkey disease; he simply had ingested C-4. True to our usual fashion, we all had a good laugh—except for Freddie, of course.

Relaxing near Quan Loi's main gate.

For a few days, we were in a daytime ambush position at an intersection much like the one we occupied on 12 August. The scenery was the same—rubber trees—but locals would visit us so we surmised the NVA were in Cambodia licking their wounds. Short-time girls would come by, and along with them came an older woman who brought her small children. She arrived bearing baguettes for sale. Baguettes! The French influence—c'est magnifique! Before long, she was making us tomato sandwiches and using her wok to cook us French fries. We provided the heat source—C-4, but only enough for the fire; she took none home. She made us very tasty food, a real delight. Surprisingly, we remained in place there for a few days, and she returned to feed us each day.

We were required to take an enormous orange malaria prevention pill every week. While we remained in the area of Quan Loi we also had to take a small white one every day. Even with precautions, malaria was still a problem. Back when we received orders to Vietnam, we had been preached malaria control. In-country, the medics chased us down to ensure we took those pills. What a job! Although Lynn Claybaugh took all his pills, he still contracted malaria. He was sent to the hospital at Quan Loi to recover and was away from us for several weeks, maybe a month. Upon his return, he appeared visibly unaffected by the disease and appeared to be very well rested. He advised not to fight a hospitalization—the nurses were pretty and smelled great.

We continued to work with the 1st Air Cav, RIFing during the day and ambushing at night. Periodically, we located a few enemy bunkers—some fresh, some old. We also found fighting positions, bodies, booby-traps, mines, Hoi Chanh (surrendering enemy combatants), and we engaged small units in firefights. Several times an RPG team stepped out of the jungle onto the trail we made and fired at us, then melted back into the bush. Frustrating! It was just another reason why I preferred working within the rubber trees; the visibility was much better.

The first week of September I found out Top had again said nice things about me, and that I was in for a promotion. However, there was a problem: I did not have enough time in service, nor did I have enough time in my pay grade. I had been in the army only fifteen months and a buck sergeant for only eight. The army allowed one of the two requirements to be waived, but not both. There would be no promotion for me until one of those qualifications was achieved. Oh! The best part? My PMOS (Primary MOS)—my main job classification—was changed from a school-trained 11E40 (tank commander) to 11B40 (infantry squad leader). Did you notice? Infantry! Really? Had that happened to me? All the hard work and planning to avoid Vietnam, to avoid infantry, and most of all to avoid the infantry *in* Vietnam was then, with one simple stroke of a clerk's pen, totally shot to shit. I was squarely in Vietnam, a member of a celebrated infantry division—*The* Big Red One—and they went and made me a grunt. I was already a part-time grunt, since I lead dismounted night ambushes every few days. (I commanded an armored vehicle, so not all was lost.) With the change of my PMOS, it was made official. So much for my best-laid plans!

Squadron HQ assigned a captain as squadron historian and sent him to ride with Alpha Troop. I recall his RIFing with us in second platoon, as he intended to do with each platoon in each troop. Fate dealt a different card to him and to Alpha. We were in Quan Loi basecamp on a quick afternoon visit. We were crowded into a temporary and borrowed troop location, very close to the airstrip. A field mess had been set up, and we were about to scarf down a hot meal. What a treat! We were lying about, napping, reading, and writing letters home while awaiting the call to mess. I was lying in the shade of an ACAV twenty feet from the mess tent. Our vehicles were lined up, side by side, close in. The sky was clear blue, not a cloud anywhere—a beautiful day in, ahem, paradise. Not far from the north end of the airstrip, we heard a "swoosh" followed by a loud boom. Someone yelled "incoming," and we dove for cover. In my case, I dove for better cover. We peeked and saw a cloud rising in the distance—we thought it was the ammo dump at first—and hoped no one was hurt.

Then came another, but shorter "swoosh" coupled with an extremely sharp and very loud boom. A rocket had hit us, landing right between the ACAVs and the mess tent. The NVA could not have aimed at a better target. Fortunately, we were not yet in line for chow. There were many injuries—ten or more. The hospital was next to us, so those who could not walk were driven. One guy was placed on a stretcher, and the stretcher placed across the passenger seat and onto the hood of a jeep. He was flat on his stomach, naked except for his boots, his ass to the world with a large, very ugly wound to one butt-cheek. As he rode by, he looked at the group of us, smiled, raised himself up on his elbows, and then flashed the peace sign. He yelled, "I'm going home, boys!" He did.

Another image I have retained is of CPT Newell, our CO, standing on his command track, his hand over a kidney with blood seeping through his fingers. He was on the radio calling for medical aid for the troop. He never returned to the field, and visiting CPT Dock assumed temporary command. After a few days, CPT Dock was officially in command of Alpha Troop.

Author's Cambodian border banana harvest.

I cringe when I allow myself to consider the slaughter we would have suffered had that rocket been ten minutes later at the same spot—our chow line. The fates were kind to us.

We continued with the routine operations that we had previously performed. Mostly RIFing and setting up mounted ambushes. On one night's ambush, we set our NDP in a small clearing sandwiched between jungle and rubber trees. The area around us was sufficiently open and clear of vegetation for us to see anyone approaching or transiting the area. With first guard of the evening in each vehicle's cupola, everyone else was milling about killing time and socializing.

"Incoming," someone yelled.

Mortars! Three rounds so close together we guessed there were three launch tubes. Shrapnel pinged off vehicles, but, again with good fortune on our side, we had no injuries. We got pissed thinking it was friendly fire from an ARVN unit nearby. We never did find out who it was, but if someone had died, *maybe* we would have known. Probably not.

Mike Armstrong, our platoon leader, having completed six months command duty, went to our Lai Khe basecamp. Promoted to captain, he became Alpha Troop's XO (eXecutive Officer); he later took over command of Bravo Troop. He was replaced as our platoon leader by LT Winters who had just arrived in-country. Our new platoon leader was thrown into the mix with very little preparation. He may have been book competent, but we knew right away that he seriously lacked command presence and meaningful leadership skills.

Most men of second platoon, from the very moment he assumed command, did not respect him much at all. He was not a problem just because he was an FNG—something we all had been and were attuned to—he should *never* have been an officer with a combat command. My recollection is that he empathized with the majority of us and wanted to be judged a nice guy, liked by his men. That is a recipe for disaster. His demeanor was not authoritative, and he appeared unable to make the simplest decisions. Certainly, he had insecurities and fears, but they were too evident. The platoon's confidence in our new leader was nonexistent. We worried that he would make a catastrophic mistake by virtue of his uncertainty and lack of command ability.

Chapter 13

Death a Peril, Dying the Fear

I came to believe the darkest fear of combat soldiers is not being killed; rather, it is the process of dying. Of course, no one I knew wanted to die. However, we were realistic about it; some were fatalistic. If "it's my time" or if "my number comes up," then we could accept our fate. We all learn during childhood that one day we will depart this life. However, we expect that ours will be a long trek unless some disease or high-risk adventure gives us a reason to consider otherwise. Combat will do that—it *is* a very high-risk venture.

The process by which a combatant dies can be quick, "He never knew what hit him," or it can be agonizingly slow, brutal, and ugly, with the outcome never seriously in doubt. To those I served with and to me, the real fear was the course itself: the potential agony and hell of clinging to life only to die in the end. We were accustomed to death and fatalistic about it. When someone died, our attitude had to be "ain't me, move on." Enough death had surrounded me by then, and I very consciously worried less about the finality. I was not unique.

Alpha Troop was released from 1st Air Cav and returned south where the environmental conditions were not nearly as pleasant. We no longer expected to encounter large enemy units as around Quan Loi. We continued thunder runs along QL13, escorted the occasional convoy, RIF'd, and provided Rome plow and nighttime FSB security. The other platoons did the same independently of our operations.

We continued sending dismounted ambush patrols out every night. An NCO would lead a squad-sized element away from the NDP to set the ambush. The rotation for NCO and patrol member alike was every fourth or fifth night, depending on the number of NCOs available—exempted were the platoon leader, platoon sergeant, and medic. Everyone else took his turn when due. I was living the nightmare of my lost plan.

On 11 September, I finally got a tank. It was Danger Dragoon Alpha Mike Seven. It was my standard luck that I commanded the oldest, most jungle worn, most road worn, and the most failure prone tank in the platoon, and maybe in the entire squadron. It was nonetheless a tank, and it was my tank. The main gun ammunition consisted of a few HE rounds, one or two beehive rounds, and the remainder was canister rounds. We did not carry HEAT rounds since we did not expect to see enemy armor. Several nights during my tour, we heard tanks moving near us, but Higher swore there were no friendly tanks in the vicinity. Whose were they?

Canned Heat–KIA 12/23/69, mine.

I cannot remember all of my first tank crew. I remember Terry Valentine was one of them, and I think he was the only armor-trained crewman besides me. We decided to name our tank "Canned Heat," so we painted the name on the main gun barrel in red. The rock group Canned Heat had songs, "On the Road Again," and "Going Up Country." That is what we did, so it was a natural for a tank—"Canned" for canister round, "Heat" for the HEAT round (even though we never used them) and the heat we brought our enemy. We thought our name was cool. Yeah, we were in Alpha Troop with a name that started with the letter C; we never gave it a thought. The first time we busted jungle after painting the barrel, we fired a few canister rounds to make going easier. The barrel was hot, and our new name quickly disappeared, brushed off by jungle vegetation—it was just gone, vanished, nothing left but a smudge of red. We decided that painting the name on the barrel had not been worth the effort, but we continued to refer to our tank as "Canned Heat," however.

A Chinook came out almost every day to provide fuel and ammo resupply, so we often received a hot meal. It was usually delivered by one of our cooks, a nice guy who was a temporary soldier just like most of us. Although he worked mainly in the rear, he was not a REMF, not that guy. He was the type of soldier to help us—even when he was out in the field. After completing his cooking duties, he always joined a crew overnight and pulled guard. That gave a crewmember a break and the whole crew shorter guard times. He did not have to do that, but he did—that was not the behavior of a REMF. We teased him that because he did not qualify for a CIB (Combat Infantryman's Badge), then he should get the CCB (Combat Cook's Badge, which we just made up). I do not recall if we had any enemy contact any time he was in the field with us, but he was the type to have joined the fight.

We discovered bunkers and tunnels frequently during our daily RIFs. I reveled in blowing them up, although I no longer had the demo chest responsibility. When we found a tunnel, we deployed our own tunnel rats. They were not trained, not official, but some of our smaller, adventurous guys enjoyed it. (Yeah, they *were* insane.) Occasionally they would find an interesting item like an SKS carbine or Chicom (Chinese communist) 9 mm pistol.

Knowing that there were weapon souvenirs we could take home, I got a wild hair and checked out a few tunnels—*only* to the first level and *only* behind someone else. After the two I ventured into, I was spooked. Claustrophobia is not an affliction, but I just did not like being in tunnels, even at that shallow depth. My desire for an SKS overcame my fear for a short while, but my terror soon won out. We did not know it at the time, but there was a massive tunnel complex under the area around Cu Chi and into our AO. We were on top of them. Did I ever imagine they were there? Nope; no one did.

One mission we were given provided us a departure from our usual and mundane routine. Had it been successful, our unit may have become famous for a day. We were put on the hunt for a particular "Chinese advisor." I can still hear the radio traffic the morning we were told of the mission.

"How the hell will we be able to tell if he's Chinese?"

"He'll be the one wearing size ten shoes."

"He'll be the one *wearing* shoes," said another.

We found nothing and no one, but that was not for lack of trying. A reward of three days in-country R&R at Vung Tau, a coastal resort city, was promised. We only needed to snatch the "Chinaman," and the prize was ours. There was a lot of talk going around of Chinese and Russian advisors, and I am sure they existed, but I never saw one. No surprise.

Later in September, we stood down again at Lai Khe for our quarterly maintenance service. As was the case with many bases in Vietnam, the regular residents referred to Lai Khe as "Rocket City." Our troop area was located very close to a 105 mm artillery battery, and it took me a while to discern outgoing 105s from incoming rockets. Either could wake us out of a sound sleep at the worst time—such as when we dreamed about a beautiful girl. One would think we would become immune to the deafening sound of outgoing artillery, especially after so much FSB security, but I would always awaken, if only briefly. I never did get used to loud noises.

The artillery unit closest to our troop compound usually showed recently released and classic movies. They even had bleachers for comfortable viewing—oh, the disadvantages of life in the rear. We would join them any chance we could. The battery continued to receive fire missions during movies, and the interruptions seemed to happen just when the plot was unfolding. They would stop the projector, step into their firing pit, fire their mission, and then come back to the movie. We did not mind at all; they were helping someone in the field, and maybe American lives were being saved.

I recall watching a movie one night titled *If It's Tuesday, This Must Be Belgium*. It was a fun movie, but not a great one, yet we enjoyed ourselves in spite of its lack of naked women. We were relaxing—otherwise fat, dumb, and happy. We heard incoming rockets splash, but they were not close enough to worry about. Whenever there was incoming, REMFs usually jumped headfirst into their bunkers—without weapon, steel pot, or flak vest. Our artillery guys grabbed their flak vests, M-16s, and helmets, and then they made for the bunkers. However, they turned off the projector as they always did. We did not mind that they wanted to hide, but we were going to watch that damn movie, right then. One of our guys turned their projector back on, and we continued to watch. "Superior field knowledge" indicated we were safe from that round of incoming rockets.

On 8 October 1969, I was "selected for promotion to Staff Sergeant" under the primary MOS of 11B40—infantry squad leader—without the burden of a review board and without any points required. My promotion was referred to as accelerated. Either my time in service or time in pay grade requirement had been waived; I never found out which. I had been selected, but I was not yet promoted. I was not yet privy to the army's reasoning and timetable, despite my extensive experience of seventeen months. I would get higher pay when it was official, and for a guy that could not spend much that was good. I would be able to save more for the new car I was going to buy when I got back to "the World."

We began to work with the ARVN more frequently as part of the Vietnamization program. We would accompany a straight-leg ARVN infantry unit for a few days, then we would work alone or with an American unit for a few days, and then we would work with an ARVN mechanized infantry unit. The cycle would repeat, mixing up the rotation. I never delighted in working alongside the ARVN. Did I say *working* alongside? I should have said *trying* to lead the ARVN and pushing them to defend their own country. We felt we did all the hard work while they just watched us—and sometimes probably aided our common enemy.

How many of those guys were really VC? I was always suspicious, especially of the officers. Corruption was rampant in their country, both in the government and in the military—I think especially so in their military. A high number of the lower ranks wanted no part of the war at all, and it was very evident. They just wanted to farm for sustenance. An ARVN infantry unit that was with us one day included criminals and deserters, and I was not sure who was who; maybe they were all criminals *and* deserters. The regular ARVN soldier, the non-criminal conscripted one, had a casual approach to their war. We, the Americans, saw it as their war; we were helping them retain independence (or retain their corruption). Every temporary American soldier I knew was just fighting to make it back home; the career soldiers were busy building their warrior-credibility and punching tickets.

The ground turned to dust in the dry season, covering everything with orange, including every pore of our bodies. During the time when Vietnamization began we did not get north on QL13 for FSB security very often. A visit to our basecamp at Lai Khe did not happen very often either. It was the dry season and we had no natural bathing shower from rainfall, no basecamp or FSB showers, and only rarely a shower from a canvas bag hung from our elevated gun tube. I was used to my stink, and everyone else was used to theirs. We grew to tolerate each other's smell. There was a fifty-three day period when I had no personal cleansing other than washing myself out of my steel pot, very infrequently. That "bath" was not worth the water I dedicated to it. We were all very ripe, indeed. I still carry the smell-memory of my flak vest. It was awful.

When we had an American infantry unit with us, they

complained of our stench. Of course they did, they were able to catch a shower several times since we had.

"Man, do you guys ever bathe?" one asked.

"Where? We're always in the field. We sometimes get to a firebase, but not very often. Even then, sometimes there's not enough water."

With exception, most infantry units were able to visit basecamp or an FSB for cleanup and rejuvenation after an operation—certainly more than cavalry troopers, mechanized infantry, or tankers were. Frequent visits to the rear just were not practical for us. We remained in the field after operations; our life was a constant military operation. We were resupplied almost daily with necessities: ammunition, fuel, potable water (drinkable), food (hot meal), and mail. What about a shower? It was not considered a necessity at any point. Chafing and jock itch were rampant among FNGs in the field; the rest of us had built up tolerance.

The ARVN ate anything, and that was perhaps the single benefit to spending much time with them. They enjoyed the C-Rat meals we would not eat, and chief among those was ham and lima beans. They were nasty. ARVN rations included quick-cooked rice, canned sardines, and hard candy in a tin. Any food I did not like was good for swapping with the ARVN. I liked the ARVN hard candy and rice. Heat water, add it to the rice, wait a few minutes, then eat it or add something. A special meal for my taste was rice added to a C-Rat meal such as beans and franks, meatballs in sauce, or the chicken or beef dinner. My favorite was rice and meatballs. We were very food-creative when we had time. Occasionally, we would have a tanker's stew. We used a steel pot to cook a combination of just about anything. C-Rat cheese (it may actually have been Velveeta), salt, pepper, and hot sauce improved a multitude of otherwise offending mixtures.

My platoon was running Thunder Road one afternoon and stopped by FSB Thunder II. We were not the designated security force, but we must have been working with elements of the 11th Cavalry who were, and we stopped by to coordinate efforts. As we pulled in, I noticed the perimeter was ringed with tanks and no ACAVs. It was the 11th Cav's M Company, where my friends from the Armor School, Butch Tidwell and Dwight Humphrey, had been assigned. I asked around and I learned Humphrey was on R&R with his wife, and Butch was with their medic. We met up as he returned to his tank. He had wounded his pinky in a firefight earlier in the day, and he was pissed about the aggravation. Most of us felt if we had to be hit then make it something that would get us out of the field—the proverbial million-dollar wound. His was not one.

"How do, Street?" he said.

"Surviving. Seems you are, too. They had me worried a bit until I found out it was just your finger."

"Yeah, no biggie. Just pissed me off royally, though. Why not the million-dollar wound?"

"So far, knock wood, I've had nothing but scrapes and cuts...the wait-a-minute vine." It was like concertina wire.

"It's not fun, is it?" he asked.

I shook my head, laughing. In the prior few days, I made the mental shift from worry about dying and carping about the inconvenience of field life, to one of biding my time as safely as I could, taking one day at a time. We laughed about our luck and chatted a while longer until my platoon readied to move out.

"Give my best to Humphrey," I said.

"I will. Take care."

"Let's get shit-faced after we're done."

We each made assurances we would. Usually, promises like that were never kept.

One morning, we traveled north on Thunder Road soon after the daily road clearing was finished. Within a few klicks, we would head west to go get our daily dose of jungle busting or RIFing. The roads in the area were not paved, nor were they entirely secure. Of course, we hardcore cavalrymen, we combat-hardened field troops felt relatively safe. We were a little surprised to see a fuel tanker alongside the road as we made the turn to head west. We were cautioned to approach carefully; there was no word out about the truck. Why was it all alone? The cab appeared empty, and we wondered where the driver was. As the lead tank cautiously approached the truck, he gave the truck a respectfully wide berth. As he passed abeam the cab, the platoon radio net exploded with hooting and hollering from the lead tank commander; he was straining mightily to see inside the truck's cab.

"Woo hoo! Get ya some, boy!" He motioned to us to look in the truck's cab. "Man, check this out!"

A short-time girl was orally servicing the truck driver. He was not at all bothered by the interruption of noise, road dust, or voyeurs, and he continued to enjoy the fruits of her labors. He just smiled at us, flashing us the peace sign as he reclined against the passenger door. He was wearing his steel pot and flak vest, and had a walrus mustache. It was quite the sight. Each trailing vehicle passed extremely close to the truck to get the best view. Crews made catcalls on the radio net for the next few minutes, until each had checked out the action and passed by. A fuel truck stopped, a solo driver, a local whore—I guess that spot was considered a safe area by local units. I am not sure I would have been so bold.

ARVN infantry was riding on my tank, and we had six to eight of them on board including the platoon leader. He was looking sharp in his spiffy uniform, but a bit too formal for combat. His men were the usual ragtag bunch of peasants, appearing more like VC than ARVN. (Hmm, I wonder.) None of those guys was comfortable as we rolled cross-country across previously defoliated jungle. The ride was rough, and they scowled at me. Maybe they would have appreciated being on top while we busted jungle. I was not paying a lot of attention to them until I noticed a commotion, and then I turned to see what was going on. The ARVN officer was in the face of what I thought was probably a private, and he was aggressively dressing him down; the private was shamed. I began to feel a little empathy for the kid and wanted that officer to stop what I assumed was chickenshit harassment. I was shocked when that officer struck him several times. Different army, different culture, but as long as the officer did not draw his pistol, or one of his men raise a weapon, it really was not my business. We were on guard, just in case. The officer turned to me and smiled, and I thought it very strange—until I saw that private produce a cold can of Coke and return it to our marmite can. Then *I* was ready to hit that private. Sodas were as precious as whatever ice we were lucky enough to have them in. Do not mess with my stuff, Luke the Gook!

Tanks broke their torsion bars frequently, sometimes in the middle of the night, jolting the guards. It was the same when a tank's hydraulic pump kicked on with its screeching whine (only) at "oh-dark-thirty." When a torsion bar broke, we would replace it ASAP. Our field maintenance guys worked miracles: they replaced our road wheels, torsion bars, tracks, and they could pull the pack (engine and transmission) out of a tank to work on it—all while out in the boonies!

One broken torsion bar on my tank proved very difficult to remove. It was not unusual for one to be difficult, but that one was more stubborn than most. It would not budge. We were told to get it changed immediately, we would be moving out soon. I do not think I would have appreciated very much being left behind. Then I had a brainstorm. I went to the demo chest and pulled a chunk of C-4 off a fresh block. I grabbed a blasting cap and some fuse. I pressed C-4 onto the head of the torsion bar at the opening, using just enough so the blast would not damage the road wheel arm—I hoped. I cleared people from that side of the tank, and then I lit the fuse. There was no boom, just a muffled pop. The torsion bar was promptly removed and replaced. I used the smallest charge I calculated (guessed) would do the job. I was lucky that I had been correct that time, and there was no damage to any part of the tank.

First platoon was on a thunder run along a route that took them straight through a small village. We were behind them traveling at normal road speed. Each village hooch was lined up along the road. When the human residents heard us coming, they always came right up to the edge of the road, waved, and begged as we passed. The non-human residents, at least on this day, were not smart enough to stop, however.

A large pig, no doubt a prized possession of a villager, darted in front of one of the first platoon vehicles—advantage armor. Restitution for the loss must have been made, because I do not recall an indignant Vietnamese chattering angrily at us as we passed through. Well, not any more than normal. Owing to the delay and late afternoon, first platoon began to set up an NDP several hundred meters outside the village. We joined them to facilitate evening resupply. I visited with guys in first platoon, and they told me their pig was going to be roasted for their evening meal. Hell, I wanted an invitation to that dinner, so I went to make nice to their platoon sergeant and his pig.

When I arrived, I saw an enormous pig hanging by its heels from a tank's main gun. The animal showed no trauma from its run-in with Quarter Cav, except for its gutting wound, which had been made with the skill of a surgeon; someone knew what he was doing. That someone was SFC Kaeka—The Great Kahuna—Lima's platoon sergeant. He was dressing the pig to pit-roast it, and had ordered a few pounds of butter to be flown out with our daily resupply.

I sensed that pig would be a real treat, and I wanted some. I attempted to endear myself to the decision makers, until I realized not a single one of them was very keen on sharing their bounty. I did not blame them at all. Who was this interloper? They were all my friends, but we had never tested our friendship over a Hawaiian-style, pit-roasted pig, especially when we had not seen a mess hall in quite a while. I wanted to dine, not just fuel myself. Before I could figure a way to get myself included, we received orders to move out in response to an American unit needing support. I almost cried as I watched The Great Kahuna cut the line from which his pig hung. Then it just laid there—our mouths still watering—in the sandy soil awaiting recovery by the villagers as they scavenged our site after we departed, the hard work already done for *their* feast. For weeks while I was on night guard, I contemplated what might have been, and I salivated freely.

There was another pig. Second platoon was RIFing an area adjacent to a field of tall grass. Someone spotted a pig or a boar, and one vehicle gave chase. Soon the entire platoon was making nonsensical tracks all over the high grass as each vehicle maneuvered to see the target and tried to get a shot. One person caught a glimpse, and our entire platoon gave chase in that direction. Our prey would be spotted once again and, when announced on the radio, all vehicles changed direction in unison. We were moving like a flock of starlings at sunset, flying first one way, and then making a sharp turn another way—and on it went. Our prey eluded us.

There was yet another. We smelled death one morning while RIFing an area next to defoliated jungle. Usually, that meant there was a victim of H&I fire nearby. Since a body count was an important item to Higher, any dead body was reported, whether the death was a result of our efforts or was merely discovered by us. We searched in a pattern similar to the other pig sighting; we assumed that our subject would not be moving and that it was human. After about five minutes of very foul smelling search, we spotted the smell's source. It was not a human victim of H&I at all, but a porcine victim. Another pig! Decomposition sets in fast in that part of the world, and that thing was not in very good shape. We moved away quickly, upwind.

Periodically we would find human H&I victims, in ones and twos. We would search the bodies, our thoroughness a function of their state of decomposition. We did not find H&I victims daily, but it was not unusual to stumble across them. It was difficult to determine exactly how many there were if there were more than one. The gallows humor reporting method was to count the feet and divide by two. At least once there was an odd number; we assumed that rounding that number up to an even one was acceptable to Higher.

We found a body once that did not appear to be an H&I kill since there was no noticeable trauma. He was bloated from decomposition, so no one checked his pockets. Since we did not find any weapon or other equipment, we concluded he had not been alone. We also assumed our find was male—no one checked, and it did not matter. I worried that any second he might explode on us as the heat of the day built.

Someone, certainly an FNG, but I cannot remember who, decided to poke the body to get it to deflate. Why did he do that? Those of us who knew better were not fast enough to stop him. As a result, we all got an extra-large dose of the death-smell headed our way, one that would remain with us for some time. The FNG who did the poking got very nasty blowback, learning a critical lesson. I do not know if he ever got clean again. For weeks, though, he suffered barbs from us about still smelling.

Either that same day or a day later, we were about one hundred meters away and spotted another body. That one was not as bloated, so we reasoned he was a fresh kill, and probably from overnight. I did not dismount and one of the guys landed a souvenir, an NVA/VC officer's belt buckle with star. Once again, my standard luck was evident; someone took home a coveted belt buckle, and I received peripheral blowback from a bloated corpse.

On the subject of smelling, I was told very early on that some guys learned how to smell "Gooks in the area." At first I scoffed, but in short order I became a believer when they could often predict contact. Later, there were times when I thought I could smell them also. Today I cannot describe the sensation, but something hit one's olfactory senses, and it set off internal alarms. It was suggested that the smell came from living in tunnels. That made sense to me.

Assigning one Kit Carson scout per platoon was the norm, but second platoon had two of them for a while. Chum had been with us for several months, and a new one, Phoung, had been with us for only a few weeks, finishing his training on-the-job. I do not think Phoung had bathed since *before* he was in the tunnels as an NVA/VC. He did not bathe even when we went to an FSB. We all smelled bad, but were used to those we worked with. We joked Phoung was planted by the NVA, a secret chemical or biological weapon. He was told to bathe immediately; we threatened his life. He did, and we never had to threaten him again.

Our Kit Carson scouts Chum and Phoung.

We made a rare trek west of our AO to Cu Chi, where the 25th Infantry Division was based on top of the largest tunnel complex found in Vietnam. Of course, no one had a clue at the time. While officers did the officer thing, we peons milled about and checked out the scenery. The more curious among us soon spotted some LRRP (Long Range Recon Patrol) rations stored by the pallet full—in the open, unguarded. A couple of our guys liberated a few boxes. Consuming that type of ration was new to us, and they were a very special treat. The meals were dehydrated and we prepared them for consumption without much effort—just add hot water. My favorite meal was rice with beef and gravy. Adding hot sauce made it into a field-gourmet meal. We ate well for a few weeks.

We began working in the Iron Triangle, an area that had

been almost completely Rome plowed and defoliated in years past. We were in two columns RIFing when one of the lead tanks fell into a hole. I did not see it fall in; I was looking elsewhere until I heard the radio commotion. There it sat—its back end in a hole and its main gun pointing at the mid-day sun. Another tank got into position, hooked up and pulled it out. It had fallen into a weapons cache—a very large and timeworn weapons cache. There were about a dozen machine guns, other assorted rifles, and thousands of rounds of small arms ammunition. Most of the weapons were still in crates. Of those that were not, many were still in waxed paper and cosmoline. For the next few days, all of our vehicles sported extra (and antique) machine guns. That is, until they were all ordered to the rear. I never heard any more about that cache, but I believe those arms and ammunition were stored much earlier, during the Vietnamese resistance to the French or the Japanese. Its location was probably lost to the enemy when the area was resettled and Rome plowed.

We moved to an area northeast of Lai Khe, one that had jungle and open, flat, grassy areas. There were long stretches of red, dusty road, an intersection, and a village nearby. With the exception of a small patch of jungle, there was very little vegetation. Squadron HQ was with us—in full complement with its antenna farm and special purpose vehicles. There was also a field mess, and as long as we were nearby, we would receive better rations. We RIF'd the jungle and areas surrounding it by day. At night, the line platoons switched off securing HQ and the NDP. Units not securing HQ were in night ambush positions nearby. We believed that something big was going on, because infantry was shuttled in and out by Huey, the Rat Patrol was with us, and HQ was secure and well-established. As usual, we had no clue.

The Rat Patrol was fashioned after the TV series of the same name. The show was about the campaign in North Africa during World War II and was popular in the middle sixties.

Our version of Rat Patrol was a small and very mobile unit of jeeps with mounted Fifties and M60 machine guns. I am not sure what hit and run accomplishment the new Rat Patrol may have had, but their TV counterparts, Hollywood heroes all, were always successful. At the time, I thought it was an easy way to get heavy and light machine gun fire to an ambush, or respond to a need quickly without the liabilities particular to armor and/or infantry. The Rat Patrol appeared to be a useful complement to armor and infantry, and at a low cost in terms of personnel and equipment.

Tommy Mathis' mine damaged ACAV.

Tommy Mathis was a track commander in first platoon whose ACAV encountered a planted mine while the platoon was maneuvering in darkness. We were told the FO (Forward Observer—an artillery liaison) riding with him lost his legs. I saw Tommy's track the next morning and remembered Joe Chiacchio's damaged ACAV back in June. Tommy's crew and the FO were fortunate to survive.

The next day broke routinely, a fall morning with skies of clear blue, a very intense blue, and without a cloud in sight. The air was still relatively cool. I loved the mornings. They were like summer mornings at home, enjoyable before the heat and humidity sapped all strength and energy. As any morning in Vietnam, I eagerly anticipated breakfast—it was always a special treat. The menu that day included powdered eggs. Real eggs were always preferable, but by adding a little ketchup and hot sauce to powdered eggs, they were palatable, *almost* tasty. We knew we were fortunate to receive hot meals as often as we did.

My driver, Nick Wolf, and I sat directly across from one another at the end of a picnic table next to the CP. I was ready to chow down and had my quart of Foremost milk, cold and refreshing. Life was good. We could see in the distance a jeep approaching, a large cloud of orange dust in trail. It looked like a pick-up truck driving the back roads of north Georgia, the omnipresent dust flying. It was the Rat Patrol. They had been working the surrounding area for a few days setting nightly ambushes.

Someone nearby yelled out, "Here comes Hollywood."

Nick and I concurred.

"Those guys watch too much TV," Nick said.

"Somebody did, that's for sure. I see a point to the effort. Probably makes sense on paper," I said.

"Maybe not."

"I wouldn't want to be out there...just two jeeps...a handful of guys...no way. Are they medal hunting? Or is somebody upstairs using them as bait?"

As the jeeps came into our NDP, we saw two NVA/VC bodies on the hood of the lead jeep. I was again reminded of home and struck with an image from deer season. I do not hunt and never have, except for what we did in-country, and that game returned fire. One does not grow up Southern without seeing deer on the hood of a pickup truck during deer season. The Rats that morning were the image of Bubba in his pickup with a buck on the hood, driving through farmer Brown's barbed-wire gate out to the main road. The Rat's job overnight was well done—two fewer bad guys to shoot at us.

Then we saw that the body closer to us suffered an open head trauma, having been introduced to the advantages our .50 caliber weapons gave us.

Coming up fast and about ten feet from our table, the Rat driver hit his brakes hard. When he did, the closer man's head rolled forward surrendering its contents—airborne. The driver, clearly astonished, pulled himself up with his steering wheel to watch. One not-so-intact brain fell to just within arm's reach of Nick and me, and there it sat. We nonchalantly peered down at it resting there, inanimate, mindless, with a tinge of crimson complementing its ghastly pale yellow-gray. The orange dust settled on it, on us, and on our breakfasts.

That thing on the ground resembled our powdered eggs. To the rhythm that a crew gains after months of living and fighting together, Nick and I looked back at our untouched powdered eggs and ketchup. We looked at one another, smiled, shrugged, and then returned to eating our breakfasts. Life was still good.

The Rat driver had intended to disturb our breakfast with an "oops." He had tried to show he was a hard-assed, cavalier combat veteran and how tough the Rat Patrol was. He was not nearly as un-bothered as he had intended. The revulsion on his face told the tale; he would have to clean up the mess he made. In Vietnam, what was a little dust with breakfast?

On 24 November 1969, the Rat Patrol tripped an overhead claymore mine, wounding three enlisted men and killing Rat Six, their leader. The unit was disbanded.

Chapter 14

The Familiar Was Never Routine

As November began, there was an increase in enemy activity. The mines and booby-traps remained at a standard high rate of aggravation. In the field, we were always at risk of triggering one, and we found too many, too frequently. Such was the case on 5 November, when an ACAV hit a mine and the driver, Eugene Jenkins, was KIA. Our new medic took one look at his body and spontaneously projectile vomited. Ours was a brutal business; deaths were rarely clean. There was nothing anyone could do for Jenkins except to put him in a body bag and send him home.

Thereafter, though, we had precious little faith in our new medic. He was sent to us as Doc Witwicki's replacement when he was promoted to Alpha Troop's chief medic. Wayne Witwicki left big shoes to fill. The new medic remained an FNG, and he needed time to prove himself. First, he needed to get past that day's event, his first combat trauma. In time, after he grew accustomed to the obscene experiences that such physical traumas are, he restored our confidence.

> *Wayne "Doc" Witwicki is one of my heroes. He says he was only doing his job as our medic; I contend he did it at a level beyond what other medics did. More than once, when a mine or booby-trap exploded and before the smoke had risen, Doc Witwicki would run past with his aid bag in tow, anticipating the cries of "medic," and without regard for his personal safety. We knew he would take care of us.*

I went to the rear for a day or two, and I missed what the rest of my platoon called the Turkey Shoot. They were RIFing in a grassy area with large bushes, investigating a suspected enemy location. They said their day was routine until the platoon rolled right over a bunker complex. The NVA (or VC) started running around trying to escape, and our guys picked many of them off.

Meanwhile, I had my own fun in the rear. One evening, our friend the combat cook and I served as bartenders for a party held by some rear-echelon officers. There were half a dozen women there—very real and very round-eyed women. I presumed they were army nurses and officers, too. They were paying attention to the male officers and vice versa. The army fraternization policy precluded personal interaction between officers and enlisted personnel, so my friend and I would not be among those who might get lucky that night. A few nurses flirted with us, but being only a Buck Sergeant and an SP4 (Specialist Fourth Class), we could not offer enough for them to forget the rules. Still, we had a good time opening beer cans for the lot. Yes, that *is* correct; there were no pop-tops, only the old-school church key.

Two of Alpha Troop's senior NCOs—one a sergeant first class and the other a staff sergeant, former field troopers with assignment in the rear—also attended the party. They were older than the crowd of twenty-something officers and not as sophisticated. They tried in vain to flirt with the nurses, but those gals just were not having any of it. Those two NCOs, one of whom I respected and the other I had not much use for (but did not know very well), were so out of their element that they clung to the bar all evening looking silly. One wore the rank insignia of Second Lieutenant and the other wore the insignia of First Lieutenant. The women were not fooled. I am certain a few of the actually commissioned officers were the ones who put those two guys up to it. Were the fun-loving gentlemen-by-act-of-Congress well intentioned?

As two temporary soldiers, my friend the cook and I were simply bartending while enjoying the adult show by the officers. I am sure we confided in one another lust for a nurse or two. My dim memory has nothing beyond that, except that everyone was having a few laughs, even the two senior NCOs.

Dismounted patrols came too frequently. I did not like them, and I had not been trained for them. One ambush scared me more than usual, though, but not for fear of bodily harm. There was always that fear, albeit at a low level—with the occasional heart-stopping spike. On that ambush night, second platoon was to set up an NDP outside of a village at a semi-improved road's T-type intersection. We were short a few vehicles, thus, we were short men. I was hoping our nightly ambush, my responsibility to lead, could be deferred to a time when we would be closer to full strength. It was not.

LT Winters and I studied the ambush site on his map. The spot selected appeared, in the context of my experience, not to be a very big deal. Just show up, and if someone comes ditty-bopping along blow him away. I did not think we would be near a route they might take, but that was not a certainty.

That night's dismounted ambush mission, however, was problematic from the get-go. There were only four of us going out, and two were from my tank. Our mission that night was to engage any interloper until the platoon responded. Yeah, right. I doubt we could have survived until the platoon—what there was of it—traveled to us. Our ambush site and the NDP site were half a klick apart; the route was treeless, over rolling terrain and required crossing a stream. I pointed out to LT Winters that the distance and that creek would delay their efforts to get to us.

I was not happy, but I knew we had to do it, so as usual I registered no complaint. Too soon, it was time to move out. We departed with only steel pot, flak vest, poncho, M-16s and one bandoleer of ammo each, a couple of frags each, a "prick twenty-five" (PRC-25 radio) with an extra battery, and several claymores, detonation cord, and clackers for the kill zone.

As dusk settled in, we moved out across the road into the field of low grass, much like un-mowed zoysia grass. Along the way, we crossed the stream, noting it was only about a foot and a half deep by two feet across. (Small, yes, but it *would* have slowed them getting to us.) The locals had driven bamboo into the streambed across its width to trap fish, and on that night there were a few in the trap. We took a circuitous route to mask our destination from onlookers—a feeble attempt; the only logical place to set an ambush that was not clearly in the open was where we were heading.

Ahead I saw the remnants of fencing, long unused. There was scrub brush, and very little of it, surrounding that old fence. I thought we could settle in there after clearing it of booby-traps; I allowed myself to think that things might not be too bad that night, after all. That little bit of cover atop the small knoll would allow us to see along avenues of approach, and it would afford us cover. With only about one hundred meters remaining to the knoll and cover, the sky fell in a sudden, violent deluge. It was not a storm, but very heavy rain—a rain unknown since the rainy season had beat down on us, a time when we often could not see for more than two feet. We had been walking single file spread twenty meters apart when the visibility had been good. With the restricted visibility, we needed to be closer together. We put on ponchos, but were already soaked. When I peeked out through the hood, I counted only three of us.

"Shit! Where's Freddie?" I asked no one in particular.

The little guy who looked like the love child of Wally Cox and Woody Allen, a veteran of 12 August, the monkey killer, the shitter killer—a guy who always appeared scared—that guy was gone. He was there with us, and then he was not. He had simply vanished. So much for my expert planning and skillful leadership. As always seems to happen at inopportune times, the boss called.

"Six wants to know how soon we'll be set up."

The radio handset was held out for me. I declined.

"Ten to fifteen mikes (minutes). Tell him we're a hundred meters short...do *not* tell him about Freddie...we'll find him."

We started to call Freddie's name, probably too loudly. He could not have heard us, though, even if he were only five feet away—it was raining that hard. After ten minutes without success and anxious, I decided we would plant ourselves right there on the spot, even if we did not have the high ground or cover. That was perhaps the most dangerous place for an ambush ever; it certainly was the worst one that I ever selected. We did not put out claymores for fear of killing Freddie. Once we were established and settled in, I notified command of our location and coordinated artillery support. It was the worst possible scenario—other than Freddie had been captured already. If we made contact with the enemy, there were a hundred ways he could have been killed by friendly fire.

    The three of us lay there prone, weapons at the ready with our boots touching—a security blanket of sorts. After a long while the rain finally slowed, finally stopping altogether after about an hour more. We had a steam bath inside our ponchos, so we removed them right away. Naturally, that meant we would freeze. I reminded the other guys that in the dark Freddie would look like an NVA private. It would not be too cool for us to blow him away thinking he was a bad guy. Although it was a long night, I had no trouble at all staying awake. My mind raced, and I pictured an NVA snatch team that had Freddie half way to Hanoi. I worried our perimeter might be infiltrated because someone fell asleep on guard, thus allowing a dedicated NVA soldier to slit everyone's throat but mine—only because he had not gotten to me yet. No, please, no hand-to-hand. My ear began to hurt because I held the radio's handset to my head tightly—our hourly sit-reps were the comfort of home and safety.

    Dawn broke and with its arrival came light tricks. I was convinced I saw a platoon of NVA marching toward us—it was actually several clusters of grass sticking up at high points on the slope. Then the cover we had wanted to nest in appeared to have NVA within; I was so convinced, I almost fired at them. I could not discuss my insecurities with the others; strangely, they were counting on me for confidence. We held our lookout for Freddie. Nothing. There should have been enough light to see him by that time, so I stood up to a crouch and took in the three-sixty view. Still nothing. Since nobody shot at me, I slowly stood taller. Something caught my attention. Was it a puddle? No, it was on a slope. Could it be Freddie? It had to be. I alerted the guys, and we moved in the direction of what I saw, very cautiously. I was as much worried about NVA as I was a nervous, cold and pissed-off Freddie, armed with a full magazine and his M-16 set on rock-n-roll.

Softly I called out, "Freddie!"

The form on the ground moved, and an arm reached up and pulled back the poncho hood—it *was* Freddie!

"Where the fuck have you guys been all night?" He was pissed and yelled at me in a whisper. "I've been lying here, freezing fuckin' cold...waiting for instructions, dammit. I was right here in this fuckin' water."

Freddie stood up slowly; he was stiff from not moving.

"Is this ambush over? Can we just go on back home now? Jeez...home...I wish."

"We had you covered the whole time, Freddie. You were never in danger." I lied. "But this thing isn't over until we're back safely in the NDP."

I called the command track to inform them we were on the move, returning to their perimeter. I asked them not shoot at us.

On 15 November, we pulled into an NDP one afternoon to resupply and RON (Remain Over Night) with troop HQ. Awaiting evening resupply, I was meandering the perimeter when First Sergeant Poncerella hollered at me.

"Sergeant Street!"

"Hey, Top, what's up?" I turned to join him.

"You are! Congratulations." He threw a fatigue shirt at me. "You've been promoted."

I checked out the shirt and there were chevrons and rocker on the sleeves. My new rank of staff sergeant—that felt good. Top told me my promotion had been effective ten days earlier. He had no copies of the orders, telling me they would be coming—in army time.

"Thanks, Top," I said with sincere humility. "I appreciate you pushing this for me."

"No, son, thank you. The army needs more like you. You and those like you are the future of this man's army."

If one of my friends had said that, we would have gone off on a five-minute laughing fit. We did not want to be in "this man's army." No, not us—not back then. I accepted Top's compliment and silently vowed to ensure he would not be disappointed in me. About a month later, the paperwork finally caught up to me. My orders were dated 6 December, and the effective date of rank was, in fact, 5 November. The army—go figure.

RIFing yet again, we worked an area near a river where the ground was softer than we usually encountered. Someone spotted movement as we approached the river, and a firefight ensued, which resulted in four enemy dead—two female. The females had documents indicating they were nurses. After a search of the surrounding area, it was time to move out. When the lead tank attempted to get under way, it became stuck. Efforts to free it only mired it more. Another tank was sent to retrieve it, and it too became stuck. Ultimately, a *third* tank and a VTR were needed to pull the two tanks out—one at a time. Later, along an improved road, my tank slid off the road into a ditch, throwing a track. I was embarrassed. It only took one tank to pull me out.

On Thanksgiving Day 1969, we were in the Iron Triangle riding around, bored, and awaiting a fine dinner of turkey and all the accompaniments. I hoped they would bring some chocolate milk for the holiday; that would certainly be a treat. We had not been in that area of the Iron Triangle for quite a while, indicating to me the area was reasonably safe. There was no jungle, only acreage where the jungle had been Rome plowed years earlier. We moved atop a bluff that overlooked the Saigon River and began RIFing, in search of anything that might be a sign of activity, either above ground or below. The area was historically active with insurgents, and problematic. It was along the infiltration route that ran from Cambodia to Saigon, a route taken by insurgents fighting the Japanese, the French, the Americans, and the South Vietnamese.

There was evidence of habitation from years before, but only scattered remnants. The population had long ago been resettled and the villages razed, leaving behind at least one graveyard, complete with headstones resting flat. It was not very long before an ACAV detonated a small charge, breaking its track. The explosion was probably caused by a booby-trap or a small mine that was ancient, and it did not cause serious damage. We set up a security perimeter, and then swept the area for other explosives while the ACAV's crew repaired their track. Our fortune was good that day—resupply would bring fuel, ammo, water, *and* Thanksgiving dinner out to us at that very spot.

Tired old Canned Heat with a thrown track.

While we waited, I sat guard in my cupola enjoying the view. Down about two hundred feet and a half-klick away, the Saigon River crooked just below us. Within that crook was a marshland that covered about one hundred meters from the river's edge to the wood line. Nothing was out of place in my world, as I only existed in the temporary bliss of a beautiful fall day. The temperature was hot but tolerable, and the sky was brilliant blue and cloudless—Carolina blue. The only concern we had was the timing of our evening meal.

Someone spotted NVA/VC walking along the marsh at the wood line, traveling rapidly. Before long, a pair of Cobra gunships arrived, and they were directed to the target. The NVA/VC ducked into the wood line when they heard the choppers coming. The Cobras lit up the area with rockets and grenades and ended their mission with mini-gun fire. I loved the sound of mini-guns; they purred. As the Cobras were making their final run, an OV-10 Bronco arrived on station. He was there to coordinate the fast-movers (jet ground attack aircraft) that were en route. The Cobras departed, and then the Bronco began to dive and ascend in nearly perfect vertical racetrack patterns right above the moving target. The fast movers, a pair of F-4 Phantoms, came into view and earshot quickly.

We did not often get such prompt service. Most of the time we had to wait for quite a while—if we received *any* help. When the weather was not keeping ground support aircraft grounded, then other units usually had priority over us. We would complain, but on reflection we realized we were last on the list because we could take care of ourselves most of the time. We were 1st Infantry Division's fire brigade, so it was us who usually responded to others' need for firepower. We could respond when the ceiling was overcast and low, unlike the fast movers.

That particular Thanksgiving must have been a slow day for infantry units since ground support aircraft responded to our request promptly. The Phantoms flew a horizontal pattern at around fifteen hundred feet, circling the Bronco as he flew his vertical racetrack. The Bronco spotted movement in the jungle below and fired a Willie Pete (White Phosphorus) rocket to mark the target for the Phantoms. Those three pilots were dancing to the same music: as Phantom A released his first bomb, Phantom B was on the opposite side of the racetrack; as each Phantom was turning, the Bronco descended to mark another target and ascended to spot more. Those guys had danced together before—they were good.

We watched and cheered each time a bomb exploded. Then the napalm fell. We had all seen napalm dropped before; we knew what it would do. We had also worked on occasion with our squadron's Zippo tracks (napalm dispensers), so we had intimate knowledge of the effects. That day our view was from on high, and it was as if we were doing the dropping. Our Thanksgiving show was spectacular entertainment. I was in awe of the coordination and skill required to perform at that level of flying *and* fighting. I felt much as Corporal Bruno Stachel, George Peppard's character in *The Blue Max* did. He was muddy and tired in a World War I trench and vowed to improve his lot by becoming a flying officer.

I was impressed, yes—yet, I made zero effort to go to flight school.

> *As a commercial pilot and flight instructor today, I have had the opportunity to fly with veterans who were WWII, Korea, and Vietnam combat pilots. I made it a point to tell them I appreciate their ability to fly and fight, and that I have done both, but never done them at the same time. My favorite response came from a WWII vet in his 80s: "We were kids, just dumb kids." I can relate.*

We continued RIFing during daylight and secured FSBs at night. We delved deeper into the Vietnamization program, increasingly working with ARVN infantry, both straight-leg and mechanized—usually a company-sized element. We were none too happy to be so close to them, and often wondered what they knew that we did not. With an ARVN mechanized unit one day, we established an NDP in a small clearing after busting dense jungle for several hours. We observed light and noise discipline whenever it was possible, although anyone around us was surely aware of exactly where we were. At night, that discipline was critical. After it was dark for a while and long past when noise should be at a minimum and lights should not exist at all, I could hear the sound of Vietnamese music playing from across our perimeter. When I looked around trying to locate the source of the noise, I saw that two ARVN tracks had their internal white lights on. Fortunately, their ramps were up and the rear doors were closed, but the white light was still visible through the hatch opening.

What the hell were those guys thinking? Were they the locator beacon for that evening's entertainment, an assault on our perimeter? We suffered no probe or attack that night, but neither could we get the ARVN to be more careful. The damn lights stayed on for hours. The ARVN troops were in no hurry to protect themselves, day or night. One day we took a break to rest and grab food, and so did the ARVN. After lunch, the order was given to mount up and move out. But wait—the ARVN were not yet finished. Really? Yes, we had to wait until they were.

Contrast the ARVN's approach to the war effort with our own: I received a package from home containing a few canned daiquiris, a canned ham, cheese, and canned pineapple rings. I was ready for a feast. We halted our RIF, and I expected a break of about fifteen minutes and began to prepare a special lunch. I set up a stove using track end-connectors and C-4. Then I opened the meat, and using the lid as a skillet, began to warm up some ham chunks. When they were beginning to brown, I added pineapple chunks. My crew rolled daiquiris in ice to get them cold. I added cheese in small bits so it would melt a little and make a sauce. The ambient temperature had given the cheese a head start. Just as I was ready to parcel that magnificent treat out to my crew, I was informed of a movement order. I knew it was coming—the other tracks were already moving. We enjoyed our meal later that evening.

During a night movement in the Trapezoid, we were in our standard two-column formation, and I was the lead tank on the left column. Our platoon command track was the first vehicle behind the lead tank in the right column. Our platoon leader, LT Winters, was still very much an FNG. That was a problem: he was the authority that should be leading us. Our movement was painfully difficult and slow, owing mostly to the darkness that night. During the march toward our NDP site and, after many corrections from LT Winters, he stopped both columns to gather his wits. None of us knew where we were, but we did not have a map or know our destination—he did, and he did not share.

He called me.

"Mike-7, Mike-6, where are you?"

"7...I am just one vehicle ahead of you in the left column, the same relative position I was in when we moved out. Left, forty-five degrees."

He should have seen our silhouette against the night sky, even as dark as it was; he was lower than we were. There *was* sufficient ambient light, not much, but enough.

"-7, -6...I know that. *Where* are you located?"

"Mike-6. Look to your left, about forty-five degrees and twenty-five feet away. I am the one on top."

I was trying not to be a smart ass, but to that point, the guy had not shown us very much. I, for one, was losing my patience. Someone would be killed if he were not careful. I searched to my front left, then right, sweeping the darkness and hoping I would not find any movement. If there were bad guys around, I hoped they were smart bad guys who did not want to pick a fight. That is when I was bathed in white light from my right rear. Instinctively, I grabbed the handle of my .45 pistol, but did not bring it up—I knew our guys were back there. The light was concentrated on my face for what felt like a lifetime.

"Hey! Which one of you fucking idiots is shining that light? Turn that goddamned thing off, NOW!"

I was not pleased. If I had thought about it, one of the regular guys would never have done that—they knew better. They were in-country smart. I assumed it was the boss.

"This is Mike-6," he responded. "It's me. Now I know where you are."

"I gotta tell ya, sir," I started, "that's one of the dumbest things I ever saw an FNG do. That'll get someone killed or fucked-up something awful...and I don't think you want that."

The only response, delayed a few seconds, was two clicks of a microphone. I found out later that night that the clicks did not come from Winters, but from another track commander agreeing with me. Winters never spoke of it again—at least to me.

On 1 December 1969, the first draft lottery since WWII was held. Draft risk thereafter was a function of birth date and order drawn. The first drawn was sure to be drafted, the last considered safe. On that date: (1) I was over twenty-one; (2) had number 208; (3) was in Vietnam; (4) my MOS was 11B40—infantry squad leader; (5) I was a combatant. The draft lottery was the exclamation mark on my failed plan. What could I do? I chuckled at the irony. Once again, I was reminded what a dumb ass I had been.

Chapter 15

A Painful Fall from Grace

Sergeant Nolan left the field, and we were assigned a new platoon sergeant, SFC Kamai, a Hawaiian. Someone said he and The Great Kahuna were cousins. I thought that to be literally true until a West Coast guy suggested that all Hawaiians called themselves cousins. SFC Kamai was a good leader and brought to us the experience of a prior tour. He was mission oriented, and he was very concerned about everyone making it home, and in one piece. Coincident to his arrival we returned to convoy duty on QL13 for several days—Lai Khe to Quan Loi. Nothing to complain about for me; I liked it. It was cooler but dustier, but there was that always present danger of ambush.

Christmas was approaching, and Nick's family sent him a small artificial Christmas tree, complete with two bulbs and a length of paper rings to drape over it. There was something comforting about seeing that tree on top of our tank; it was homey. Every time we would halt, Nick would emerge from his driver's hole and put it up.

A week later we relocated to the road to Song Be. Along the way, we passed through a village that I did not know. On the other side we moved as quickly as an armored cavalry unit can move straight into the jungle. We busted jungle for a few hours, searching, but finding nothing major. At least one RPG team appeared and melted away after firing and missing; the usual stuff. We broke out near another village and then made a thunder run through it. As we departed, I noticed a stretch of barbed wire that had a severed arm dangling from it. There must have been an action there very recently, or the locals would certainly have cleaned it up by then, and there were no kids nearby.

Then we went back off-road again and RIF'd. We were

working a free-fire zone—we were cleared to shoot anything. Anything, that is, except the villagers. SFC Kamai instructed us not to fire any weapon unless we were receiving fire or he instructed otherwise. In a large Rome plowed area with only low scrub brush for ground cover, we halted, shutting down our vehicles. We took a break and sat there quietly for about ten minutes. From near the rear of the column came a shot, followed in seconds by one more, then followed by many more—a whole M-16 magazine's worth.

"Cease fire...cease fire! I told you guys to hold fire."

I, for one, was glad I was not in close proximity to the platoon sergeant; he sounded pissed.

A few seconds later we heard, "I don't hear AK fire...who fired, and what the hell were you shooting at?"

"A snake," someone said.

"A snake? What? A *snake*? Why?"

"Because it was a monster and was coming at us."

There was silence, soon broken.

"He's coming back there. It'd better be a fuckin' big one...I sure hope he don't shoot y'all."

Kamai was charging through the scrub brush, flak vest, and steel pot on, his M-16 in hand and .45 strapped to his hip. He looked intense. His command had been ignored, and he was not about to stand for it. We all waited, but no word was forthcoming; SFC Kamai's walk back to his tank did not seem so agitated. Those guys back there must have said the correct things to him.

When Kamai passed my tank, I grabbed my camera and ran back to get a look. The snake was a giant constrictor of some type, probably a python, about twenty feet long and about as round as a softball. It might just have attempted to devour one of us, but I doubt it would have been from atop an ACAV. I resolved right then that whenever I was sleeping on a cot or stretcher on the ground, I would remain on full alert for large snakes. Prior to that day, the thought of such large snakes had never entered my mind.

Just before darkness set in that night, I shaved. The act

of shaving was an abnormal activity for me, one that I avoided until I was uncomfortable. That night it was a particularly terrible shave, much worse than usual. After shaving, my skin was itchy and stinging. While I pondered ways to make my face better, track commanders were called to the platoon leader's track. He announced the Bob Hope show would be in Lai Khe in a few days, and our platoon could send in two men. He told us to make our selections. A night or two in the rear would be nice, but I did not really care if I saw the show or not. I believed anyone who had been in-country longer than me should go before me. Joking, I remarked that I was already shaved. I got that unique look, the one that said, "You selfish, self-centered prick." Two deserving field troopers were selected and sent to the rear to see the show.

On 23 December 1969, while we were working with Troop HQ, I was ordered to take my tank and one ACAV to link up with an ACAV having mechanical problems. Since we were not very far from an improved road, the trip did not take us very long. Once the mission was accomplished, we turned around to catch up with the troop, following the fresh tracks our vehicles left. Halfway to catching up, the ACAV following me hit a mine. It was a big enough charge to break the track and remove a pair of road wheels, but not sufficiently large to cause any other vehicle damage. The crew reported injuries only to their hearing; a phenomenon I had often seen. I knew it would be temporary.

I needed to get to their track to check their injuries and get a close up view of vehicle damage. Remembering 9 June, I hesitated before I jumped down. I considered whether it was a trap and told everyone on my tank to stay put—on guard. First on my mind was a possible ambush, just slightly ahead of concern that we had no method to sweep for secondary mines. I stepped cautiously, fearing the worst with each planting of my foot. The area was unstable with logs from trees felled by Rome plows. I thought I checked out everything adequately, but I had not. I was 9-June-myopic looking for mines, but I forgot that I was in Vietnam—there were many other ways for us to die. I checked the ACAV crew, and they were OK except for their hearing. I asked for a Dustoff.

Within minutes of my request, a Dustoff chopper was on station, seeking guidance to land and pick up the patients. As I guided the pilot into a hover and signaled him to settle his aircraft down to the ground, he shook his head no. I repeated the gesture to settle the Huey down from its hover. Again, no go, and he remained in a four-foot hover. Just as I was about to go and ask him what the hell his problem was, he pointed to the ground right in front of his Huey. I stepped over and onto logs and brush to see where he was pointing. Yikes! There was an unexploded 155 mm artillery round. I was shocked. The pilot had seen it clearly; I had not. I sidestepped his hover until he was comfortable enough to set the chopper down and board the ACAV crew. The Dustoff then lifted off, turned, and flew away. (The ACAV crew returned to the field within two or three days.) We prepared the ACAV for towing, showing proper respect to the unexploded round. Then we moved the disabled ACAV back where we had just come from and to a rendezvous with our maintenance folks. Because our demo track was with the remainder of the troop, I could not blow the 155 mm round, our standard procedure. I notified my platoon leader of the location, and he assured me it would be handled. We continued on our way, a solo march to join the troop. We caught up with them, and they were traveling in two columns. I was told to join the left column as the last vehicle.

Moments after rejoining the troop, my tank hit a mine, much larger than the one the ACAV hit. How? Everyone else *must* have already ridden over it. A flash fire from the blast climbed up beside me, crawling along the slope of the turret, where it dissipated as it reached me. In my peripheral vision, I saw debris sailing through the air right over the head of CPT Dock and his topside crew. I do not think they ever saw it coming. I checked with my guys, and each man was without serious injury, suffering only temporary hearing loss. Unlike the ACAV crew, my guys could still hear me. I wondered if those other guys had been faking. The doctors did not think so. Nick was semi-protected in his driver's compartment, and the rest of my team was on the left side of the tank and away from the blast. The mine was just a loud noise to all three of them. It was *very* loud, and the flash gave me a sunburn on my forearm for the next few days.

Canned Heat was towed back to Lai Khe, and I rode along with it. I viewed the mine damage as an opportunity; I really wanted a new tank for Christmas. Canned Heat was an old rag, the worst tank in the troop—it *always* had some kind of problem. I did not believe it was worth repairing, but to get a new tank it would have to be declared a combat loss. The next morning I checked with our maintenance NCO; I was trying desperately to talk him into doing so, and I harassed him over it. He told me he would check as soon as he could and get back to me. I was anxious. Mid-morning he called me over and showed me a hairline crack in the hull—damn!—I had combat lost a 52-ton tank. That was fun to know, but it was more fun to know I would get a new one. He had already started the paperwork. I emptied old Mike-Seven of weapons and personal stuff. Arriving back at the troop area, Mike Armstrong, who was Alpha Troop XO, was getting into a jeep with another officer.

"Wanna see the Bob Hope show?"

I was surprised at the invitation, since I had forgotten all about it.

"Sure!" I exclaimed, "Got nothing else to do."

"Hop in."

What a journey into REMF-dom that was for me. I am not *that* person, the one with the mindset that my existence deserves more than others merely because I exist, but why did REMFs get all the good seats? During the show, I stood with other non-officer field troopers way back at the very rear of the audience. Not only was the stage a long distance away, but the cameras blocked much of our view.

I estimated there were probably about fifty in the crowd brought in from the field; of the remainder, certainly some were former combatants. The tip-of-the-spear trooper usually gets less than those who support him. That is just the way things are, have always been, and probably always will be.

The greater benefit of the show, I believe, was to those best described by "they also serve who only stand and wait"—our families. I think tip-of-the-spear veterans would agree that it is the exceptional REMF—forgive me, the exceptional rear-echelon soldier—that had no trouble doing what was necessary for a *fighting* man. They deserved a show.

> *During my tour, I never saw a Donut Dolly. I did hear that they might visit a fire-base, but they never did when I was at one. I thought they—and Bob Hope's celebrities—were detrimental to field troops' morale, leaving us wanting them and home more. An attractive, clean, regulated, and medically tested corps of women who provided services to the men would have improved field troops' morale more than Bob Hope's shows or a steak would have—and we certainly craved a good steak; army steaks were lacking. A woman is, well, a woman.*

Merry Christmas to me. I got a new tank. It was clean, green, and we would make it mean. My crew came to the rear, and we loaded it up with our personal stuff and remounted radios, machine guns, and a full basic load of ammunition for all our weapons. My tank had an unopened crate full of new equipment, most of which we had not seen since training at Ft. Knox. My new tank was wonderful—a real tool to help us get the job done. As we left Lai Khe to rejoin Alpha Troop, we tested its speed; it was fast. We made our own solo thunder runs, several of them on the way out. When we operated on roads, our platoon movement speed was lucky to be fifteen miles per hour—the new tank could go thirty. We learned quickly we would only be going fast when my tank was in the lead and not off road. Enjoying the spanking newness of it all, we knew that our brand new tank would look as shopworn and tired as all the other tanks in our unit in a few weeks. Temporarily, we reveled in the freshness of our fifty-two ton steed.

A few days later, we received word that CPT Dock was hurt. His wound should be classified as an injury, since it was (accidentally) self-inflicted—a rookie mistake. He had been with us a few months and seemed competent. I liked him—he was the first officer I knew who attempted to get to know the first names of all the men in his command. Most NCOs and officers referred to everyone by rank or last name; his approach was more personal. My view was that CPT Dock considered us as all in it together and treated us accordingly.

The HQ command vehicles had been with Lima platoon when they discovered a booby-trapped grenade. Typically, the enemy would place a grenade in a can and attach its pin to a tripwire. CPT Dock attempted to throw the grenade instead of blowing it in place. As I said, rookie mistake. He survived his wounds and Alpha Troop was assigned a new CO.

CPT Dock's replacement, CPT Wanna B. General, was an unfortunate selection for Alpha Troop. Second platoon missed CPT Dock's injury and departure, and we missed CPT Wanna B. General's highly memorable (and quite astounding) assumption of command speech. The men of Alpha Troop, at least the ones I spoke with, regarded the captain as the wrong one to lead us. Alpha Troop's esprit de corps was never the same after that speech.

Several of Alpha's troopers, mostly individually, told me of his fine introduction to the troop.

"My name is CPT Wanna B. General. I tell you now, I plan to be a general," he was quoted as saying.

I asked them, "Really, he actually said that?"

"Hell, yes he did."

"How does he think that will motivate us to perform?"

"That man must *not* be thinking. He's too busy with his general fantasy."

"That blows me away. Un-fucking-believable,"

"Fucked-up," another guy said. "It's just fucked-up. But

this is the army, what would you expect?"

I do not think anything else needed to be said to us. My friends told me he said it, and I believed them. I could hear his message, "My career is totally at your cost." The officers whose leadership I respected recognized true leadership is not the issuance of a command; they understood very well the shared risk and were willing to accomplish missions together. Some officers did not get it, and I suspected CPT Wanna B. General, was just such an officer. I would soon be certain he was.

On New Year's Eve, we watched the fireworks off in the distance celebrating the arrival of 1970. The next day we went back to platoon sized RIFing and jungle busting in an area south of Di An, the 1st Infantry Division's rearmost basecamp. The area was a well-known rocket staging area used by VC to harass U.S. basecamps and FSBs within range. Boring duty, certainly, and we hoped it would stay that way.

On one of the first nights back in the field with my new tank, it was again my turn to lead a dismounted ambush. We had RIF'd all day, just our platoon, and we joined the rest of the troop at an NDP for resupply and a meal. It was just after dusk as a Chinook brought supplies out, and by the time our vehicles had been topped off and reloaded, it was fully dark. LT Winters called the platoon into a group. Usually, he would call a mission meeting with his track commanders only—that was standard practice. If SFC Kamai were with us that night, he would have guided that young, still cherry lieutenant.

"Gentlemen," he said, "when we move out, we'll go about one- and one-half klicks back down the road we came in on," he said, pointing to his map, using a flashlight with a red lens, "...about half a klick off the road is where we'll establish our NDP. Tonight's ambush patrol will be led by Sergeant Street and will depart on arrival. Their ambush will be out about two hundred meters farther. We have a good distance to cover in darkness, and we will not be using lights. Stay alert...we make a lot of noise."

There was general bitching and moaning from the

crowd. I quickly did the calculations to determine what time our dismounted ambush would be leaving the safety of the platoon NDP, and I did not like the results at all. That was Charlie's time—he owned the night. Those whose turn it was to go out with me would be trained tankers pretending to be infantry, at night, in a free-fire zone. The crowd around me was just as displeased as I was. I heard in hushed tones, "Is he fucking serious?" and, "This goddamned cherry's gonna get our asses blown away. Fuck him."

Someone spoke directly to LT Winters.

"Sir, do you realize what time we'll set our NDP?"

That was immediately followed by another.

"Sir, do you realize what time it'll be when we set up our dismounted ambush?"

"Yes, I do, but we have our orders."

LT Winters was not moved; the speaker was insistent and no NCO did anything to stop the guy—we all agreed.

"I think it's foolish, sir. I know you didn't decide this, but did you challenge it at all? It's idiotic."

"We have to follow our orders, men," he said. "We must perform the mission as it's assigned."

"Why don't we just stay in the NDP and call our sitreps (situation reports) from there? No one'll know we didn't go."

I was mute, but the idea had merit, and it would keep us in the relative safety of our NDP.

"I was just about to suggest that," the lieutenant offered. "Let's talk about it more when we get there. Now, mount up, let's move out."

At ten o'clock on a very dark night, off we went, traveling very slowly. A little after midnight we arrived at what was the platoon's NDP location. I had no confidence that our still-FNG lieutenant was precise on his coordinates, but what could I do? Surely, he would have someone double-check his work. The ambush team gathered, and I went to the lieutenant for orders. He told me to stay within our perimeter and call in sitreps as though we were in our assigned ambush location. Our platoon frequency was always monitored by Higher, so he reminded us we must be sharp about it. That is just what we did. Our platoon leader made an executive decision without threat or substantive protest. As I said earlier, he should have met with only the track commanders.

By first thing next morning, the scratchy neck I suffered had fully blossomed into a red and itchy rash all along the right side of my neck, with raw spots on my forehead, and likewise on my ass cheek—the right one. My R&R to Sydney was coming up in a month, and I was fully expecting that ass cheek to be privately available. I needed to lose the rash, so I asked Doc to inspect it. He sent me back to the squadron aid station for diagnosis. The medic told me I had ringworm and gave me a powder to clear it up. (It did clear up in time, but it took two more visits to the aid station over the next three weeks.)

Returning to the troop area from the aid station, I was met by Alpha Troop's XO, Mike Armstrong, my former platoon leader.

"What did you do?" he asked me.

"About what?"

He appeared serious, but I was not sure whether he was or not. I tend to lead with humor, so I was ready to return in kind. All my humor was lost in an instant.

"Squadron HQ told me to confine you to the troop area. Do you know what it's about?"

It took me a second or two, but then I realized he was not kidding—I was floored. I could not think of anything that was a problem. The dismounted ambush patrol we did not go out on was not anywhere near my mind—Sydney was the main thing I was thinking about of late.

"No, not at all."

"You are to report to Major (MAJ) ActingCO at eleven."

MAJ ActingCO was *acting* squadron commander while the squadron commander was in Hawaii. Just a few months earlier in his capacity as squadron XO, his regular job, MAJ ActingCO had written my parents a glowing letter. I am sure we all got the same one, but I think my parents thought I was the only one in Vietnam ever to receive such a letter. I never tried to straighten them out.

"Eleven? Okay, I'll be there, on time."

I was perplexed, but the only way I could find out what the hell was going on would be to report to MAJ ActingCO. I gave a thought to the reason being something good. I was having good fortune lately, but then reality set in. Why would I be confined to the area if it *were* good? I could not imagine what the problem was.

"When you're through, find me," Mike said, "and let me know what's going on. This isn't usual...it doesn't bode well."

At five minutes before eleven, I walked into HQ. I sat quietly and waited for the appointed time, my mind racing, exploring all considered possibilities. The sergeant major, who normally was a very warm and genial man to me, ignored my presence. Every clerk in the room who was not required to talk to me avoided eye contact with me. Hell, those that *did* have to talk to me avoided looking directly at me.

At eleven, the clerk said I could go in. Inside, there was the major sitting at the CO's desk and looking as officious as any REMF could. Maybe he was the best combat leader around, but at that moment, I did not know that, and I really did not care. He had information that I did not, and I felt the whole thing was going to make for a bad day for me. When I reported to him, he never gave me "at ease," keeping me braced. Although my eyes were straight ahead, I could see he was referring to blue index cards in his hands. He began to read from one, saying I had the right to remain silent, the right to counsel, the provision of counsel, et cetera. It was the UCMJ (Uniform Code of Military Justice) form of the civilian Miranda Warning.

"You are suspected of being guilty of Article 99, Uniform Code of Military Justice—misbehavior before the enemy...."

I heard nothing after he said, "misbehavior before the enemy." I was very confused, and my face flushed from that confusion—or maybe from fear and anger. Had I once again been confused with someone else? No, it had been meant for me, but it was not the truth. He accused me of "balking"—refusal to carry out orders in combat. My troubles *were* all about the previous night, the dismounted ambush that did not happen. Somehow, they found out about us staying in the NDP, and they were blaming it solely on me, as if that damn cherry lieutenant had not played a role.

The media had recently reported soldiers balking as if it were occurring in every unit and on every single mission. The media did the very same thing with drugs and war crimes. None of those activities was anywhere near the norm for field troops, of course, but they played in the U.S. media as though they were. Critics of the war took that germ from the media, planted it, and cultivated fields of fully blossomed half-truths and sprinklings of absolute falsehoods. Tragically, the competent warrior was swept up in the one-size-fits-all mentality of the media and the anti-war movement.

In retrospect, I believe MAJ ActingCO panicked, thinking he was losing control of the squadron. He must have worried that he would not be returning the same great outfit that he had been given. (If so, he was correct.) Maybe he was using me so his record would show his toughness. Whatever his reason, the facts of his case against me were all wrong—way off the mark. I wondered where he got his information. From our new friend CPT Wanna B. General? That might explain it; the fool worried most about his general's stars. No one asked me anything prior to being charged. The whole thing simply snowballed out of CPT Wanna B. General's desire to make a bold statement to Alpha Troop—to establish himself as its supreme ruler and not just its commanding officer. Damn the facts, just kick ass, and they will get the message. MAJ ActingCO must have agreed with him, or else CPT Wanna B. General intimidated him. They each failed to realize there was a great group in Alpha Troop, and they were screwing it up.

"Would you like to make a statement, Sergeant?"

I wanted a JAG (Judge Advocate General) officer before saying squat to him. So, I declined any comment.

"No, sir, I'll wait until I'm represented by a JAG officer."

"In that case you are restricted to your troop area."

I saluted smartly and departed—dumbfounded. What happened? Although I was in still in Vietnam, my life was good—all things considered. I was respected by my peers, combat soldiers who had confidence in me. Good things had been happening to me, and I liked my unit and the company of my friends. When I returned to Alpha Troop's orderly room, Top was there, and he questioned me. I told him the truth as I knew it, in detail. He was demonstrably displeased with me and did not accept anything I said as valid. He had been my champion, but he turned on me with a vengeance. Why? Why did he not give me a fair shot at defending myself? I believe he had put such stock in me (and a few others) and, given the nature of the charges, he believed I betrayed his trust. That hurt—I had not betrayed him at all. I respected him and was extremely embarrassed by his perception of my failure. I have never known whether he was upset because he thought I balked or he thought that I should have overruled the platoon leader and carried out the mission. The former hurts me if true; the latter I would understand and be disappointed in myself for letting him down. How could I overrule the platoon leader, though? That alone could have been a court-martial offense.

The troop XO and I met, and looked up Article 99 in the UCMJ. I was astounded to read the penalty was death. Since he knew me well, he offered to assist in my defense, telling me he had been involved with a few courts-martial. While that gave me a little consolation, I was stung by the rebuke from Top. Hell, I hated even being thought of in that way. I *was not* that way, and it *is not* in my character to behave the way I was depicted.

Sadly, the next afternoon seven men from Alpha Troop's second platoon, every single guy who would have been on the ambush patrol with me, arrived in the rear. We were sent to other Quarter Cav troops. Lacking evidence of wrongdoing, yet punctuating CPT Wanna B. General's statement to Alpha Troop, we were traded. I went to Charlie Troop, along with

Nick Wolf and Clifford Payne. Others went to Bravo Troop and HQ Troop. There was a little poetic justice for us, though, as LT Winters was relieved of his combat command and assigned to the POL (Petroleum, Oils, and Lubricants) dump as OIC (Officer In Charge). He suffered the most.

I found out all the problems began when a member of the ambush team fell asleep while manning the Prick25 radio and failed to answer a sit-rep call. The next morning, while I was in the rear and unable to defend my ambush team or myself, a knee-jerk reaction mistakenly pointed at much more than was there. A few answers to calm, intelligent questions would certainly have kept our team together if the *actual* squadron CO had been in command, or, if Alpha Troop's CO had been someone who was a true leader, or, if LT Winters had *resembled* a leader. It was a perfect storm of very poor leadership.

On the night of the ambush that was not, I was not the ranking NCO. I was second ranking NCO, and I was *not* about to argue with my lieutenant as he offered us an out to the mission we disagreed with—one fraught with extra-normal dangers. Should the ranking NCO have stepped in? I do not know, maybe. Had I told LT Winters we should perform the mission and then let him talk me out of it, maybe things would have turned out differently. The absolute truth is I never refused *any* mission. We were engaged in a serious business, and we knew it all too well. I was extremely proud to be a small part of Alpha Troop's success while I was with them. I thought ours was the best troop in the squadron, and that our squadron the best in-country unit. After the mass transfer, second platoon could not have been nearly as good a unit. About twenty-five percent of the platoon, the best and most experienced, were forfeited because of an ineffective and dangerous platoon leader, and two career-at-all-cost officers.

> *I softened my view of LT Winters during the years after returning home. Distance from the events and concentrating on making a good life for my family*

helped. When I made a second visit to the Vietnam Wall, I found a name in the panel locator book that I believe is his: First Lieutenant Edwin T. Winters was KIA 10 June 1970 in Cambodia, while serving with the 25th Infantry Division.

In the early 1980s, I requested my service records to determine what remained of the Article 99 debacle. I found only the nominal notation of reassignment.

Chapter 16

Respite from that Beastly Business

Because each troop worked chiefly on its own, and so their platoons, I never gave a great deal of thought to the other troops in the squadron. Each unit, whether platoon or troop, might be temporarily assigned to another 1st Infantry Division unit, the 11th Cavalry, or to the 1st Air Cavalry for either a combined operation, to rescue a friendly force, or pile on during enemy contact.

My new in-country home was to be Charlie Troop, and I was not looking forward to it. I do not recall ever seeing them in the field or at Lai Khe prior to reporting to their orderly room. I went to the field and found my new platoon; Nick and Clifford were already assigned to other vehicles. I wanted them on my tank ASAP so I requested that the platoon leader reassign them, stating we would be a better team having worked together for so long. He thought a second or two, and then told me we would make the change when I returned from R&R. I was happier—until I saw my tank, another rag. I had such bad luck with the Big Boys. The tank he assigned to me was even worse than the one that was a combat loss in Alpha Troop. I gave the lieutenant a silent, "Do I have to?" He introduced me to my new (and hopefully temporary) crew. I pulled myself up and shook hands, saying the usual stuff to get acquainted.

It did not take me long to wonder about them: Charlie, M.C., and Carli. In full view on top of the turret were two emptied C-Rat meal boxes full of Mr. Zig-zag rolling papers. I really did not care what they did in the safety of the rear, but the quantity of rolling papers indicated to me constant use—even out in the bush. They may have placed them in the open to gauge my tolerance, or maybe they were merely flaunting their total lack of respect for authority—mine foremost. Only briefly at a loss as to how to handle the situation, I suggested they put the playtime boxes with their personal possessions, but only if they thought keeping them on the tank was wise. I never saw the papers again.

Duke (ACAV TC), M.C., Charley, author, Nick, Carli, Clifford.

The crew and I became better acquainted as we RIF'd and busted jungle. They accepted me, if not as a friend, then as their tank commander and a senior NCO in the platoon. Either way, I could deal with it. Carli, my new driver, was quite a talker; we could not get him to shut up—ever. He could go on for hours about anything or nothing at all. On a couple of occasions, I had to tell him to shut up or "I'll Article 15 your ass." (Article 15 is an administrative punishment.) He was not bothered by my threat, but he *would* get quiet for a while. All my crewmen performed fine, but I still wanted to have Nick and Clifford. We had been in battle together.

There were a few firefights with NVA when we would stumble upon them, but they mostly kept out of our way.

There remained the ever-constant danger of booby-traps, however. Almost every other day we would run across one, and sometimes we had wounded. I do not remember anyone in my new platoon being KIA around that time. There may have been—I did not know those guys as well as I had Alpha's guys, and I have probably suppressed memories of Charlie in favor of Alpha. There was nothing terrible about Charlie—but it was not Alpha Troop.

The day arrived for me to go on R&R—one glorious week in Sydney where I would be far away from the battlefield, safe, and comfortable. I managed to score some clean fatigues and a shower. The troop clerk arranged my transportation to Camp Alpha in Saigon—a deuce-and-a-half full of guys, all 1st Infantry Division soldiers, and all going on R&R. The party started. I was the only one going to Sydney; the others were going to Bangkok and Taipei, and one guy was meeting his wife in Hawaii. We all wished him luck. Everyone was in good spirits and getting increasingly full of beer.

My R&R orders stated we were to depart for Sydney the next morning. Checking in at Camp Alpha, I was assigned a bunk, and I showered again. Of course, I did—I could have taken a shower every thirty minutes and still not felt clean. Nor would I feel any cooler two minutes after drying off. A few of us decided to get some food, so we flagged down a taxi, a Lambretta. Those contraptions were ubiquitous and scared the crap out of me. Their drivers rushed through traffic at speeds that were excessive for the volume of cars, motorbikes, and pedestrians. Lambrettas were always a wild ride, indeed.

We went to the USO to get a burger and shake, and kill time. I was bored at the USO, but the stateside-style food was a treat. Later we found our way to the air force compound and managed to get into the Officer's Club. (Or was it their Open Mess?) Nobody confused us with officers, though. Our entry must have been an air force courtesy, or someone in the army—no REMF—had done a good job caring for the average soldier heading out on R&R. The reason they allowed us in did not matter to us—we were in. I loved their bar, and the round-eyed women were attractive, if only by comparison to Mama-San. However, I did not care much for Saigon warriors; REMFs were always REMFs wherever we went. I do not recall what we did for our evening meal, but we probably ate there. It did not matter how fine our meal was that night, it was overshadowed by what we anticipated to come in Sydney.

The next morning came after a fidgety sleep—I was too safe to be comfortable. Ironic, huh? At the appointed hour, we went to the Tan Son Nhut terminal to board our aircraft. After our plane had taken off, at first inspiring a fair amount of hoots and hollers throughout the cabin, everyone became quiet. Those of us who were in from the field grabbed more sleep, keenly aware of how precious it was. I assumed those who were REMFs either read, played cards or played grab-ass with one another. Descending into the Sydney area, close enough to the ground to grasp what we were looking at, I marveled at the homes below. Most had red tile roofs, and their lawns were lush and green. I was looking at something I had not seen in quite some time: a modern suburb.

Once on the ground, I expected the standard cautions from the cabin crew about waiting for the aircraft to come to a complete stop. In Sydney, though, they added that we were not to leave our seats until instructed. When we stopped, the cabin door opened and a few folks wearing surgical masks stepped aboard, spraying aerosols over our heads. They told us it was their insect control program, an effort to keep all non-native critters from entering their country. I understood their reason, but I felt dirty. *We* were non-native critters, but perhaps were desired—for our money.

The next order of Aussie business was clearing their customs process and being allowed into the country as a guest. While I stood in line to be cleared by an agent, another agent randomly selected three of us from my line and led us into an inspection room. We were told to unpack everything; the agent wanted to inspect all of our baggage thoroughly. Once satisfied that we brought no contraband, the Australian Customs service allowed us entry. Then it was off to the R&R

in-processing center. We listened to several officers warn us to behave; we were guests of the people of Australia. We were to abide by the laws, customs, et cetera, of Australia. They advised us that if a woman said to us, "Please knock me up tomorrow night," it did not mean to impregnate her. It simply meant to come over and knock on her door. Of course, that elicited a good bit of anxious laughter.

We were antsy to move things along and join the fun ASAP. After what seemed an eternity of horrendously boring do-this-and-don't-do-that babble, and too many bad jokes, multiple double doors at the rear of the room opened. Inside was a fully stocked men's store. We were invited to come in and shop for civilian clothes. Talk about a captive market; I wanted to own that store.

It was January 1970, and the trend for young people not in uniform was to wear sandals and serapes, or perhaps clothing influenced by Carnaby Street fashion. I purchased a John Serafino, double-breasted, blue suit—baby blue. (Take a moment, and laugh if you wish.)

Serafino was at that time the preeminent Australian men's fashion designer. (I had never heard of him either.) I did not know what influence Serafino had on men's fashion on the world stage, maybe none, and I did not care then. Along with the suit, I purchased two dress shirts, tie, shoes, belt, underwear, socks, and Australian flag cufflinks. They fitted my new suit, and made the alterations in minutes. I have only the cufflinks today; that ugly blue suit was long ago relegated to the trash heap of fashion history. It has been said to hold on to your fashion clothing that it will come back into style, that everything old is new again. My baby blue suit was the opposing argument. I do not do fashion, but at that time of my life, when I was so lost, it gave me a sense of belonging again to my generation. (My friends were probably wearing serapes and sandals.)

I found a place to stay at King's Cross, a nice room in a hotel full of American servicemen. I would feel right at home. As I checked into my room, I noticed several very attractive women about my age in the lobby, each busy in discussions with guys whom I assumed were also on R&R: the early birds. I went on up to my room to get myself cleaned up. Afterward, I was planning to explore and enjoy a *real* steak.

My room was clean and comfortable. I wanted to take the relaxing hot bath that I had been dreaming of for so long, so I filled the tub by using only hot water. When the water had cooled enough to immerse myself, I lay back and slid down beneath the surface. My muscles turned to mush; I was relaxed, and I had never known such relaxation. My mind drifted off into a fantasy of girls from around the world, alone with just me on a Sydney harbor night cruise. How nice it would be. I sat up enough to rest my wet head on the tub's surround. I must have been exhausted in spite of catching up a little on my rest because I promptly fell fast asleep.

When I awoke, my water was only room temperature, not anywhere close to being warm. Clinging to the tub and to me was eight months of dirt and grime. I was reluctant to move lest my pores recollect it, but I was too chilly to remain in the water any longer. I did not step out of the tub cleanly, but I did try. I could not have been the first GI to be so filthy. When I checked what time it was, I realized I had been in the tub fast asleep for several hours. I took a routine warm and very refreshing shower, and felt the cleanest I had since my arrival in Vietnam. It was finally time to party. I donned my new baby blue John Serafino suit (hanging out in the evening was more formal in those days) and went down to the lobby. I signed up for a cruise and asked reception to call me a cab.

"Perhaps you would care to accompany the gentlemen by the way out," she said, gesturing to two guys standing near the front door. They were Americans, and I recognized them from our flight to Sydney. I introduced myself, and they were gracious enough to share their cab. Ken hailed from northern California and Daryl from a farming community outside of St. Louis, Missouri.

"Where are you from?" Ken asked me.

"Atlanta," I said.

I was from Atlanta's northern suburbs of Chamblee or Dunwoody. My parents' home was not technically in either but lay in a then unincorporated area of the county. The post office kept changing the zip code, so I was never sure which I should claim. Early on in the army, I learned that no one knows where either Chamblee or Dunwoody is. Some people did not even know where Atlanta is; I always claimed Atlanta.

"Georgia?" Ken said, as if I would consider there were more towns or cities with the same name. There are some, but I did not know them and if I had, I would never admit it.

"No, *Atlanta*." I was definite. "It's a modern city, a virtual island of twentieth-century population smack in the middle of a nineteenth-century state."

Daryl perked up. "I have kin near Waycross."

"Way south of me...down where it's even hotter,"

There were to be no REMFs, no Gooks, no senior NCOs, and no officers to ruin my days during this R&R week. I was hell-bent on forgetting what I had left behind in Vietnam. I did not want to think about what I was going to face during my final months in-country. My focus was on fun, just girls and fun and more girls. The young women of Sydney were from all over the world and delightful. I spent my first full day at Texas Tavern, a bar and grill right around the corner from the hotel. Along with Ken and Daryl, we had our first lunch and dinner there getting the lowdown on Sydney and the local girl-life from other soldiers. Then we went hunting. We had a dilemma that repeated itself each night. No, it was not finding a girl—it was choosing a girl. Wow! What an incredible and international selection.

I slept late my second day in Australia since I had been out late the night before. I went to lunch where I met some guys and drank away the afternoon, after which I returned to my hotel to prepare to meet Daryl and Ken. We wanted to go on another chick-hunt. Before I left my room, I thought it might be a good time to phone home—I gave no consideration to the time difference. Dad answered my call genuinely happy to hear from me. Mom got on an extension and asked all kinds of questions. Some were innocent and ignorant, and some I found offensive. They each expressed the pride they had in me, though. Neither Mom nor I knew it, but she gave me a heads-up on a serious affliction I would suffer for years to come: there-is-no-way-you-would-understand syndrome. I caught up with what was going on at home with friends and family. Then they mentioned the high cost of the call. (I had called collect—shame on me.) As we said good-bye, I was told in a pleasant but unmistakable way, that it was the middle of the night in Atlanta. They had been sound asleep, and I felt shame I had been inconsiderate.

For the next few days Ken, Daryl and I hung around with one another searching for our evening's entertainment. Not once did we speak about where we had arrived from, what we had been doing back there, or what might await us upon our return. Instead, days were spent eating, drinking, and chasing women who were not working days or in school. At night, we partied heartily. We checked out the harbor and the Opera House. The building had its distinctive multiple roof design in place, but it was not yet open. It was even then spectacular. Sydney's parks were beautiful, and the city was the cleanest and greenest I had ever witnessed. The only blemish was we were unable to walk out of the hotel without being stopped in the street by some slick Aussie guy carrying a briefcase.

"Yank, are you looking for a girl? Wanna get laid? I've got prime stuff...here, mate, take a look."

Their question was always the same, and they produced albums full of women. Of course, our curiosity got to us the first time we listened to the sales pitch, and we viewed the photos of naked and very attractive women. It was ironic that the ones we pointed to were not available, and they had no pictures of girls who were. We may have been crazed combat veterans and voraciously horny, but we were not *complete* fools. We did not want—or need—to pay for a companion; there were enough *free* young women. The Age of Aquarius mindset gave many young women a non-peer-judged sexual freedom that was new to me—I learned a lot from those girls. What a voyage of discovery!

We tried to prevent being taken, but I believe we became a victim on the final night. Jose Feliciano was in Australia playing at a supper club. He was an international star, whose star may have been fading. The restaurant required a cover fee, and we paid it. Halfway through our meal, and well into the show, our waiter discreetly announced that we had paid only part of their cover charge. Embarrassed in the company of our new lady friends, we did not question him; we paid the additional amount demanded. (So naive.)

> *Weeks later when I was back in-country and on night guard, I was replaying R&R in my head. I got really pissed that I was exploited so easily. Not that someone tried it, but that I fell for it. The waiter was an Asian immigrant, so my bruised ego fashioned him an NVA spy gathering funds for their war effort.*

Our week ended too soon. I returned to the place where we had in-processed and did the requisite army paperwork for departure. The tone of the room was the opposite of what it had been a week earlier. When we sat around—a serious army pastime in any war in any time—we swapped stories of our week. The mood was very light in the beginning, and we were all in very high spirits. By the time we were assembled to depart, we had told all our stories and bragged about our conquests. Then we became reflective about our return.

Outside, though, on our way to board the bus to the airport, a wonderful thing happened. Standing nearby and formed into a receiving line was a group of Aussie men and women of our parents' generation. As we passed them to board, they offered each of us a firm handshake.

"Go get 'em, Yank," and "Give 'em hell, Yank," was how they bade us farewell. A shocked, but appreciative "Thank you" was all that most of us offered in response. Giving GIs a sendoff was probably a regular thing for them, but whatever their motivation, I am very grateful, and I was truly touched. I have had a strong affection for Aussies ever since. They were kinder to us than our own countrymen were, as we were to find out.

After takeoff, most men on board were either lost in their newest memories or contemplating what awaited them on their return to war. My conscious thoughts were of what lay ahead in my final months, but when asleep I dreamed of all the fun I had in Sydney. My memories are special and have lasted a lifetime.

Chapter 17

Death Loomed Ever Larger

---

*M*y R&R was over, and I would not get another unless I reenlisted or extended my tour. I was *not* about to do either of those things. I was prepared to get into serious survival mode and get myself back home, back to "the World." I needed to get my education finished and get on with life. Knowing my days in-country were rapidly dwindling, my base fears made an about-face. The former possibility of my imminent death soon became a conscious and every-waking-moment *probability*. I was no longer in the comfort groove I had established, relative as it was. I felt like an FNG—I had achieved combat maturity, but my mind made me act like a new guy.

There came into view a glimmer of light at the end of my tunnel and a promise of brighter days ahead. I was short—a double-digit midget—only "eighty (days) and a wake-up" yet remained. My first objective was to ensure that I became a physically intact *zero*-digit midget. To get there I had to be careful—but not overly cautious—and pay enough attention but not agonize over every little detail. The consensus was the greatest danger for a field trooper was his first three months and his last month in-country. When we were FNGs, we were too stupid to survive on our own. During the middle months we found sufficient comfort to settle in; we were duly attentive and mentoring. Those were the months that soldiers were most useful within their fighting unit. Yes, our comfort was indeed relative. Nearing the end of a tour, we did not want to screw up. We had survived that far, so why not all the way?

In a combat environment, many things can kill or maim besides the enemy. Merely being a member of an armed force is inherently dangerous to life and limb. As a service person in a combat theatre, even a REMF, there is a high level of danger. We field troopers were always at risk from someone out there, some sixteen-year-old with an AK, who was trying his best to kill us. One of our running gags was the army was a collection of ne'er-do-well nineteen-year-olds who were in battle against a group of drug-crazed sixteen-year-olds, all because some forty- and fifty-year-olds told us to.

Infantry unit extraction after mission.

I held no animosity toward the Vietnamese of either side, but I admit to a few types I could easily dislike. On the friendly side were malingerers, thieves, bullies of the locals, and corrupt leadership at all levels. On the enemy side, I can count only those who were shooting at me and only *when* they were shooting at me (or my friends). The conflict was measured as him or me, and I planned to depart for home one day—that poor bastard *was* at home.

How could I improve my chances of seeing the U.S. again? Simple: do not make any big mistakes and have a healthy dose of good luck. I endeavored to ensure no one around me made any significant mistakes. The seasoned guys did not worry me, but those damn FNGs would sometimes kill or maim others as well as themselves. I increased the wide berth I gave FNGs, preferring to be with seasoned veterans I already trusted with my life. I thought about trying to get a rear job for a short while until I realized they received too many rockets back there and were not able to fight back. (My luck would be to survive the field only to be KIA in the rear—it had been known to happen.) We never worried about the round with our name on it; we worried about the ones that were addressed "to whom it may concern." The nature of rocket attacks was rather impersonal—they were addressed "occupant." I decided to reduce the random odds against my survival by remaining in the field.

Back in Charlie Troop after R&R, Clifford and Nick were my crew, along with Forrest Carli. The army announced The Big Red One would be going home in April, but the news meant very little to me since my DEROS was late April. The official word was if we had two months or more left, we would receive an in-country reassignment. Carli, Nick, and Clifford would not be going home early; they would be reassigned. Nick complained he would probably be assigned to defend Nui Ba Den (Black Virgin Mountain). Friendly forces held the high ground as a communications relay station, but the VC owned the rest of that mountain and were active in the surrounding area. I suggested to Nick that he would probably be driving a water truck at the DMZ. He did not like either scenario. I knew I would be going home earlier than I had expected, but I did not yet know when. The division made its preparations to redeploy, and its combat elements prepared to draw back into our Di An basecamp, turn in all its equipment, and relinquish the AO to others' responsibilities. Quarter Cav was assigned as covering unit for all other division units' redeployment and withdrawal from the AO.

For the remainder of February, our efforts were business as usual—we RIF'd. Occasionally, but not as frequently as earlier, we would bust jungle or carry ARVN infantry along with us. Our jungle busting effort was not as aggressive an activity as it had been previously. It seemed to be more of a defensive effort to keep the enemy off balance. Jungle busting remained, however, the same as always: slow, hot, tedious, and nasty work—even without enemy fire. We did not receive much early benefit from the division's pending redeployment.

I recall one very special and heartwarming NDP during that period, though. We had performed our routine task of RIFing and jungle busting that day without incident. Our mission was to set up an NDP outside a small village of about five hooches. We were told to establish a dismounted ambush several hundred meters from the NDP, and just outside the village. As our platoon entered a field next to the village, we circled and turned our vehicles out from the center as usual. Over the platoon radio, I heard yelling and started to pucker up, just in case.

"Sheeeeeee-yit!" Someone was excitedly yelling. "I am in heaven, boys. Know what we gots right here?"

What? I saw nothing but weeds. Then I realized those *weeds* were cultivated.

"Boys, these are peanuts...goobers. I'm gonna boil some up. Man, what a treat."

"Boil? Are you serious? Yuck. Hell, no." One of the West Coast guys was incredulous.

"You ever tried some, hippie? Back yonder in my parts it's good chow."

He jumped off his track to inspect the plants closely, and I walked over. We were both from Georgia: I was from the big city, and he was from a South Georgia farming family. I knew boiled peanuts. They are an acquired taste, one that I had acquired. He took a few empty ammo cans, some C-Rat salt, and boiled up a couple of batches. Not many of the guys were keen on them, saying they were slimy, but I, too, was in heaven. I was reminded of home.

Tensions must have been high between the troop CO and squadron CO a few mornings later. We were busting our way through a patch of jungle and found nothing. Perhaps that was our mission, merely a show of force. HQ platoon was with my platoon in a one-column formation, and my tank was immediately behind the lead tank. Occasionally we would switch places with the lead tank because the leading crew and their equipment would need occasional relief from the heavy workload. (Single column formation was unusual for us; we were normally in two columns.)

The lead tank halted. Sometimes a lead tank would hang up on a stump or termite mound and need a few minutes to maneuver back to good movement. Everyone in the column would know what was being done, but that was not the case that morning. After halting and understandably failing to notify command, the lead tank's entire crew was standing on the rear deck—stripped naked—and beating one another with anything useful and within reach. Ants! Biters. Nasty little critters. Soon, we heard from Higher.

"What the hell is this column stopped for?" The call came from the troop CO, back in the column somewhere and on our platoon frequency. He bypassed the platoon leader on their common frequency or maybe did not like the answer he got. I do not know if the source of the concern was the CO or his boss, the squadron CO, who was flying high and cool in his C&C (Command and Control) chopper.

"Ants. The crew is naked trying to get rid of ants," I said.

I had the best view of the scene and knew the intimate impact of the source of the standstill—and standoff.

"*Ants?* Goddammit, tell them to get moving...now!"

"Well, I'll try, sir, but I can see from here that those ants have them pretty well covered up. They do sting hard...very hard. A nest fell right on top of them."

"Get them moving...*now!*"

I forwarded the message to them. I received a single-digit reply. The platoon leader started yelling at us, actually me, since the ant-battle crew did not have on their helmets. After an ant-combative five minutes, the lead tank was on the move again. They had used every can of bug spray on their tank and a few we threw to them. Until they began to move, the CO continued to scream at me on the platoon frequency—as if I could change the outcome.

A few days later, about a klick north of Lai Khe's north gate, we were RIFing an area that had been Rome plowed years before. We discovered the recently deceased body of a VC male, clothed only in Ho Chi Minh sandals and shorts. We speculated the death was attributable to H&I fire. There were no apparent deathblow wounds, and we were not about to look for any. The guy was nasty and rapidly decomposing. The death bloat was gone, the fat had melted, and the skin was turning to leather. Yet, given all that, I felt the need to relieve him of his sandals. They were something I could take home, a souvenir. How I wished I had never laid eyes on them. We carried those stinking sandals on our back deck for the remainder of the day. We were in hopes that heat would help to cook them clean. Of course, that did not happen, not even close. It was a very bad idea. When we were resupplied later that afternoon, I built a stove of track end-connectors and C-4, and I tried to boil them clean. I used the salt from our C-Rats thinking maybe, just maybe, that method would work even though it had not with the skull. It did not work at all with the sandals, either. The smell would not go away, yet I still held out hope.

That night when I awoke for my early morning turn on guard, I could still smell them. I knew then it was time to let them go. Using C-Rat toilet paper to pick them up, I hurled them as far away as I could. For the next few days, though, I could still smell them. Exasperated, I took some bar soap and wiped the inside of my nostrils with it. That only relieved the smell a little, but the discomfort from the soap was utterly worse than the death-rot smell. One would think I would learn. Nah—not me.

Our dismounted ambushes were reduced dramatically; I was grateful, I hated leading them. It was a manifestation of the change in mission from offense to defense. Yet, there were still some very crazy things done. One example was what we referred to as an automatic or mechanical ambush. Upon reaching the evening's RON/NDP, a patrol would depart the secure perimeter to install an ambush device, placing it along a likely enemy route. The mechanical type was nothing more than a string of daisy-chained claymores to be detonated by enemy tripping a wire strung across the trail. That was the theory. In my recollection, animals more frequently set them off—as did a drizzle or the morning dew.

Those devices were best left to non-cavalry types. None of us wanted to disarm and recover those monstrosities. I never set one up, nor did I retrieve one, nor did I want to. We preferred to blow them in place, as it was infinitely safer. All the fun ended for us one morning with a bang when a unit nearby lost a few guys when they attempted to disarm their mechanical ambush. I think the very idea of field-expedient mechanical ambushes was insane from the get-go.

We were in the area of Thunder I FSB RIFing when my tank began to show signs of engine distress. We were not far from the north gate at Lai Khe, and I thought we could safely drive the remaining few miles to get to our motor pool. I made a call to our motor pool for them to expect me. Along with an ACAV escort, we were on our way. The going was agonizingly slow. There was not much power and our exhaust was very smoky, but at least there was no detectable fire. The Lai Khe north gate had an uphill slope into the basecamp, and I thought we would be wise to get a running start. In our sad and dilapidated condition, it would not amount to much. About three-quarters of the way up the slope, just where the level ground was within reach, my old tank slowly ground to a halt. That rag refused all exhortations to continue. Then my ACAV escort advised me large flames were licking through my exhaust grates. Yikes!

"Grab your shit and get out...we're on fire," I yelled.

Nick heard the ACAV and was already bailing out, after locking the brakes so our tank would not roll back down the hill. I called our motor pool requesting firefighting assistance, and I grabbed the personal items I kept in an ammo can. My crew and I walked over to our ACAV escort, still back down the hill and away from the burning tank. We needed to be at a much safer distance—there was a full basic load of main gun rounds and .50 cal ammo on that burning tank.

We heard a siren in the distance grow louder when the fire truck came rushing to our aid. As it came to a stop in front of the tank, its siren's sad and melancholy wind-down seemed to signal the death of my tank. I was elated; I would get a new one, or I would get out of the field and maybe go home. The shiny, well-waxed, fire-engine-red, slick truck was a sharp contrast to our weathered, beaten, and left-for-dead tank. I noticed it was a Vietnamese civilian fire truck. Where were the American pros? The smoke, dense and black, was billowing from the engine compartment through the grates of the rear deck.

What followed is best described as the Keystone Cops meet the Three Stooges, as written by the Marx brothers. The *empty* hose required two men to encourage into position. Once water started through the hose, those two guys needed a third to aim it correctly. A fourth man put a chock under the tank's track in an attempt to keep our 52-ton behemoth from rolling backward out of control—and on fire—and with thousands of pounds of explosives on board. That was the very moment that the brakes gave way, and the tank began a slow roll backward down the hill. The chock man stood there watching the rolling tank as his buddies were laying water on him, just as if he were on fire. He was repeatedly knocked to the ground by their water blast, but each time he would rise and replace the chock, only to have the tank slow-roll over it again. Each time a chock was rolled over, the fireman calmly retrieved it from uphill and put it back, precisely where he had it before—while the tank was moving.

Our chock-hero tried one final time, doing exactly the same thing and getting exactly the same result. Why did he think that his single chock would hold a rolling tank if it would not hold a stationary tank? Then he had his moment of clarity and ran back to his truck. That was itself a hysterical sight to see—a slight Vietnamese man in American-size fire gear, running. He grabbed two more chocks from his truck. Amazingly, three chocks did the trick, after he made them a pyramid. While all the comedy was unfolding, the fire boss, standing thirty feet away, directed his crew with a whistle and hand signals. The whole scene was bizarre.

We were taken to safety uphill, outside of the range of exploding rounds—we hoped. Had I known Vietnamese, I would have asked the commander if he knew what exploding main gun rounds might do to his men. They were either the bravest firefighters around or the dumbest; they seemed oblivious to the danger. Perhaps their superiors lied and told them the tank was empty and safe—it was not. Once my tank stopped moving, the firemen began to gain control over the fire. They remained a while to ensure it was completely out, and the danger of exploding rounds was past—but only after we suggested that they place plenty of cool water on the main gun rounds, and from a safe distance. (Evidently, the word "boom" followed by frantic hand gestures is universal for an explosion.) Once the fire was out for certain, and the rounds had cooled, the motor pool sent a VTR for my tank. Alas, it was repaired; there was to be no new tank for us, and I did not get to go home.

A week after that ants debacle we RIF'd all day and, much to our appetites' chagrin, were told there would be no resupply that day. The REMFs must be going farther to the rear. We were OK for ammo, but fuel, while not critical, would limit our RIFing in the morning. We only bitched about not getting a hot meal, of course. We worked some areas of low brush islands amidst grassy fields located next to jungle growth, one of the most beautiful areas I experienced. In the early evening, we made a cross-country thunder run of about half a klick to a patch of jungle and quickly dove right in. We were in a single column again. Driving into the jungle about a hundred meters, we began to make increasingly wider circles, knocking down trees and opening up an area to set up our NDP. We stopped when there was enough room for us to face out to the jungle with twenty-five meters between the jungle and us.

Duke, an ACAV commander, and I were on my rear deck

talking. I had nobody in my cupola on guard—very much an uncommon oversight. An RPG harmlessly swooshed into the center of our perimeter. I dove into my loader's hatch, head first, in a panic, and dropped the five or six feet to the floor. I landed hard. Clifford followed me in and landed squarely on my back, and then immediately scrambled up to the loader's hatch and started firing his M-16. Duke immediately manned my .50 cal machine gun and began to fire.

"Gook at the wood line," he yelled to me. He did not have on a CVC, nor did I. "You want to come up here?" he yelled to me.

No, I did not. I could not move. Unlike the many other firefights I had been in, that time I was frozen stiff, virtually catatonic. I could not think clearly for a few seconds and did not respond. All I could think was I did not want to expose myself. I did not intend to die that day.

"No, you keep firing...I'll load."

I looked through the gun tube at the wood line and thought I saw him. I loaded a canister round and took the gun off safe.

"Canister up and aimed." I had to wait for a break in his .50 fire. "Fire this thing."

"How?"

Oh, shit. He was not a tanker.

"That trigger on the TC override. It's red."

I could not get to it from the loader's position—the main gun recoil would have seriously hurt me if it went off—if it did not kill me first. I was already in pain from the place-in-space possession fight I had with Clifford.

"This?"

KABOOM!

Thankfully, I was clear of the recoiling breech.

"Yes, now move it left while I load another...then we'll go back the other side."

Together we fired three rounds from the main gun, and Duke fired about two hundred rounds of .50 caliber before we were told to cease-fire. When all was quiet again, I climbed up into my cupola. My visitor jumped down and sprinted to his own track, no doubt to get off the rather large target. (Tanks tended to be RPG magnets.) I surveyed the area to my front, and I saw only the vegetation damage from our three canister rounds. There was no sign of anyone ever being there, but we would check it out the next morning.

We remained on alert, but after nothing had occurred for thirty minutes, we started to relax and left just one or two men on guard. We had a tightly quartered NDP, and we were not very happy about it, especially since we had been probed. Again, the thought of hand-to-hand entered my mind—please, no hand-to-hand. Someone yelled incoming and we received a single mortar round. What had he heard? The round leaving the tube? Were they that close? The platoon leader called for a Mad Minute. Surely, nothing close by could have survived our lead assault. We stayed on alert.

I heard yelling behind me, from directly across our tight perimeter. The mortar round had landed on the front slope of the platoon sergeant's tank and instantly killed one of his crew. When I looked back to that tank later, he had been placed on a stretcher and covered with a poncho liner. He was merely a heaping mound of flesh and bone—there was no discernible human form. There were no other injuries from the incoming, just one KIA. His crew would have his remains keeping them company overnight, giving them plenty of time for reflection. It had been an instant, an incredibly violent one, and he was gone in an easy—he never knew it—but very ugly manner.

While up on guard in my cupola, I reviewed my actions, rather, the lack thereof. I was short; I feared death; I froze; I could not function. Diagnosis: short-timer's disease. The cure was home; there were no good treatments in-country for the symptoms. I accepted my disease and vowed to overcome it.

After darkness, we stayed at full guard with maximum pucker factor and periodically held a Mad Minute. No one planned on much sleep. We ate C-Rats cold, because we did not want to show any light from a fire. There was no need to aid the enemy in targeting us, since they already knew where we were. Later, a visitor from one of our ACAVs was on my tank's rear deck, and I was leaning half out of the cupola chatting with him. There was a muffled explosion within our perimeter. I thought it was from a hand grenade or another RPG that lost most of its effect within the scattering of downed trees. It was not much, and nothing followed it. My initial reaction was to grab the .50 cal to start firing, but a check of the wood line offered nothing to shoot at, just the blackness of night in the jungle.

"I think I'm hit."

"What?"

My visitor's right arm was straight down by his side, not moving. Blood was pooling on the deck.

"You have been."

I climbed out of my cupola and raising his forearm, I could see he had a deep, clean cut from his elbow to his wrist. He was not spurting blood—that was a good sign. We needed to stop or slow his bleeding.

"Press here and bend your elbow...tightly. Raise your arm above your heart."

Doc was two tracks over, and I yelled for their guard to alert him and call for Dustoff. The blood slowed. I opened a field dressing and applied it lightly to protect his wound from dirt. Doc arrived and we walked him to Doc's track. I heard Dustoff calling inbound, and pickup was uneventful. Dustoffs were always a vulnerable target, but ours departed without incident.

I was confident the wound was not life threatening, and I hoped it was not limb threatening. I have often wondered what happened to that man's arm, and I hope that my initial non-medical assessment was correct. I wish we had routinely known the disposition of wounded friends after they left us.

Our lone KIA was placed on board also.

The enemy must have been too small a unit or too ill equipped to do us much more damage. The remainder of that night was quiet. They had made their statement, and perhaps that is all they wanted. As we prepared to move at daylight, Doc was scouring the area for body parts to ensure our KIA would go home complete. I do not know why, there was no way that lump on the litter could ever be reconstructed—his could never be an open casket. Doc found only a two-foot length of large intestine. Whatever would he have done had he found significant remains? The body was already gone.

Once on the move departing the NDP, we took a look around and found no signs of enemy. There were also no wounded, no blood trails, and no bodies. Had I really seen someone? I wondered. The enemy scored one KIA and one WIA. We scored nothing that we knew of. That was the bad news. The good news was I did not die.

I was counting down my days to DEROS and well aware that I had a year left until my ETS (Estimated Termination of Service). What orders would I receive for the upcoming year? Where would I be sent? Very briefly, I considered extending my tour in-country by six months. Why would I consider such a thing? Simple: the army would have discharged me early for extending, and I would have received a six-month reduction to my sentence (um, enlistment) in exchange for six more months in-country. I would also get another R&R. I seriously considered doing that, and was aware that my extending would prevent my brother from being sent to Vietnam. I had the experience, he did not, and I could probably get a job in the rear. I considered the odds that Bob might get an infantry gig, and then I regained clarity. If he were sent to Vietnam, his MOS would have him so far in the rear that he would have been in air-conditioned and concrete structures several stories high. He would not have had the field danger I was worried about. It would make no sense for me to protect my little brother, then and still taller than I am. After deciding to forego an extension, I realized that my adjustment to civilian life during the remainder of my enlistment would be beneficial to me and to those who knew me.

We were still screening division redeployment as March began. The work got easier as we moved south a little more each day. We continued to work QL-13, which by then was being paved from Lai Khe northward. Running vehicles on pavement was pleasant—much less dust was ingested. Our Squadron XO, my very special friend MAJ ActingCO, was in the field. Why? He summoned me to one of the Thunder FSBs one afternoon, along with two ACAVs. Again? Was I going to end up my tour in LBJ (Long Binh Jail)? To my surprise, when I reported he gave me a mission.

"Good afternoon, sir," I said.

I was polite and offered a smart salute. He returned it.

"Good afternoon. I have a mission for you today."

"Yes, sir."

He turned away and referred to a map sheet.

"Take your section north on Highway 13 to the village of Chon Thanh." (One tank and two ACAVs composed a section; a platoon was made up of three sections.) "Wait there until an ACAV arrives under escort. You will then bring that ACAV back here, and return to your unit."

He studied his map sheet a few seconds and then he turned to face me.

"Any questions?"

"No, sir," I said. "It's straightforward and simple."

I saluted again and departed.

I do not recall ever seeing a single ACAV, or any other U.S. land vehicle, traveling alone north of Thunder I FSB. (The fuel truck described earlier was south of Thunder I.) It made good sense to travel in force—it was an Ambush Alley along that part of Thunder Road. Our little mission was to be a cool walk in the park. My crew was aggravated that we had to go *anywhere*. We had been on perimeter guard, easy duty, with the ability to catch up on sleep. They changed their tune quickly when they saw the possibility to buy ice. That alone was worth the risk and the inconvenience.

The next day our platoon repositioned west of QL-13 and into the jungle, but not for routine busting purposes. Our mission for the next few days was to provide security for Rome plows as they maintained a unique cut in the jungle:

the 1st Infantry Division patch. Carved out of the jungle was a Big Red One patch, visible only to passing aircraft. Aviators would be suitably impressed—right? Was it public relations or a seal on a job well done? After crisping up the division's patch, we relocated to QL-13 (Thunder Road) to secure it as army engineers were paving it northward. It was cooler and safer duty. The downside was the dust—we were roaming the unpaved portion of the road as well as off-road RIFing.

Author: a hardcore dragoon.

By then the ARVN had assumed responsibility for most of our AO in concert with remaining American units. Our equipment was to be turned over to the ARVN. Therefore, we were not surprised with a big stink over keeping it in top shape until that happened. No problem, we always took care of our equipment so that it would take care of us—we *were* still a combat unit. The word came down from Higher that air cleaners were to be cleaned daily. Well, duh! Of course. Our work required more frequent cleaning due to the conditions we worked in. After we made a thunder run several klicks north through our usual dust complement, we pulled into Thunder II to secure it overnight. My crew and I maneuvered our tank into our place on the perimeter, and we began to set up for overnight. Nick was still in his driver's compartment when someone raised the alarm.

"Advancing major at six o'clock."

I turned to see my favorite squadron XO, MAJ ActingCO, still in the field, making tracks toward us—rather, toward me. From about twenty feet away he commanded, "Let me see your air cleaner."

My crew scattered.

"Yes, sir," I said, reaching to open the door to retrieve it.

Of course, my filter was still filthy. We had just returned from a thunder run and had just shut down.

"Dammit, sergeant." His face and neck were red. "You were instructed to clean these daily. Obviously, you don't care to follow instructions."

With that, he yanked the filter from my hands and threw it on the ground, in the process snapping it against his knee. He was pissed, and his starched and pressed (to a fine crease) jungle fatigues were dirty. I was wearing a pair of pants that had not been cleaned in a month. Hell, I had not taken them off in a month.

"I personally cleaned both sides this morning...sir. We cleaned them again mid-day. Now that we're in our RON and preparing defenses, they will be cleaned yet again...making that three times today. That's our standard behavior when we run dusty roads."

I was being singled out. What had I done to him?

"Sounds like bullshit to me. Take them out and clean them right now, I want to see how you do it."

I wanted to ask him if he did not know how to clean them, and if he would like a lesson—but I thought better of it. He might have been looking for the perfect excuse to make me a private. I did not want that at all, and I certainly did not want him to have that satisfaction. Therefore, being the good soldier that I was, I grabbed the cloth filter and began to beat it clean. From the corner of my eye, I could see him quickly step back to avoid residue from my cleaning, but he did not move quickly enough. Dust settled on his pristine fatigues. I cleaned the filter well and asked if he approved. I never acknowledged that he had gotten dirty. I stifled a smile.

"See to it that you clean these filters often, because I'll be checking on you."

Maybe he had gotten bad news from home. What a jerk. I had been in the army long enough to know the difference between instructional criticism, ignorant criticism, and just fucking-with-you criticism. His criticism of me was surely the latter. Luckily, we were to have no further encounters.

Knowing we were returning to "the World" or redeploying in-country, no one wanted to be the last, or even one of the last men of Quarter Cav KIA. Until we were safe, we would remain alert and field-smart. That said, there were areas we RIF'd that were no doubt more for show than for anything else. One such area was heights from which we could watch Freedom Birds (homebound airliner), inbound full of FNGs, on final approach to Bien Hoa.

As we RIF'd along the heights, the squadron CO was overhead in his C&C chopper. "Get a steel pot on your head," was the message relayed from on high to anyone seen without one, or not wearing a flak vest. What had been a group of men staring danger down daily, were by then a bitching and moaning mob being reformed into REMFs—garrison troops—of the familiar police-call and spit-shine army. Ours had been a good run.

I learned I was to get an eighteen-day drop and go home on 6 April. Just ten days remained. Nick received orders to report to the 25th Infantry Division where he would be driving his water truck very close to Nui Ba Dinh. It was uncanny how we each had an element correct.

We went to Di An and stripped our vehicles; everything had to be cleaned. We used a washing station like none I have ever seen. The water spray could peel paint, and it did exactly that if not kept constantly in motion. We were extremely careful, but accidents will happen. One poor guy, the last to be hurt in any way in my platoon, lost control of his spray wand. The water jet sliced open the skin near his wrist, filling his hand with water. It was grotesque, but had that stream remained stationary more than an instant, it would have removed all the meat on his hand. Instead, it blew the skin of his hand up like a balloon. I hope he kept his hand.

Once they were cleaned thoroughly, we drove our tracks down toward Saigon to a depot where they were to be turned over to the ARVN. I was lead tank and an ABC film crew ran ahead of us in a jeep, filming the whole way. I have never seen the footage, nor has anyone that I know. Our final duty was to clean all our weapons and turn them in. When I cleaned my M-16, I kept the firing pin. I have it today along with my boonie hat as the only souvenirs of Vietnam besides my pictures. I surely hope those weapons were checked for serviceability before the ARVN took them into battle. I would hate to be responsible for the fall of South Vietnam.

Weapons cleaned and logged in, we went to 1st Infantry Division's out-processing center. We collected orders, listened to lectures, had an exit interview, and completed more forms. We received current editions of the division's magazine and newspaper, and each of us was presented a 1969 yearbook of the division's units, with summaries of each unit's activities during the year. I was surprised also to pick up two Bronze Star Medals and another Army Commendation Medal. Later, I would be awarded the Combat Infantryman's Badge since my primary MOS was 11B40.

Quarter Cav—1st Squadron, 4th Cavalry, "Prepared and Loyal," had been the final 1st Infantry Division maneuver element to depart the field.

On 15 April 1970, the 1st Infantry Division's colors were redeployed to Ft. Riley, Kansas.

Part III

Finding the True Measure of Self

*Did you ever feel like the world is a tuxedo,
and you're a pair of brown shoes?*

—*"Lonesome" George Gobel*

Chapter 18

Troubles in "the World"

Those of us going home were assigned to the very same 90th Replacement Detachment we had passed through upon our arrival in Vietnam. Again, we found the food, bars, steam baths, and massages to be a good method to while away the time until our flight. That place still smelled of urine. We did not know when our flight would be—one day or several days. Who knew? There was a schedule somewhere, but we were not told what it was. We contented ourselves with local amenities, relaxation, sleep, and the satisfaction of knowing that nobody was shooting at us.

Freddie—the NVA shitter-fragger, monkey-killer, and the guy I lost in the rain—received his first ever massage. The room was full of tables with very young girls giving massages; I was on the table right behind him. We were all dressed in towels having just come from a steam. I was on my stomach, enjoying the touch of my young masseuse, and chatting away with the guy next to me. He pointed to Freddie, who had turned over and was sporting a full-on erection, concealed under his towel—but oh, so obvious. All the young girls for several tables around were having giggling fits. While he tried to recover a little dignity, his masseuse pointed to his erection then to the draped rooms along the wall.

"You go short-time," she giggled.

Freddie was not about to do that.

Our first morning back at 90th we awoke to a rumor that a guy went into the bar with an AK, killed a few guys and wounded many more. I was not so sure, and I never did hear anything official at the time. I believed it to be only a rumor initiated and perpetuated by REMFs. If something like that had occurred, the media would have been all over it. There were too many guys around and too many were going home to keep something like that under wraps for very long.

On 6 April 1970, just as I had been informed I would be, I was on a manifest out of Vietnam and scheduled to fly to McGuire Air Force Base, New Jersey. I wanted to see some of my friends from the Armor School before leaving, and there were plenty of them there at the 90th. Two very good friends were missing, though—Steve Sapp and Marc Sievers—and no one knew anything about them. Among those I did see were a few who had also been promoted to staff sergeant, a few who were busted in rank, and plenty showing physical scars of their yearlong effort to stay alive. Only one indicated any sort of emotional scar. He had been in a firefight where the enemy involved civilians as cover. I hope he has done well over the years.

> *I lost track of my friend from the Armor School, Mike Mitchell, shortly after we arrived in-country. He was the fellow I shared a cab with in California. He had been assigned to the 25th Infantry Division and our sister unit the Three-quarter Cav. On 19 July 1969, he was KIA just one week before my friend Joe Chiacchio. The song he so often sang, "Get Back," is linked forever in my mind with him. When I hear the first two or three notes, I say his name.*

DEROS arrived and I was about to go home. I needed to hear Simon & Garfunkle's "Homeward Bound" right about then, just to have order in my universe. Unbelievably, I did hear it a few hours before our manifest was announced. Shortly afterward, we assembled for transportation back to "the World." We were giddy, ready for home. There would be no more 365-and-a-wake-up, not even thirty-and-a-wake-up, nor even one-and-a-wake-up—we were *past* the wake-up. We were the ultimate definition of "short."

After our Freedom Bird was airborne, we all—and I do mean all—let out hoots and hollers. The party continued for a while, especially when the pilot announced we had just left the territorial waters of South Vietnam. Shortly thereafter, everyone was relaxed and pensive. We were an exhausted lot, even the noncombatants. I decided I should sleep—there was still a lot of catching up to do.

When we landed in Japan for refueling at Yakota Air Force Base, I was again struck by the beauty. I wondered if it was just the American base or the whole country. The snack bar was my immediate goal—I remembered it being very good. Standing in the line and minding my own business, I was bumped by a guy behind me. At first, I ignored it, but more bumps came in rapid succession, one being truly intrusive. I turned to tell him politely to knock it off, and there he was—my friend Steve Sapp. We visited for a while then we departed on separate flights: his to the West Coast, mine to the East Coast. I have never heard from him again, nor did I ever hear from or about Marc Sievers. I hope the two of them have done well over the years—I hope they all have.

It was a long, boring flight, but we finally arrived at McGuire Air Force Base in New Jersey, USA—"the World." The date was 6 April 1970, the same day I left twenty-some hours earlier (due to crossing the dateline eastbound). Several of those on board kissed the tarmac, but I thought it silly—just get on with it and go home. A deep nasal inhale worked just fine. I was breathing American air—no shit burning, no Asian incense, no charcoal, no human decomposition—just the sweet aroma of automobile and jet emissions. Yep, I was home.

The first order of business was to clear customs, and there were sufficient stations for us with little waiting. Some of the agents were checking all returnees very carefully and others not so much. I joined the closest and shortest line, hoping for a "not so much" agent, behind a captain dressed in khakis. I still had on jungle fatigues, and they were squeaky clean compared to what I had worn the preceding twelve months. I was unkempt compared to the captain. The agent required him to unpack everything in his possession for a visual inspection. The captain registered his complaint with remarks about the agent's use of time. The agent's attention was quickly drawn to a model of a Vietnamese peasant hooch.

The customs agent told the captain, referring to the model, "I'll have to take this from you. You will not be able to bring it in."

"Why?"

"It has dirt and dust...it's crumbling. Not allowed. This sort of thing is on the list of prohibited items."

The captain was angry.

"I'll be damned if it is. That was a personal gift to me from a U.S. Army three-star general. I *will* be bringing it in."

"Not today; your general doesn't decide what's allowed."

"Who can I talk to? Where's your superior?" He paused, calming himself. "Look...the general gave it to me when he came home. I would like to keep it."

No doubt the captain usually got his way with those who did not outrank him, and he must have realized the agent was not at all impressed by his captain's bars. The agent had seen a few before.

"Sounds like your general was smart enough to know he couldn't get it home."

With that, the captain began repacking and, shooting one final glare of contempt, moved along in the process. He removed his partially packed bags from the counter, leaving his model behind. When I arrived for my inspection, the agent was gracious.

"Welcome back, sergeant."

He asked a few routine questions and was satisfied with my answers. He stuck his hand, only his hand, into the top of my duffle bag and brought it right back out. He indicated I was good to go and directed me to the next station. When I walked past the captain, he was still struggling to repack.

Next up was the issuance of boxer shorts, T-shirts, and towels. Then we encountered a gauntlet of new trashcans; each one was assigned a clothing item, wherein we relieved ourselves of Vietnam wardrobe. Boots went in one can, shirts in another. Pants had one, and underwear (which I still did not wear) had one as well—whatever we had that was not personal was to go into its own can. I chose to keep only my boonie hat and the M-16 firing pin; I wish I had kept more. At the next station I took a shower with actually *heated* water. So nice. So very nice.

After cleaning up and in only our just-issued skivvies, we were like brand new recruits again, except many of us had a great above-the-waist-only tan. Much unlike our induction days, there at McGuire every effort was made to put us in the correct size. A room full of women made custom alterations for a good fit. Our unit patches, individual ribbons, and awards were attached to our jackets in another room. I was amazed the clothing segment of our arrival process was so fast. I was still in the army, however, and there remained plenty of paperwork and a few lectures. The initial fast pace soon began to drag, and we were all getting more impatient by the moment. Finally, we were finished and released. I said good-bye to friends, got some addresses, and promised to write. Those of us remaining on active duty had a thirty-day leave prior to our next duty station. Then it was party time. We scattered into the wind, anxious to get back into whatever groove we had departed a year earlier. Many of us were going straight home and immersion back into a world that had changed; there would be no decompression. How well did they assimilate?

I hooked up with three others and shared a ride to the Philadelphia airport. As speed increased in the limo, I found a brand new fear—going fast. We were not going fast by normal travel standards, but my mind and my body would need to adjust. One of the guys purchased a bottle of Chevis Regal, and he took a long drink. Then he offered to share the bottle with the rest of us. We passed the Chevis around and were soon getting mellow. There was not much left in that bottle upon our arrival at the airport; the owner took the last pull and wished us all good luck.

At the ticket counter, I was given the one seat remaining on an Eastern Airlines flight to Atlanta. On my way to the gate, I stopped at the first public phone I saw and telephoned home. The line was busy. I tried again after waiting a minute. Still busy. I walked to my gate cursing my luck. The airplane was loading, but I wanted to try phoning one more time; I preferred to be picked up if I could. Still busy. I remembered I had a sixteen-year-old sister. I boarded last.

The army's process at McGuire, customs, and everyone along the way, including stewardesses, treated me well, just as anyone would expect to be treated. I did not interact with any passenger around me; they initiated no conversation, and I was lost in my own thoughts. I was a veteran-virgin, without expectations beyond family and friends. At that moment, my recent experience did not matter one whit to me; I was on my final leg home. On the ground in Atlanta, I again attempted to call home using the first pay phone I found available. Still busy! I tried one more time using the phones near baggage claim, and I got through. Finally!

"Oh...hi...hang on," my sister said, just as casually as if I had been gone only overnight.

I wanted to give her some sort of good-natured, sibling grief about living on the telephone, but thought better of it. She called my mother to the phone, saying nothing to me as she waited to hand the phone over.

"It's for you," she advised, matter-of-factly.

"When did you get in? Where are you?"

She seemed to be speaking to an old friend in town for a few days. My parents treated Bob and me as friends after we were in the service. Was she just uncomfortable, not knowing what to say? I was her firstborn. Why was there no emotional reaction to the confirmation of my survival?

"Go get the limo to Lenox. Your father will pick you up."

So that is it? I finally get home, cannot get through on the telephone in time to be greeted at the airport, and I have to spring for a limo? I was not a kid anymore, and I did not care crap about a parade or party, but damn, how about not quite so casual? Did they even notice I had not been around for a while? Such thoughts should never be spoken, and they never were by me. Although I do not have thin skin, I was stung a little. The limo dropped me off across from Rich's on Lenox Road. I stood there looking very much out of place as if I were on display. I was recovering from a scary limo ride at expressway speed, and steeling myself for more expressway speed with Dad. An unidentified discomfort fell over me. I did not understand it, but things just were not what they once were—I was no longer who I had been, and I knew damn well my youth was behind me.

Dad showed up in about five minutes, and I threw my bag in the back. I slid into the front seat, and he stuck out his hand, which I shook heartily. He never was an emotional sort with his kids, but right then I wanted to be a child of five again, and I sorely needed some emotion from him. That would not be forthcoming. Did my parents finally consider me a man? Men do not cry; men suck it up and move on. Yes, I know—but they *were* my parents. I wanted validation of my experience from them. When we arrived at the house, my mother and sister came out to greet me. The busy telephone and tepid welcome conversation were quickly forgotten. I went inside and reveled in the familiar smells of home, those family smells I had known intimately. I was amazed how much my two younger brothers had grown; they were ages six and two and had grown like weeds. I sat down in a chair and had a beer—I was relaxed, so very comfortable.

After catching up a little with my family, I took several naps trying to adjust my body to the time change. My friends could wait. That first evening my mother's very close friend, Wini Hull, came over to welcome me home. That was a very special moment for me. Her embrace and comments told me so much about what my parents had endured with two sons in the service, than they ever could or would divulge. I have always appreciated her for her unintentional enlightenment.

> *Years later, just after my father's funeral, when everyone was gathered and telling tales on Dad, Wini leaned over to me and in a hushed voice, said,*

"You know...your father won me in a poker game." I laughed so hard I thought I would wet myself, yet I knew that was the truth. The nut does not fall far from the tree.

On my second day home, I received a shock that kicked me in the gut, on two fronts. My sister's boyfriend came over and we renewed our acquaintance; I liked him, although I did not know him very well. As my sister and he were leaving, my mother was extremely rude to him, borderline nasty. She was mean and said hateful things directed only at him. My sister just glared at her but remained silent. He did, too. That was wise—Mom could show her temper. After they left, I had to say something to her.

"Wow! You sure jumped all over him."

"He deserves it...the bastard," she exclaimed, shaking her head. "You have no idea what he's done to this family."

"You're right, I haven't been here for quite a while."

I did not understand, but we had a lengthy conversation that was enlightening. I consoled my mother, assuring her my sister played *the* major role in her life events. It was a rare moment of maturity on my part, non-parent that I was.

It was in those moments, though, that I realized my year in Vietnam, given that I had survived physically unharmed, did not really mean squat to anyone but me. I understood it, and I could and would deal with it. The world would still turn.

I got together with a few friends, the ones who were not still away at college. They made fun of me when I asked them to drive slower than the speed limit. I wanted to buy a new car right away, so I worked hard on getting past my fear of speed. To the new car end, Dad helped me get a bank loan, warning me, "Bankers don't view the army as employment." He was right; he had to cosign. My loan approved, I went straight away and bought a new 1970 Chevelle SS, 396 cubic inches, 375 horsepower big block, cowl induction, triple black with white rally stripes, 4-speed, and posi-traction rear end. My parents drove me to pick it up. After the paperwork was done and I owned the car, the salesman presented me the keys, and we all went outside for the delivery. My mother looked my new car over very carefully.

"What are these things?" she asked, pointing to the hood pins and cables.

"That's what'll keep his hood down when he's going a hundred and fifty mile an hour."

"Oh, my," was all she said. Dad shook his head.

The moment needed something, so I addressed my folks.

"You do realize, don't you, that I no longer think I am invulnerable," I said. "I learned that lesson the hard way. I won't be killing myself in this machine, thank you very much. I feel like the rest of my life is a gift...I plan on dying in bed many decades from now. Besides, I'm still a little too scared to drive fast."

I got in my car, cranked it up, and revved the engine a few times to torment Mom. With thanks to the salesman, I told my folks I would be home by dinner. As I attempted to leave, I stalled the car. Embarrassed much? Yep. My new ride was a powerful machine, and my lack of familiarity almost caused me to run into one of the unsold cars. I decided to be patient, so I found a large and empty parking lot to practice in. By the end of that afternoon, I was comfortable enough to take my new chariot anywhere. The next day I added an eight-track tape player and stereo speakers. I was driving the Skunk, a very fast muscle car. My fear of speed had been overcome.

My war was becoming more distant every day, but I was still far from normal. Daily, I thought about Vietnam and my friends. Many of my in-country habits were hard to recognize and break. Adjustments have been made over the years, some consciously, some not. Language was a primary adjustment for me; I needed to clean it up a lot, lest I offend my parents. Actually, lest I offend my father. My mother would not hold back with her adult children. I consider that a normal adult thing. On the other hand, I would not hear my father utter anything any worse than 'damn' or 'hell' until five years later.

When my mother would have a rant, cursing and sometimes throwing things, Dad would calmly say, "Helen, if you will not speak any more intelligently than you are, perhaps you should not speak." That would leave her speech paralyzed and incensed—as if she had never heard him say that before.

There remained a conditioned response suffered by men who spent quality time in the field. In Vietnam, the field was the bush, the jungle, or any place not thought relatively safe by combat troops. We were often in places where we might experience booby-traps, ambushes, and/or incoming fire. We were always on edge, and our anticipation of horrors not only wore on us, they became ingrained in our psyche. I was not alone in that experience.

My first notice of being affected came within one day of returning home, and the condition would last many years. Even today it comes back, albeit less frequently and with much less instinctive impact. Every time I started my car, opened the refrigerator door, turned a door handle, opened a beer, or flipped a light switch—anything like that—my mind would race, questioning my wisdom while steeling my body for the inevitable explosion. The expectation was visceral and terrifying—but for only an instant and only in my mind. My body did not miss a beat and simply performed the task; my mind played out the dilemma, very pronounced. When I heard a car backfire, I would recoil into a protective posture, lasting only the instant until my racing mind met reality.

Mom often described an incident occurring soon after I came home. The site for Perimeter Mall was being prepared, located about two miles through the woods from our house. They were blasting for several days and had advised all the affected homeowners in advance. Someone forgot to tell me, or did not realize what the effect would be on me. I was out all morning far from the house enjoying my new car and trying to find friends to skip out of work. Around lunchtime, I came home and began to fry some onion rings, one of the items I had missed so much. My mother was watching her mid-day soap operas, and I stood next to her, chatting, while my onion rings cooked. There was a massive boom, and the house shook—it was reminiscent of an Arc Light strike, but much abbreviated and without the rolling thunder. In an instant, I hit the floor and scurried five feet to get behind the sofa. My mother was completely freaked out. By the time she asked if I was all right, I was—no big thing. She swore it happened, but I do not have much memory of that day beyond the onion rings. They were tasty. I am sure I sought cover, and my loss of memory is probably my mind protecting me. I wonder what unpleasant experiences I have forgotten over time or blocked out altogether. Our minds can cause us serious pain, but they are wonderful healers, also.

There was another incident; one which I think was the result of my in-country mindset and its residual effect. Late one evening I was taking a date home when a car pulled up behind us. We were being followed too closely, and I was a little put out about it. At first I tried to ignore it, hoping the car would pass me or turn off onto another road. That did not happen. I soon grew tired of the nonsense and stopped my car smack in the middle of the road, thinking my follower would pull around me. He did not, so I walked back to the driver's window. I firmly rapped on the window with my knuckles; I had no clue who it was inside that car.

"Open this fucking window now, asshole," I demanded.

In a flash, the window was on the way down, revealing a high school kid all alone and in shock. I reamed him out for following so closely and not backing off when I demonstrated I was disturbed by his behavior. I suggested he get the hell out of there quickly before he really pissed me off. I displayed similar reactions other times, also. I attribute them to a very well-learned lead-with-violent-offense response to a "fight or flight" situation. I had brought mine home, and I might have gone out of control; some of us certainly did. I was learning what it meant to be a "deranged Vietnam vet."

A serious incident occurred in downtown Louisville, KY, about six months later, while I was still on active duty and in civvies. I turned my car onto a single lane, a one-way street only to be confronted by a car going the wrong way. We were in a standoff. When the driver stepped from his car and walked toward me, I stepped out of mine. We exchanged a few words, and I allowed as how I was not about to move, I was in the right. (Still needing a rock to the head.)

"Let me see if I can persuade you," he said, reaching into his car and producing a pistol that he pointed squarely at me.

As I returned to my car, I let him know that I was not very impressed with his gun, but the truth is I was—it could have killed me. The police at the local precinct would not even talk to me. Since that time, my response to confrontation has been measured and calm, for the most part. There remains a point I do not usually allow myself to go past.

Friends invited me to a few local soirees, and I visited the University of Georgia to attend parties there. They were great fun, but girls were the real reason for my visits. I hit it off with one young lady and was shocked when she invited me to her room. No, not that she invited me; my shock was that her room was in a dorm that had been a men's only dorm the last time I was there. My world had indeed changed.

During the time I was out of touch, everyone must have become a hippie—or so it seemed to me. In that environment, I felt as if I stood out like a sore thumb. No one said anything to me about Vietnam, good or bad. They were all preoccupied with flashing the peace sign and scoring pot, peyote, and the like. I readily admit to some exploration of my own. Maybe they were also preoccupied with school, but I could not tell.

I joined friends on a spring break trip to Myrtle Beach, SC. I was envied for my tan, but still no one said anything to me about where I had gotten so dark. No one showed interest in what I had done or as much as queried my experiences. They were my old friends. Why did they not care? I expected them to be either concerned or curious; they were neither. I thought maybe their demonstrated apathy was out of respect, but more likely apathy or fad was their politics. I needed to talk to someone about my experiences, but no one wanted to hear. I wanted to make them understand—it was not what they saw on television. I did not realize that my experience was valuable to me and to nobody else. Only those who shared similar experiences could understand or empathize—only they could relate.

The anti-war movement had taken a serious foothold in the Southeast in the previous two years. While I was in the army and generally sheltered from society, the world as I had known it broke apart. I no longer knew where I belonged. At a party, a friend of a friend of a friend was very much in my face about his opposition to the war. He wanted to question the morality, but I did not want to discuss the politics. He certainly had no standing to debate its military prosecution. My response was that he should understand that the war he saw in news reports, and the war that was a reality on the ground were two different things. Yet, he could not accept there was any view other than his own.

He was speaking only to impress those around him, and he was following the script of the then-current fad of trashing war *and* warrior. I have little tolerance for those who preach the unreasoned, illogical, or an untrue position as if it were an absolute. Worse, are those that spout faddist oratory. That friend of a friend of a friend is today probably *the* most vocal of veteran's supporters—and still a phony. I know people who hold that same position, yet they listen to and respect the views of others. I respect their views, as well. Today, those who were listening and respecting while debating Vietnam may be at a peace-at-all-costs rally someplace, but I wager they still listen—and learn. Why is it that so many begin a conversation only to skip over intelligent discourse and go straight to argument, meanness and hate?

My leave was almost at its end when Nixon announced the U.S. incursion into Cambodia. There was no doubt in my mind the guys I had served with, those who had not come home already, were going in, thus the evening television news was my obsession for days. Where were my friends? I knew the reason for the Cambodian offensive; it was abundantly apparent the public did not, nor did most of them even care—

they were war-weary. The entire country was.

The enemy we fought often escaped across the border and into Cambodian sanctuaries to lick their wounds, only to come at us later. The NVA command and control center for the lower part of South Vietnam, COSVN (Central Office for South Vietnam), was located just inside Cambodia. The prior year's "secret" bombings and ARVN's cross-border operations did target them, but evidently had not hurt them much. The ARVN that had been inserted across the border the previous August were blunted, no doubt by forewarning and a large well-established protective force surrounding COSVN. Nixon's secret bombings of Cambodia (and secret cross-border raids) had not been so secret to those with whom I served.

Responding to the incursion, or Cambodian Campaign, American college campuses witnessed massive anti-war and anti-military demonstrations. A few suffered terror bombings at the hands of militant anti-war factions, whose targets were on-campus military sites such as ROTC (Reserve Officer Training Corps) buildings. The national reaction to student deaths at Kent State University punctuated the already ill will aimed at government in general and the military in particular. Most of America's youth and a sizable portion of its mature population looked upon the U.S. military with disdain, and very few were able to make the distinction between war and warrior. They treated draftees, draft-avoidance enlistees like me, lifers and career soldiers as the guilty parties—the cause of America's woes.

As I readied to return to my final year of active duty, I realized many of the friends of my youth—all very intelligent people—were at that time also unable to discern a difference.

I welcomed myself home.

Chapter 19

Celebration of Survival

*M*y orders were to report to Ft. Knox, Kentucky, on 11 May. Just before midnight, I arrived at overnight quarters, nothing more than a roomful of enlisted guys in bunk beds. There were about fifty bunks in the room, and I grabbed the first open one I saw. Glancing at the top bunk, I saw my overnight bunkmate was still awake, so we began a short, quiet chat.

From a few rows away I heard, "Man, you need to shut up and crawl in that bunk."

Surprised, I did not respond right away. I did not intend on disturbing anyone.

"I'm serious, goddammit...don't you make me come over there and shut your ass up."

A second round of protest had come from my newest fan. Why? Since I had not made a peep since his first protest, I headed over to see if I could smooth things over. If not, I hoped to outrank him. (That might have worked if I had been wearing my uniform.)

"Damn you, you Roll Tide motherfucker!" I probably did disturb someone with that announcement.

It was Butch Tidwell, one of my roommates at the Armor School. I had last seen him at a Thunder FSB several months earlier. We chatted a while, regaling one another with our leave exploits and catching up a little on our experiences in Vietnam. Butch was with the 11th Armored Cavalry, and their AO was almost the same as ours. We agreed we might have worked together often without ever knowing it. The next morning after chow, we discovered that we had bought the same model car (his was red with black rally stripes). We left to report to our new units, and agreed to meet up again once we were settled. I had been assigned to the 4th Basic Combat

Training Brigade, but did not yet know in what capacity. My new home was a *basic* combat training unit—guys just in the army. Recruits and trainees; I had no choice, so I reported to the 4th brigade sergeant major. After pleasantries, he was all business.

"Sergeant Street, we have a very serious need for combat veterans to impart their experience to these young recruits," he began. You are an ideal candidate for that role. What you have accomplished is exceptional, and the army wants to benefit from your experience."

"Thank you, sergeant major, but what's the role you see me in? What would my job be?"

"Drill sergeant, the backbone of the army. We'd like you to attend Drill Sergeant School. You'd remain attached to the 4th BCT (Basic Combat Training) Brigade, but your temporary duty station will be the training school."

"I don't think I want to do that, sergeant major. Besides, I only have one year left until ETS...what good can I do in just ten months?"

The sergeant major was none too happy with me, and we discussed and debated the issue for several minutes.

"Hell, I'll send you on down to 13th Battalion, they can figure you out."

With that, I departed for battalion where I was to hear the same speech; I wondered if the brigade sergeant major had phoned ahead.

"Sergeant Street, you need to go to Drill Sergeant School. It'll be good for you and good for the army. You've had thirty days at home getting soft...the job will keep you fit."

"I really don't want to do that...and I have no intention of attending unless and until you give me orders to do so. Please don't do that."

"What's the problem?"

"No problem, I don't want to be a drill sergeant. I would rather do something else my last year. I just want to go home and get back into school...college that is." I hoped he would understand and accept my request.

"I am really disappointed." He engaged me squarely with his eyes, and I think he meant what he said, that it was not just his sales pitch. "I think I'll punish you, make you regret turning down the army's request—Charlie Company has an opening for Training NCO. That's going to be you."

I was a little worried. I had no clue what a Training NCO did. I knew it was not a drill sergeant, and that was fine by me. When I stood to leave the sergeant major's office, I thanked him.

"Son, I hope you don't regret your choice," he said.

"Thanks, sergeant major, I'll live with it…or come back."

A few minutes later at Charlie Company, I met my new boss, First Sergeant Rodgers. He was short and wore thick glasses, and I took an instant liking to him. He did not seem at all bothered with my turning down Drill Sergeant School. He assigned me to a room with a company cook, and told me I would get a room by myself or with another NCO within a week. People were leaving, including the current training NCO and the senior drill sergeant. The next morning I joined the departing training NCO to learn my duties. They were well within my abilities, even untrained. I was to keep training records on each trainee (about two hundred), each platoon (four), as well as the company's permanent personnel. The records were physical test schedules and results, weapons' qualification and recurrent training scores and all mandatory MOS-specific classes for the company's permanent personnel.

Additionally, I would ensure each venue was scheduled and all necessary equipment was ready for each day's lesson plan. I would arise before trainees when the drill sergeants did, to begin performing my routine duties. I was also to be available until the last lesson of the day had begun, or until the senior drill sergeant agreed everything was in place. On Saturday mornings, I would be required to stand by until the company commander's weekly inspection was finished. I was usually free from mid-afternoon until early the next morning on weekdays, and from late morning Saturday until Monday morning very early. My work for the next year was easy, and I was not required to march a gaggle of newbies everywhere—or run for miles along with them—all day, every day.

Within ten days of checking in, the senior drill sergeant left for his second tour in Vietnam. (He returned home the next month having lost both legs.) His replacement was SFC Wabbs, a late twenties or early-thirties career soldier. He was a real character. He was always drill sergeant loud, typically degrading, abusive, instructive, and downright mean to a trainee. It was all about building team. He was hoarse from yelling at them. At the same time, he was always professional, polite, and considerate to those who were not trainees. We were both single and ended up sharing a room, but rarely would we cross paths there. We were usually both partying, but with very different crowds. He was country music and I was rock-n-roll. We were hard partiers. I am confident his partying was borne of a drinking problem. Mine was borne of catch-up fun.

When he signed into his brigade and battalion, Butch Tidwell received the same welcome I did. When I told him I turned down Drill Sergeant School, he exclaimed, "I wasn't given the chance!" I got lucky, I guess. Butch and I hung around a lot when we could and visited Louisville every chance we had, each of us driving his own car and often in formation. We dated two girls who were best friends. Gas prices were cheap. I could fill up for six or seven dollars—a twenty-two gallon tank, too. Amazing, huh? I cannot recall actual mileage, but we joked that we got gallons-per-mile not miles-per-gallon. We had a lot of fun. When we were not working or the girls were not available, we would wash and wax our cars, repeatedly, chatting about women, Vietnam, and our lives after ETS.

During one of our marathon waxing sessions, Butch told me of his new senior drill sergeant, and that he had been in the 1st Division. He casually mentioned his name—Kamai.

"What was his unit in Nam?"

Butch shrugged and smiled. Was he the same Kamai I knew? In Hawaiian, Kamai may be as popular as Smith is on the mainland; I did not have a clue.

"I don't know, but he's a thin guy, my height, leathery skin...next time you're over, we'll find him."

A few days later Butch was without trainees, and we set off to wax our cars in the shade of an off-post tree. We waxed them twice, and they looked great. When we were finished, we decided to make a jaunt to Louisville and see the girls. On the way to clean up, I thought I would stop by and see if his new senior drill sergeant had been my former platoon sergeant.

"Sergeant Kamai, how are you?" I asked.

"Hey, how've you been?"

He shook my hand, and we began to catch up. I was glad to see him, and he seemed genuinely pleased to see me. He was a competent NCO—a good leader. My time with him was only a few months, thanks to the Article 99 aftermath. After chatting a while, it was time to go, and I felt the urge to say something else.

"You know, Sarge...I didn't refuse the patrol...and I wasn't the ranking NCO that night."

"I know. It's a shame what happened, but luckily the whole thing ended before it became serious. If I was there, none of that would've happened. You *would* have taken out your patrol." He was emphatic.

"Even after Winters said we didn't have to?"

"Hell...he wouldn't have said that. Higher gave us the mission...it would have been done...period."

He would have ensured we went, and I accept that. He would have found a way to get our FNG platoon leader to get the mission done. I knew he was correct.

Later that afternoon, Butch and I were chowing down on cheeseburgers at the Dairy Queen, when I was tapped on the shoulder. I was floored to see CPT Dock standing there, not much worse for wear. I would have guessed, given what I had heard about his wounds, that he would be suffering some very serious long-term medical problems. He claimed to be fine, albeit with a dueling scar on his cheek, and the heavy scars from what must have been a virtual rebuild of his arm.

He was one lucky man and still on active duty.

A few months after arriving at Charlie Company, I ran into SFC Kinnard, our TAC NCO at the Armor School. Over mess hall coffee one morning, I let him know his guidance had served me well, and that I was certain it helped others. He dismissed any contribution to our welfare as merely doing his job. Doing his job: he had performed his mission as well as he could, irrespective of his personal thoughts. Therein lay the lesson he taught me. To my thinking then and more so today, he embodied the very best of an NCO. He was a career soldier, not a lifer. The army I knew back then could have used more like him—and like SFC Kamai, the Great Kahuna (SFC Kaeka), SFC Nolan, and First Sergeant Poncerella.

Enjoying muscle rides—and girls.

Butch and I made a visit to the Halftrack Club, located across the street from the Armor School, where we ran into Jon Laird and Rocky Granziano. Rocky was in first platoon with Jon in Vietnam. He had been wounded during the time Alpha Troop was op-con to the 1st Air Cav, back in August when we were working along the Cambodian border. I was glad to find out he was OK. He showed us his scar, which ran from his neck to his waist and was about two inches across at its widest. His was a horrendous reminder of how close he came to being KIA. Rocky is lucky to be alive—and normal.

Within a month of arriving back at Ft. Knox, I began to experience severe ear pain. I ignored it. When my pain was bad enough, I took aspirin, but it did no good. I jokingly asked Top if he had something stronger than aspirin. He nodded yes and then opened his desk's bottom drawer. He retrieved and placed on his desktop a half-full bottle of pills—Darvon-65s. It was not a small bottle; rather, it was a bulk container like pharmacists use. There were several hundred capsules remaining in the jar.

"Here, you take these. Since I am retiring I don't need them anymore," Top said.

I started to take the Darvon for my pain, and I was pain free—and probably Darvon addicted. There was something wrong beyond a minor ear infection. My hearing worsened, my ears continuously drained clear fluid, and they stuck out perpendicularly to my head—I was the living image of our Supervising NCO from OJT, Sergeant Pistolgrips. The whole area surrounding my ears was grossly swollen. After a few days still without pain, I went to the ENT clinic at Ireland Army Hospital where they checked my hearing. I suffered from a slight hearing loss that was a consequence of armor service at Ft. Knox and of the field in Vietnam; there were no surprises. Then the doctor inserted a scraping instrument deep into my ear, and I yelled loudly—*very* loudly. "Oops," was the only thing he said. He left the room and returned in about five minutes with a small bottle of eardrops.

"Insert these four times a day and return in two weeks. We think we know what it is."

"What is it?" I asked.

"We aren't certain. Let's see what the drops do."

I wondered why he was so mysterious. Since I had no medical training and was not an ENT specialist, I would just have to wait. He did not prescribe anything, even knowing I must be in excruciating pain. I did not think to ask for any; I had my own self-prescription: Darvon 65s. They did the trick.

Two weeks later, I was once again on the ENT doctor's table and with the same instrument as before, he reached deep into my ear. I braced for the pain. Although I could feel him down in there, there was no pain. Withdrawing his probe, he inspected whatever it was he dug up and uttered, "Cool." Really? The doctor thinks it is cool? With that, he stuck a tube down in my ear and began to vacuum, retrieving a green and black slimy mass—and a lot of it. It looked like mold. Yikes! I could not believe that crap was inside me. The other ear was the same. He followed the procedure with an ear cleansing solution that was very soothing down deep.

"You have a jungle fungus we've seen a few times, but only in soldiers returning from Vietnam," he began. "There should be no long term effects, but you may drain for the next few days. After that your life should be back to normal."

"Doc, I assure you if there are *any* effects, you will be the first to know about it."

I felt great, wet ears and all; I was cured, finally. All the pain was gone and the swelling soon went down—my ears no longer stood out ninety degrees. Today my ears drain a clear fluid periodically. My doctor finds nothing but eczema; he is not impressed whatsoever.

Days became a routine of doing my lesson plan tasks, updating records, and recycling problem trainees. I was also responsible for managing the workday of, and processing out of the army, admitted (or faking) homosexuals, drug addicts, and those otherwise deemed unsuitable for military service. That was interesting—draft boards filling their quotas with anything they could intimidate into induction, and the army sending many home, contending they were not fit to die.

My duties, when performed correctly and on time, meant I did not have much to do with SFC Wabbs. We were different ages from different places; he planned to be in the army until his retirement, and I was on a one-and-done enlistment plan. We had different social agendas, and we rarely slept in our shared room at the same time. I only remember once; it was a

Sunday morning. The previous night I had been partying with friends in Louisville and had too much to drink; I slept hard. About eight that Sunday morning I awoke slowly, stretched, and tried to clear the previous night's crap from my head. I heard Wabbs snoring and glanced over to his bed. There, as glorious as a fresh and bright spring day, was a woman, very naked, and not under the covers. I could not help myself—I stared—hers was truly one shapely derriere.

They were each sound asleep, so I eased myself out of bed to take a shower. When I came back to the room, they were gone. As much as I liked her show, and I would dearly have loved more, I was curious how Wabbs had sneaked her out. To get her inside in the middle of the night, all he had to do was distract the CQ (Charge of Quarters) or make some sort of deal with him—easy enough. In the daylight of early morning, there is sufficient activity to make it difficult to hide her exit. I can still see her in my mind.

I applied that fall for an "early out" to return to college, because the army would let me leave ninety days before my contracted ETS. My application was approved. The army knew by then I was not going to be a career soldier, but they still tried to get me to reenlist. I was not the only one, though.

I knew I would do fine in college, finally; I only had to make an effort. My friends, the ones who were smart and who managed to stay in college, were close to graduation or were already in graduate school. After I enlisted in May 1968, most guys I knew did whatever they could to avoid the draft. Some were exempt for a physical reason, but education deferment was the most popular method of avoidance. It is curious how many advanced degrees are among my former friends.

On 15 March 1970, it was finally my turn to depart the army. I reported as directed on the morning of my release, checked in, and my name was marked as being present. About twenty-five of us were there to out-process that day, and we sat in a room listening to the usual lectures and filling out paperwork. We were told to break for lunch and as soon as we returned we would pick up our completed paperwork, get our final pay, and be on our way. REMFs—they could not have worked their schedule so we did not have to wait until after lunch? Some of us had long drives home. Typical.

Humphrey, Conyers, Tidwell and author celebrate ETS.

After lunch, a new clerk came in and began to read the names printed on the large envelopes, handing the responder his paperwork. There were only two of us remaining when I noticed there was only one envelope left. Yep—my luck, I had no envelope. The clerk advised that I should see some other clerk in an office a few buildings away. I did. I was told I would not be getting out until 19 March, four more days. My question—why all the paperwork indicated *that* day, the 15th—was met with a shrug.

"It's the army," he said.

Fuck the army, I wanted out. Goddamn REMFs!

I started up his chain of command only to hit a wall. I was scheduled for the 19th and they could, or they would, do nothing. They admitted one of their people screwed up, but they could not rectify it. I got nowhere, so I accepted my fate.

On my way back to Charlie Company, I made a stop at the IG's (Inspector General's) office on a whim and registered a complaint. Normally, I would not do that, but I was so pissed that someone needed to pay. The reality is no single person could; my problem was surely a systemic failure. Some series of clerks, some weenie REMFs, were keeping me in Uncle Sam's Army for four days more than we agreed. Shit. I returned to my company, reported in, and bitched. A few friends took me out for a beer—many, actually.

I got over my anger and processed out on Friday, after which I was no longer on active duty. I was assigned to the Inactive Reserve Component to complete my obligation of six years. Yes, I made damn sure they paid me for those four days. I do not recall what lunch was on the 15th, my original separation date, but on the 19th my company mess hall was serving liver and onions. A strange but fitting twist, which bookended my very first day and my final day of active duty—serving my least appreciated meal. It is curious I had not seen those items on any other menu during my entire enlistment.

I learned many times during my enlistment why so many said, "FTA" (Fuck The Army). I was guilty of doing so more than once. Although I wanted no more part of the army at that time, I understood—even on that, my separation day—that I had gained experiences few soldiers, and many fewer people, ever obtain. Had I lived in another time I may have stayed in the army, continued my formal education, and gone to flight school or OCS, or both—but not during those days.

Chapter 20

Combatant Rehab

A few days remained until classes were to begin. I was keenly aware of the admonition the army gave me—if I did not remain a student for the quarter, I was subject to recall to complete the rest of my enlistment. That was not going to happen. I planned to attend every class, pay close attention, study, and try to get maximum scores. There was no way I was going back in the army.

The remaining responsibility-free days were filled with good times with the few friends who were still in town. We hung out at bars on the weeknights, and on the weekends, we found a party or two to attend. Mostly, though, I was alone and bored, so I returned to Athens to see friends still at the university.

I visited a previously close friend who was working on his master's degree. He recently joined the Army Reserves, trained a few months, and returned to full-time studies. He delighted in telling me of the arduous training he encountered in BCT and AIT. He was well aware of where I had been the previous three years.

"Man, let me tell you how bad it was," he began. "Basic training was a bitch. They nearly killed me. I was always hot, tired, thirsty, and never had enough sleep."

"Really?"

"They fired *live* ammunition at us...LIVE! I almost pissed myself...and...the gas chamber was horrible; everyone got sick. The full-gear marches were incredibly hard. Shit...they had an ambulance that always followed us."

He continued several minutes more, eagerly regaling me with his deprivations and hardships. I patiently listened for a while longer, silently, remaining calm at his total lack of tact, consideration, and most important, his stupefying ignorance.

"Man, six whole months? How ever did you survive that? At least nobody was shooting at you."

I could not hold back any longer. He agreed, absolutely missing my sarcasm. I realized then that my former very good friend would never get it. How could he? How could anyone without personal experience of the stresses of risking life and limb daily? His experience had only been his training. Our relationship, previously close, began to grow distant that day, after I realized that we no longer had much in common. Whether it was because we had lived totally separate lives for three years, had radically different army experiences or his irritating superior demeanor that day (and later, too) or that we had simply grown up and apart like so many before us—we would not be the same close friends ever again.

All my other friends in Athens had full class or study days and could not come out to play, so I went back home with my tail between my legs. My world was very much out of sync. I had little in common with my old friends anymore, and I began to feel truly alone for the first time. During my active duty days, I was surrounded by guys I did not know, but they were guys in the same situation I was. I realized there was nobody around who was in my situation. Everyone had moved on with their lives—without me—and they could not share their time. It was another rock-to-the-head moment for me; it was time for me to move on myself, to grow up.

On that first day of spring quarter, I was once again a college student. There were no serious distractions, other than my continuing slow decompression from almost three years living the adventure of my lifetime. I was paying close attention during class, though that was difficult at times since some lectures were still boring. I was sensitive to having nothing in common with any of those around me: they were so young by comparison, so naïve. They were normal; I was not. I was life-experienced—aged beyond years, even though I was only three or so years older than they were.

The effort I made that first quarter put me on the Dean's List. Classes were easy, no big deal at all. (Why did I not do it the first time through?) I attended almost every class, did the coursework as assigned, and embraced the subject matter. Since none of my friends were around, my concentration was focused, and with my spring quarter success, I registered for summer quarter. I had sufficient enthusiasm to complete my education, but I realized I had no money. I was living with my parents rent free, but my muscle car was a gas-guzzler. On the first day of summer session, I drove up to that very same building that I had problems entering back in the winter of 1968, and I just could not go through that door. Yes, it had happened yet again. Had my irresponsible disease returned? No—absolutely not! My problem was no longer a case of my misdirection, pursuit of carnal pleasure, or beer appreciation, as it had been so many times before. I handled those things in stride. No, the mature me was truthfully saying, "Hey! You really aren't ready for this, yet." I sorely needed some more decompression and much more stimulation. The classroom was too quiet, too confining, too limiting in scope. I needed more time. I knew I would get there one day.

I had proven to myself I could get my education, but I was not hard-driven to do so immediately. I reasoned that I had waited so long already that I could wait a little longer. I planned to get right back at it as soon as I could afford my car, gas, insurance, an apartment, food, beer, *and* school. Meanwhile, I needed to live a little—and save a little more. I left school and set out to find a place of my own. I felt strange still living in my parents' house; I did not belong anymore. I needed to be self-reliant, and I needed my independence. They deserved me gone and I wanted to be gone. I needed to find a job. I feared that no employer for whom I desired to work over the long term would be serious about me without a degree, or if they faced the prospect of losing me to full-time studies. I looked for *anything* that paid enough.

A new hospital was being built nearby, and they were advertising several openings, so I applied to be an orderly. I could handle anything they might throw at me, after all, I had been to war. The midnight shift was ideal for my situation, and I felt I could get back in school *and* move out by the fall quarter. That was not to be. Nope, not for me. I did not even get an interview. I was surprised. I experienced only slightly better failure after I applied to a new hotel opening, when they invited me to interview for an overnight desk clerk slot. That would have also been an ideal place for me. I thought my interview went well, but they must have felt otherwise. Maybe someone applied who was actually qualified and did not need training. No job for me there, either.

After a several week long and aggravating search, I found a management opening in a retail import store in Sandy Springs. I knew *that* particular job would not be my career path, since I planned to return to school soon, but I sold myself as though I were hoping for retirement at their company. The stores offered exotic items from all around the world. The company was a franchisor of their import store brand, and they needed company-owned stores to be great examples. I was hired as the assistant manager of a brand new store, the prototype of a new store concept.

I learned all I could about their operation and thought I would like to be a buyer. I could envision traveling to faraway places. Alas, the real buyers burst my first-impression bubble when they said my fantasy was just that—fantasy—and was far from their routine reality. They told me their travels were to the poorest areas of the poorest countries, peculiar places in the third world where they were not usually comfortable. I was skeptical, until I considered our prices, our products and how they were made so inexpensively. There went my hopes of fine dining in Paris.

I was becoming increasingly aware of my conservative dress and hair, relative to my age group. I was an outcast in some circles—at minimum not conforming to fads a segment of so-called non-conformists did. I did not fully embrace the hippie culture—I was curious, though, it seemed cool, but I preferred traditional, less current-faddish people. Those who used their continuing education as their means to avoid the military were not among my closest friends, either.

I grew my hair longer in an effort to fit in a little better between the hippies and the older generations. The resulting hairstyle I had has been referred to as my "hair helmet," an apt description. A new tool, the hot comb, kept it just as I wanted it. Today, I detest that look. What *ever* was I thinking?

One night, a friend and I were on our way home after clubbing, being rowdy and stupid, and racing with another car. I was driving my car and I was in the lead, well ahead. Looking back to see just how far ahead, I careened off the pavement and right over a dry fire hydrant.

> *Earlier in the day, I had seen Mr. Ridell. I never wanted to see him out walking ever again. Every time I did, I had a wreck. That was the last time I saw him and the very last time I had an accident.*

A high school friend said he was getting a divorce, so the timing was perfect for us to pool our resources. We agreed to split the rent on a two-bedroom, two-bath apartment, and party as much as we could. That was exactly what I needed. When I was not working, finding pleasure preoccupied my mind, body, and spirit almost constantly. (It did the same when I *was* working.) I celebrated my constitutional right to the pursuit of happiness every waking moment. I wanted to experience all that I had been missing for the previous three years—and I wanted it all right then.

When I went into the army, young people were not too far removed from dance cards, sock hops, fedoras, gloves, and girdles. That had changed. A club named Uncle Sam's was a favorite spot for young adults, and we often visited. Generally, there was a relaxed, albeit casual sexual culture in those days, and the female selection was astounding. How lucky young men were; not every woman was pursuing a husband. Many were asserting themselves within society in general and sexually in particular. I embraced my new world.

There was honesty—sexually free and consenting adults enjoying adult behavior. The casual-sex-no-husband-hunting concept was new to me, and I was not initially secure with it. I did not know how to act with females anymore, especially "liberated" ones. However, I learned to embrace it. It was a wonderful time to be young, independent, single, and sexually active—we knew nothing of AIDS or herpes. (We did know that penicillin could be our friend.)

Men were also changed. Earlier, in the fifties and the first half of the sixties, serving in the military was honorable. Some used it as a method of self-improvement of character and/or discipline, others for the educational opportunities and résumé enhancement. By the end of the decade of the sixties, men who were in the service, or had been in or even those who aspired to serve were often reviled as much as the war itself. It was the then-current fashion to berate the war *and* the warrior.

As a civilian, I experienced my first warrior-hate while at a party. It came from a guest whose callousness and venom were appalling to me, as much as it was personally hurtful. Had I not been so taken aback, I might have asked the reason for his anger and tried to educate him. Either that or punch him out. I was just hanging out doing the usual young man conversational competition.

One asked, "What's the most difficult thing you've ever done...in your entire life?

"I ran a marathon," one guy said. (There are many more runners today than there were then.)

Another offered, "I finally finished college...I've never been a scholar...not even a very good student."

They all looked at me next, and I was not sure how to answer. I decided to tell the truth.

"Survived combat in Vietnam."

I turned to the other guy for his input. He surprised me with a puzzled look on his face.

"You went to Vietnam?" He was incredulous. "Are you fuckin' stupid? There were a million ways for you to avoid it. Man, you aren't real bright, are ya?"

"Yeah. I went. Long story...but not because I was stupid.

Naive maybe...aimless...immature."

"Lookit, anyone who goes is an idiot. It's a crazy war, run by a few crazy, rich, old, white men. They use draftees as cannon fodder. I'd never go."

I knew that was not the place, and right then was not the time, for me to make a stand. What could I have said? He may have been correct in some of the things he said, but he was uninformed in most, and dead wrong about my being stupid. He could voice his opinion, no matter how offensive, no matter how it personally stung me, but I did not have to listen to him. My experience was still too fresh, and I was not yet decompressed enough for that form of battle—I still was too close to violence mode and did not think that would help me. I excused myself from the conversation.

Another rock-to-the-head moment: to most people my service was of little or no consequence. That is fair enough. To a few, it was offensive. Huh? Something is just not right with that. I tried my best not to be annoyed by those who felt that way, and at times, that effort was a struggle. However, over the years I would come to realize that the problem was not mine; rather, the problem was with those who were offended by my service.

Just about the time I got my bearings at my job, the manager of the Lenox Square store had a heart attack and died, leaving a high volume store manager opening. I said to an employee, "Well, at least he made thirty-one." I was not flip, but my comment was taken as such, and I was severely chided. No comparison to young men still dying in Vietnam helped. She had been his friend. I apologized and moved on.

My manager assumed the duties at the Lenox store, and I was promoted to manager at my store. I found the work easy, interesting, and preparation for pursuing my business degree. I wanted to know as much as I could and to make my store the best performing store in the chain. However, I would learn that it was not expected to be competitive—the company was testing a smaller store concept.

My performance after a few months must have been

enough to impress higher management—I was soon asked to make a temporary move to Huntsville, Alabama, to recover a failing company store. I never considered they might be trying to run me out of town, and I thought it was a step toward higher management. When our VP of operations asked me if I would go, I was reluctant at first. Huntsville? I had never been. What was it like there? I was a single guy and required an active nightlife to balance the hard work I was giving to the company.

"They roll up their sidewalks at seven every evening."

"Now, you *do* know that won't get me to say yes...right?"

"It's a nice clean town...NASA has a big footprint, lots of smart people making good money...I'd bet they have many daughters, too. They might even let you near them."

The army had undoubtedly changed me, but it had not rid me of my innate ability to find a good time when times were not so good. (I had done just such a thing in Vietnam, where I tried to have a good time by making a truly bad time better.) So, for the sake of growth, I knew I could handle it for the short term. I accepted the offer and moved, knowing that I would be coming home before long.

Once at the Huntsville store, I introduced myself to the manager and asked him to phone our corporate office. He was dismissed. The employees were shocked, but happy. They were there because they wanted to earn money, and he closed the store routinely in mid-afternoon. How did he get away with that behavior for almost a year? We stayed open the hours advertised and the employees earned more money.

The first week we cleaned and dusted the merchandise and the shelves, and we changed many items' locations for a better-organized display—very simple stuff. We washed all the windows and buffed the floor. I ordered a truckload of new merchandise and bulked up stock of existing items. Sales sharply increased, and I made a big splash back at corporate, as well as with my employees. They were being treated as if they mattered, and they certainly did to me. They all had a great sense of humor, gave good conversation, were the right age, and loved a good party. What is not to like? One evening, the same-age, non-employee aunt of one of the women who worked for me asked if I could take her home. Being such a kind soul, I obliged.

"I don't have to get home right away," she said as we pulled out of the mall parking lot.

Well, I may be a little thick at times, but there was *one* thing I did not need help comprehending. She was interested in me; I was interested in her, as well. We enjoyed several hours of adult fun that night, and our encounters continued until I left there later that year. Huntsville was a little Peyton Place—in a good way. Rocket scientists (and their wives) liked their fun, and I was glad to have been part of it.

For example, the middle of every week a petite, older, very attractive woman would come to the store and shop. (She must have been all of thirty or thirty-five.) She would spend a long time looking over our merchandise, usually that which was on the bottom shelf. Consider that those were the days of hot pants and mini-skirts—and she *always* wore a mini-skirt. She would bend over frequently, revealing, well—everything. My college-aged stock boy would alert me, and we enjoyed her show often. At first, I thought it was accidental, but soon I became aware of her pattern. She would do her routine about fifteen minutes and then buy a candle and leave, usually with one last show as she slowly maneuvered into her car's bucket seat. We named her Lucille, after the name George Kennedy gave to the large breasted, car-washing woman in *Cool Hand Luke*. I think our lady shopper had a crush on my employee. Good for him!

Corporate returned me to Atlanta that fall to run their number one company store at Northlake Mall and improve its flagging sales and profits. Using the same approach I did in Huntsville, the numbers rose rapidly. That time, though, the effort necessitated an all-new staff, as well. Although they remained open during mall hours, no one made any effort to keep the business growing. Why? There *was* a manager. I was not expecting to stay with that company for life, but I would certainly give them, or any other company I worked for, at least what they were paying for. Evidently, not everyone felt thus obliged.

I could not afford the cool apartment complex I wanted without a roommate, and I thought of someone I had known since just prior to going into the service. Maybe he would be open to sharing rent. Don Conyers joined the army a few months after I did, went into armor training, also went to the Armor School, and also went to Vietnam. When he came home to serve out his last year, as Butch Tidwell had, he, too, attended Drill Sergeant School. We all spent a lot of our free time together. He agreed to share a two-bedroom, two-bath townhome that I found. Since he was broke, I needed to loan him his half of the deposit. That should have sent a message, but it did not. We moved a building over to a two-bedroom, two-bath apartment for more room. Don became a Dekalb County police officer, but even before that time, we were not keeping similar hours or the same friends. We had not hung out together since we left Ft. Knox.

Don's police service weapon, at least what he carried when I saw him, was a .357 Magnum. I asked him once if he needed that much firepower for large game about that might be inclined to rob a bank, but he failed to see the humor. Since he had been a tank guy, he must have been used to—and needed—a lot of firepower. I cannot fault that. What I can fault was his often very careless handling of a loaded weapon. He was a cop—and combat veteran—he should have known better, much better. Finally, the day came when I had enough. He went out and left his gun on his dresser, loaded. I could not resist—I removed all the rounds and placed them all around the apartment. They were not hidden, but they were not obvious; I hid them in plain sight. The last round I placed standing up in the water at the bottom of his toilet. His reaction was quite amusing and his frantic search for his ammo was hysterical. Priceless. He called me a child, and I called him irresponsible. Maybe we were both right.

He did some other stuff that rubbed me the wrong way. The worst thing was probably when he brought a date home, a female Dekalb County police officer, and they sat on the floor listening to music while they smoked pot. I absolutely did *not* have a problem with them doing that, as I smoked on occasion also. They were off-duty, out of uniform, unarmed, and in recreation mode. The problem I did have was their conversation and mentality regarding the fifteen-year-old kid Don had arrested earlier in the day for possession of a single joint. I could not get them to understand how corrupt they were. Don never did get why I thought he should not be a cop.

I vowed never to share a place with a male again.

Six months later the evening news had a story of a police officer who, while responding to a call, lights flashing and siren blaring, lost control of his police cruiser and struck a utility pole. "The young officer suffered no injuries, except to his dignity," the newsreader said. I howled. The policeman was Don.

My brother Bob and his girlfriend, who was raised in southern Georgia, decided to get married. Her father was a big shot in the peanut business, which was huge in those parts. While my family was down there for their wedding, we were shown about town, and we took a tour of the processing plants. Who knew there were so many gazillion goobers? I was surprised to learn the company was contracted by Uncle Sam to provide peanut butter—the tin that was included in a C-Rats meal. They did not appreciate it *at all* when I told them we usually threw them to the Vietnamese children who would assemble as we passed through villages and hamlets.

We met his bride-to-be's family, including her siblings who were in town for the wedding. One sister was married to a Vietnam veteran and, as people often do, everyone assumed we would know each another; we did not. However, we were in-country at about the same time. I asked him what unit he served with, and he said he had been a military intelligence officer. Had he been involved in, or knew of, some interesting operations? I probed. We soon concluded his work covered the AO I worked in.

"So you're the SOB who kept on sending us hunting for enemy which we never found, getting us really pissed at Higher...until we'd report all kinds of bogus shit back up the chain," I said, emboldened by alcohol.

"Yep, I was one of *those* guys. And...after you gave us your info, you were sent back out on the bogus info another unit had fed us." He chuckled. "Wasn't it fun?"

I admit it; there he had me—the absurdity of it all.

While at the wedding, I suffered a migraine. No, not a hangover—a migraine. They are radically different. As much as I sometimes drank, I would not get a hangover back then—I can today. Beginning when I was pre-pubescent, I suffered seasonal allergies and was accustomed to an occasional harsh headache. Those certainly continued, but I also began to get migraines, a very different form of head pain. While I was in that horrendous pain, I was unable to tolerate light, noise, or movement. The first migraine lasted about half an hour, as I lay absolutely still with my face covered. They would become much worse and longer in duration over the next ten years.

About six months after I took over the Northlake store and with my success visible, the owners of the store next door approached me to open several new stores they had planned. The owners were not active in their business on a daily basis, but the son of one was—he was their general manager. He and I often chatted, and we had become somewhat friendly. Unbeknownst to me, he had been watching and assessing me, and he made the recommendation. I accepted their offer knowing I would be returning to school just as soon as I had saved enough money to dedicate all my time to my education. After a year and a half in non-food imports, I left for cheese—both domestic and imported. I like cheese.

After product and systems training, my duties would be

building out, staffing, training, and then supervising the next four mall stores, already in the works, and locating them in several cities around Georgia. Soon, I moved to an apartment in Marietta so I would be closer to their soon-to-be-built store in Cumberland Mall.

All my older friends were scattered, and I did not see them very much. One very notable exception was an old friend I had not seen for several years and for whom I always had a special fondness. We had never dated, but I think we always enjoyed each other's conversation and humor. To be truthful, I had lusted after her for some time. Not only was she great looking, but also she had a body that killed. I teased her about my lust for her—I was serious, she thought I was just having fun with her. Since the last time I had seen her, she had married, had a child, and divorced.

One night a group of us met at a bar, and she joined us. Nobody in the group was dating anyone, much less anyone in that night's group. I teased my old friend as always, but that night it was a beautiful, hot bodied, more mature, mother of a small child, who teased me right back. The flirt was on, she in her skin-tight, white skirt and dark tan, me looking my usual pasty-white self. She was—in the current vernacular—a MILF. I did not then want a wife, but to have her as an intimate friend would have been very nice. That was not to be—not that evening. My time came several months later when we dated a bit. I have some very fond memories of great laughter every time we were together. She made me feel special at a time when I really needed it.

As the first store was built out I spent a lot of my time on site, and I became acquainted with the neighboring stores' on-site people. The store just next door to ours was being opened by a fellow named Russ, and he visited with us often. He told me about his family—his wife and daughter. He said they would be joining him from Northern Virginia (suburban Washington, D.C.) soon, and his wife would need a job. He talked up her vast experience in specialty cheeses and asked if I would consider interviewing her.

"Of course, introduce me when she comes." I wanted to meet her. Even without her experience, I wanted to because I liked him. I felt a friendship was blossoming between us, and we did become good friends. He had also become friendly with my boss. That became a problem when Russ's wife was hired sight unseen and without even mentioning their discussion to me. My boss *informed* me she would be my lead employee. Since his family owned the operation, I was a good soldier.

After our construction company had finished enough of the build-out of the store, I began to train my replacement store management and staff, mostly women, for our August 3rd opening. I struggled to maintain staffing within our low budget. It was challenging, but more so because I had hired young, opinionated and self-important women. Russ's wife, Chrisanne, according to her agreement with my boss would be working weekdays only. She brought needed experience and knowledge, but that did not matter to the other women—it was all about *their* schedule. They were very resentful, and I did not like her so much myself. When she heard me saying to another employee something about being in the army, she asked if I had been to Vietnam. I said yes.

"Did you kill anybody?"

Her question—*that* question—was the cherry on top of my dislike for her. I just glared at her and tried to distance myself from the looming confrontation. I was fed up—she was causing me grief all around; the other women were always bitching at me about her, and my boss thought she hung the moon. I certainly did not. The truth is, though, because she was forced on me and because of all the negativity coming my way from other staff, I had prejudged her. I never even gave myself a chance to like her. I am certain I would have hired her. Over time, relationships seemed to be improving and I relaxed about her a little.

One day Chrisanne questioned me about a procedure while she was helping a customer—a woman about sixty, very well dressed, but not formal, and someone who struck me as city-southern. I answered Chrisanne's question, and as the customer began to thank me for helping, she saw my name. She cocked her head back and looked at me.

"Are you any relation to the late author, James Street?"

I was flabbergasted, and Chrisanne was astonished and looked at me with a "Say what?" expression.

"I am his grandson," I said.

"We sat next to each other on an airplane years ago," she said. "We had a nice and quite lengthy discussion of Faulkner and Mississippi writers. He was a hoot."

"Did you really?"

"He was a lovely man. Quite the character...and he had an opinion on anything...everything. He did not mind voicing it to you, either. But...he also heard what others had to say. That *is* a little unusual."

"Thank you so much for the kind words. I will surely tell my family...and for sure my grandmother."

"No...thank you for sparking the memory."

She smiled, and expressed her pleasure at meeting me, and then she left. She made my day; I was impressed and, I should say, proud. My grandfather had died almost nineteen years earlier, and she was still a fan. Later I reflected on our conversation, and it reminded me of my family's achievement; to date, I felt I had none.

Chapter 21

Traditional Priorities

The week before Thanksgiving Chrisanne informed me that she would be leaving her husband soon and may be moving. The news meant I would be left with a staff void—her depth of experience and knowledge of the industry. We spoke at length about her departure, but our discussion slowly morphed into non-business topics, and I began to change my feelings about her. I realized I actually did like her—a lot. Yet I was torn. She was about to leave Russ, and he was a friend. Also, I was not sure whether my feelings might grow beyond a healthy like. Would she feel the same if they did? By the end of the week, and after several intimate conversations, we were emotionally involved. How did *that* happen?

That Saturday several of us represented our stores at a festival in town, including Chrisanne. After spending the day together, I drove her home to the apartment that she and Russ shared. All along the way home, we discussed what was going on between us—I was in a daze, but tried to think with a clear head. When we arrived at her place, she told me Russ would be attending a company function the next day, and she would not be going.

"We should spend the day together," she said.

I did not mention to Chrisanne that I had previously made plans for the day with an old friend, my favorite MILF whose intimate company I enjoyed so much—and that she was due at nine the next morning. I decided to cancel my date with her knowing she would understand, but since it was so late Saturday night, I thought I would telephone her first thing the next morning.

Her mother answered my call and informed me she was already on her way. When she arrived, I told her what had happened. She knew me before I went into the army, and she sensed what was coming. She was gracious, as I had expected she would be. Just as she was leaving, there was a knock at my door. Chrisanne and her daughter Jennifer came, and I made the introductions. After pleasantries, my friend left. I have not seen, nor have I spoken to her since, and I sincerely regret that. She was a very *real* and good person in the best sense of those terms. She recognized the interest I had in Chrisanne readily, even as I did not yet know the depths of my involvement.

Author's future family. Who knew?

Chrisanne, Jennifer, and I spent the rest of the day at the lake enjoying warm November sunshine, and then we went back to my apartment. There was a knock at the door. When I opened it, I was startled to be rushed and pushed back against the wall by Russ. He and Chrisanne yelled at one another, and I could only stand there, mute. He departed taking Jennifer with him, and Chrisanne and I calmed one another down. She thought she should go home and I agreed.

I walked her out to her car, but it would not start. I went to get my keys, and the phone rang—it was Russ telling me how he had disabled the car. His demeanor was mostly apologetic without saying so. Mine was as well. Chrisanne's car was an easy fix, and she was soon on her way with a caution not to let things escalate at home.

That week had been a lot to process for me, and I could not stop thinking of the afternoon's events. What kind of a person was I? What of Jennifer? Would she be scarred from the altercation and so much yelling? I was not feeling very proud of myself, but I rationalized my actions because I had not sought out a relationship—one had found me. Late that night my phone rang. It was Chrisanne.

"My father flew down tonight. He wants to see you first thing in the morning...eight o'clock."

Events were getting ahead of me. Who the hell was he to command my presence? Who was that man to assume my subservience? Her father, of course.

"Okay, I'll meet him at eight in front of the store."

I tossed and turned all night wondering what he would do or say. Was he big, physically imposing, not sympathetic to the situation at all? The next morning I arrived early; he arrived right on time and introduced himself.

"Greg?"

"Yes, I am...Mr. Ives?"

"Bill Ives."

He stuck out his hand. He did not look like he was going to kick my ass, but I was still on guard. He said he had come in Sunday night at Russ's request, to get Chrisanne straight. As can be imagined under those circumstances, he was not very pleasant—he was civil, but not cordial. He asked very pointed and highly personal questions—which I deflected. His tone did not soften. Then he crossed a line and angered me when he asked if Chrisanne and I had been intimate. We were innocent, but he should not have asked.

"I'm sorry, sir. That information is on a need-to-know basis, and I don't believe you have a need...and perhaps no right...to know. That information is privileged, between your daughter and me."

He accepted my response without visible reaction but continued by telling me all of the things Russ could do for Chrisanne and Jennifer. I responded that I was fully aware Russ was a capable adult, yet he was not the only person with those capabilities.

"How much money are you making? What assets do you have? Where do you see yourself in five years?"

Once again I was floored, although that last question I expected; it is so cliché.

"Well, sir, I do believe that is one more area not of your concern. I will say this to you...I'm not making now what I will in the future. Yes, I do fully understand that you are Chrisanne's father and that you want what's best for her and for Jennifer, but it's my view that *she* has the choice to make, not you. Obviously you influence her, but in the end, it's her life, and she's the one responsible for Jennifer."

I was no longer intimidated.

"Oh, and please don't ask about religion or politics. You won't get an answer."

He was no longer making eye contact, but he continued his third-degree questioning. I continued to parry questions as gracefully as I could trying to be non-committal. After about thirty minutes, he actually smiled. Then his tone was different; he became amiable.

"I don't know what will happen between Chrisanne and Russ...or Chrisanne and you," he began. "I do know I came to this meeting expecting to meet some Lothario out only to bed my daughter. I don't feel the same now. Yes, it's her life...her decision. If she chooses you and she's wrong, she'll pay the price. I'm satisfied that in the mix, however it plays out, that Jennifer and Chrisanne will be okay. And yes, that *is* what a father wants most. You may not be best for them, but I don't think you'll harm them in any long-term way."

While it was not exactly his blessing, at a minimum, I must have allayed some of his fear that I would lay waste to the well-being of his daughter and granddaughter. I surely did not think I had won him over, but I sensed that he would give the situation time and let it play out.

The next few weeks passed quickly. Chrisanne hired herself a lawyer and began her state-required thirty-day legal separation from Russ. We established Jennifer and her in an apartment to meet a potential legal requirement, but they never stayed one night. Instead, Chrisanne and Jennifer moved into my apartment as quickly as she left the one she shared with Russ. Within a few weeks, I asked Chrisanne to marry me—she said yes. In a virtual instant, I had a beautiful and loving family. I was as surprised as anyone.

The divorce was final shortly after their legal separation ended, and that is when we announced to our families and friends that we would be married in the summer. I can only imagine what our parents, siblings, and friends thought about what we were doing so quickly. I was relieved when Chrisanne did not move out of my place immediately after her divorce, since previous positive events in my life had typically been followed by personal trauma, real or perceived. Although there had been no signs to indicate otherwise, when nothing actually happened and she stayed, I thought I had a chance at family permanence.

Learning to fly was high on my agenda. It always had been. Chrisanne, very early on, enthusiastically encouraged me to go for it. I was worried about the money it would take, but I was also harboring aspirations of flying for the airlines. I forged ahead and began flying lessons. After a few weeks, I recalled I had a high school friend who worked for Delta. His job, long forgotten, gave him knowledge of what was required of a pilot applicant, so I gave him a call. He said to be hired by Delta, a pilot-applicant must have two-thousand hours of multi-engine turbine time. I knew the best place to acquire that time was in the air force, but I still needed a degree to qualify for training. My friend was no help except to quash for good my desire to be an airline pilot.

Joe, a marine fighter pilot and Georgia Tech graduate

student, his wife, and their two kids lived in the apartment below us. Our families became fast friends when our children played together. We often swapped babysitting chores for an adult night out. Joe also helped me with aviation studies. I told him of my recent conversation with my Delta friend, knowing he certainly would qualify to fly with Delta. I asked him what he knew about the new package delivery company, Federal Express. I had just recently read an article that their qualifications were not nearly as stringent as the airlines. Joe told me many of his friends were flying for them and hated it. Their pilots were always away from home, and their flying was during the overnight hours. OK, I do not want to do that.

Chrisanne and I were still getting to know each other and sharing histories. Going through her photo albums one day, I was struck by a picture of a guy in army uniform; he had on a yellow scarf—armor/cavalry yellow. His face was one I recognized.

"I know that guy!" I blurted. "He was in the class behind me at the Armor School."

"Uh-*uh*. He was not!"

"Promise you he was. I didn't know him well, but we spoke. I never knew his name, though. Who is he?"

"That's Russ's brother, my former brother-in-law."

"Russ's brother? Shit. I wonder if he'd remember me."

He did. Chrisanne and I met him and his wife for dinner several years later. We all had a delightful evening together.

When Chrisanne and I decided to marry, we needed to decide what kind of service we wanted. I said I did not really care provided it was legal. She was raised Catholic, and she thought a church service would be meaningful to her parents. Because she had a wedding already, she did not feel the need for a production. My parents suggested we could marry in their side yard and have a ceremony officiated by clergy. We visited the local Episcopal priest and asked if he would marry us. He said he would if we took pre-marital classes from him. Then, as an afterthought, he said we would also have to get special dispensation from the Bishop. Because I had been christened, baptized, and confirmed an Episcopalian and was marrying a Catholic? Nope. Chrisanne was divorced, and that did not sit well with Episcopal clergy.

The Bishop approved our union, so on 4 July 1974, only eight months after first becoming involved, Chrisanne and I were married; Jennifer was our beautiful little flower girl. We chose Independence Day, which I suggested for the irony, and selected high noon to begin the outdoor ceremony. Again, my standard luck—the day broke with low overcast and rain. At precisely noon, though, the clouds parted just long enough to perform the ceremony. The priest, Father Fisher, was suitably impressed and asked me to put in a good word. (The truth is, I knew from flight lessons how to get aviation weather from Flight Service. They told me there would be a hole in the weather at noon and last about half an hour.)

Chrisanne's mother flew in to attend, but not any of her siblings, nor did her father. I was a bit offended at first, when I recalled that her father had previously flown down in a skinny minute. My incredulity did not last long, though, and I enjoyed our day with friends and family.

In what I consider an ironic twist, Chrisanne's father had just recently left her mother after she discovered that he was having an affair (even while he preached to me). Yes, that same guy who flew down to rescue his "wayward" daughter and that same guy who chided me for being a cad—*that guy.* He had left Chrisanne's mother for another woman. Then I understood why only her mother was there.

In October, we made a trip to suburban Washington, DC, Northern Virginia, where Chrisanne had grown up. We went to visit her mom, but we also spent time with her dad. We visited him in his new home where he had been living alone, estranged from the rest of his family. Chrisanne was their eldest daughter and had been through a divorce; she could make no judgment.

Bill had retired from the U.S. Navy over a decade prior, after twenty-something years' active duty. He and Chrisanne's mother built a catering service, and he wrote a food column for the *Washington Post* and sold life insurance. He needed to run an errand to his office one morning and, in an unusually generous mood, he decided to show me around the Pentagon. I jumped at the chance. Forget in-law bonding, I was going along strictly for my own exploration. I was not on active duty anymore, but they let me in. As each guard greeted him, Bill would point to me, saying, "He's with me." I admit that I was suitably impressed. (Can you imagine in our post-9/11 world saying, "He's with me" to get someone deep inside?)

In our meanderings about the building, I was surprised to find myself standing at the doorway of the Chairman of the Joint Chief's office—me, a one-enlistment, staff sergeant, E-6. I was star-struck. I saw "Congressional Corner," a Medal of Honor presentation on an outside corner of a hallway, where silver plaques are mounted, inscribed for recipients. I was dumbstruck by the number of awardees and how many were posthumous. I contemplated the selflessness and sacrifice that was represented in that solemn corner.

Chrisanne and I went back to her mother's to spend the remainder of our time, and we visited a few sites around the District, including the front of the White House. We stopped in front, on Pennsylvania Avenue—a section you cannot take an automobile any longer—for me to take a nighttime picture.

"I feel nauseous," Chrisanne said. "I'm not well."

"You're probably pregnant," her mom said.

She said it casually, as a mother of six might.

Within a few weeks, Chrisanne told me she was indeed pregnant. It was shortly after my first solo cross-country, and thinking flying lessons would no longer be affordable, I stopped. I was very close to completing all the requirements for my Private Pilot Certificate, but I felt I had to abandon the effort. That was a small price to pay for family. I was enjoying the role of father, and I was looking forward to another child.

We temporarily moved to Macon, Georgia, so I could

open another new store. Chrisanne kept her Atlanta doctor since she was so close to full term and so our child would be born in metro Atlanta. In July, thanks to the medical ability to induce labor on a certain date, we were back in Atlanta for my new child's birth. I was euphoric, much fulfilled, and most satisfied.

At the hospital, I sat in the general waiting room, since there was no expectant father area. I was quietly celebrating the imminent entry of my child into the world and wondering what was taking so long. Across from me, there was a quite large family huddled together. They alternated praying and sobbing. Their teenage child was in intensive care; he had been gravely injured in an accident during the early morning hours. While I celebrated my child's pending arrival without fanfare—I had big plans for my new baby, a lifetime for me to contemplate—they merely wanted survival. I silently wished them good fortune, and I cursed the lack of private areas for them and for me. My sadness at their grief was soon dwarfed by the stabbing fear I felt when I was summoned upstairs.

"The doctor wants to see you," was my command to go to the delivery floor.

Heretofore in my life, that message would mean that bad news was coming, and my concern kicked into overdrive. The nurse's tone was non-committal, but I read into her words every problem that my racing imagination could think of. What could it be? I hoped everything was OK, but if not, I hoped any problem was fixable. As I stepped off the elevator, I saw the delivering doctor beside a nurse. She was holding something in her arms.

"You'd better come here and look at this boy," the doctor yelled to me—more like *at* me.

Was he saying my child was male? My mind was reeling. Did I have a boy? Did I have a healthy child? The nurse showed me his face, and I melted. Straight guys certainly *can* be in love with other guys—when that other guy is their son. (Today that includes grandsons.) When I asked if he and Chrisanne were OK, the doctor did not say a word. He just pulled back the blanket that my new son was bundled in, and he showed me. There, in all his birth-moment glory was my new son: wrinkled, slimy, and very much an ugly mess—he had not yet been cleaned up. He had all the characteristics of healthy newborns, but I did not yet know it, despite reading all I could about pregnancy and birth. He had grotesquely swollen breasts and genitals, and I was shocked. The look on my face must have been special; both doctor and nurse laughed heartily.

"He's fine. A *perfect* baby boy. Mom is fine, too. She's in recovery, and you can be with her soon."

While Chrisanne recovered, David, as we had previously decided to name a boy, received a medical and legal welcome to the world. As common as I knew the birth process to be, I considered his healthy arrival a personal gift. A part of me was bewildered I deserved such a thing, but I welcomed it.

Once she recovered, they moved Chrisanne to her room and allowed me to join her. Then they brought in David. I fondly recall that special time as we inspected him in intimate detail. I was concerned with everything. The nurses, no doubt quite used to such new-father behavior, took my questions in stride and educated me. I soon relaxed and believed my new child really was fine.

The hospital threw me out of her room that afternoon, so I grabbed a six-pack of beer en route to joining Jennifer at my parents. Encouraged by beer, I became sentimental and began to weep. I was struck by the realization that I really was an adult, and my future and that of my wife and kids ran through my mind. When I arrived at my parents, Jennifer was very excited to see me and hear all about "her baby." I had a blast having an adult conversation with a mid-three year old. She was full of questions, silly and sensible, and the loving acceptance she displayed was truly heartwarming—she had a little brother of her very own. The standard negative event I expected never happened, contrary to my usual luck.

Before David was a year old, we returned to Atlanta and bought our first house, planted vegetables and flowers, and recognized that we had become suburbanites. In the spring, I announced my intention to leave the company to complete my education with full-time studies. Before I left the job, I was made an offer for a position with corporate headquarters in Wisconsin. Such an opportunity would have been a great step up for anyone—and for me—but that would have required a large amount of travel that would encumber my education. I would not have minded the travel, but I was on a mission to get my degree. I declined.

We fell into the suburban lifestyle easily, busy with scheduling activities for our kids and enjoying neighborhood get-togethers. We became good friends with two families whose children were our kids' ages; we shared dinners and evenings frequently. I learned the two men had also been in the service. One had been in the reserves and made no bones about his good fortune, having wanted absolutely nothing to do with Vietnam or the army beyond his reserve obligation. He respected my service, but it had not been right for him. I respected that. The other had been military police, an officer, and was in Vietnam about the time I was.

After too much to drink one night, I took umbrage at his story of arresting an infantryman one minute after curfew. He went on to tell me he had it very tough trying to police combat soldiers who were in from the field, and how being a convoy escort could be extremely stressful. OK—I did not serve where he did, but I did when he did. The alcohol had caused me to challenge him instead of keeping my mouth shut. He did not understand that a combatant would consider him a REMF. I certainly thought so, given my assumption that he slept in an air-conditioned hooch, showered every day, ate three hot meals daily, and gave unnecessary grief to combatants. Also, he surely had a great Officer's Club at his large base, a major coastal port, and resupply center that had loads of amenities that were completely unknown to field personnel. I quit being bothered about it over time and settled into a nice friendship with him. He had served, also.

The folks next door to us moved after selling their house

to a newlywed couple. When we met them, we discovered she was an RN and he was a doctor, a surgical resident rotating between several area hospitals. Chrisanne and I instantly liked them, and we were glad they were in the neighborhood. Having a nurse and surgeon right next door was comforting with small children around, and they came in handy on a few occasions over the coming years. The first time occurred on a 4th of July outing when we all went out for fireworks. David, by then four, cut his foot on a broken bottle. Our neighbor examined it and declared there was no serious problem; it just needed a few stitches. On the way home, we stopped by the Veteran's Administration Hospital, where he currently was working. After a few minutes inside, he returned with some supplies, and we drove on home. Over our kitchen sink, he put several stitches in David's foot. The best part was the personal medical care was free—it was an undocumented VA benefit.

Jennifer had not heard from Russ since he and Chrisanne divorced. He had remarried and had another child. Periodically she would hear from her paternal grandmother, though. I felt bad for Russ's mother: through no fault of hers, she was deprived of her first grandchild. From the beginning with Chrisanne, I promised I would raise Jennifer as my own. I pledged that all child support would go into a bank account set up solely for her benefit, and none would be commingled with our funds—ever. In addition, I promised I would never stand in the way of any agreement regarding Jennifer that she and Russ made. I need not have been concerned. Russ made a few child support payments and stopped.

Before Jennifer started school, I hired an attorney and petitioned to adopt her. Russ was duly sent the paperwork, complete with his right to contest. He received the notice but did not respond. For years, I thought he had been callous and unfeeling. Over time, though, I saw that he was wise enough to realize adoption by me was best for Jennifer. The adoption was granted, and she legally became my daughter. However, the reality is that long before the adoption she had become my daughter; I was all she knew.

> Jennifer has grown up knowing where she came from and feeling richer for the extra relatives. My parents and siblings embraced her as one of their own. Dad always had a special place in his heart for her; she does for him, as well. She told me that he visited her after he died to assure her he was just fine. Real or imagined, that says special bond.

By that time, my sister was on husband number two. He was my parents' age and ran his family business *without* the help of either of his two grown sons. I gave it little thought, but that should have been a huge sign of his dysfunction to me, yet it was not. I was working very hard at my education and money was tight. Knowing I was a full-time student and might have a little extra time, he asked if I would help him out of a jam. I expected to be helping him for a month or so, casually, during which I could pick up a few bucks. Before long, I was sucked wholly into the operation, mostly because he paid me well. Although the money was good, the job began to require too much of me. It was tough to balance family time with the increasing responsibilities of a full-time job *and* a full academic load.

I began taking my classes at night, and that worked for a short while. The job burdens continued to grow. My young children needed my time, and the schoolwork required of my major was increasing in difficulty. My grades suffered some, but since I was related (by marriage) to the owner, there was some consideration regarding my time away from work. The burdensome routine, probably coupled with a bit of residual stress delayed from my world travels about nine years earlier, caused me to collapse into a sniveling mess one night after work. (It was a rare night off from school.) Chrisanne did not know what to do—*I* did not know what to do. However, the event was cathartic for me. Thereafter, I handled my daily stress much better, internalizing less and actually returning to my Vietnam mindset of "just deal with it—don't agonize over it." I did my best.

My brother-in-law-boss was decidedly not one of the good guys in this life. Behind his back, I referred to him as the "horse's ass" and to my sister as the "horse's asset." He was a poster boy for "control freak." I often ran interference between him and his employees, and once or twice, I did so with customers. Despite his upper middle-class upbringing, private schools, and Ivy League education, he sorely lacked social skills. That had been known to me at the family level for a while, but I was surprised that his deficiency included business relationships and people in general. He did things over the year and a half that I worked for him that just defied reason; I wondered if he had deep-seated problems with me. He would praise me and then put me down, in an attempt to humiliate me. I was not bothered; I was paid well, *and* I was getting my education. His operation was not to be my life's work, and I knew it. I viewed it only as a means to my college education end.

He asked me to meet him for breakfast one morning. It was such a periodically routine thing, I gave it no thought. The conversation had also been ordinary; he monopolized it, expressing views on matters business and life, never once asking my thoughts, or entertaining any notion but his own. The man thought he had hung the moon. An only child, he had been pampered by his parents. As an adult, after he had taken over the business his father started, he was pampered by his employees. I consider that the fear-of-losing-my-job method of pampering. Besides paying well, nothing he did brought out the best from those around him.

We had finished our meal.

"I've made a decision—you have to go. I am firing you as of right now. I'll mail your check; you can drop off the car at your convenience this weekend."

I was surprised, but not shocked. This was actually the kind of behavior he demonstrated so frequently. He needed to have absolute control; whenever anyone in his management team showed any ability to perform successfully independent of his micro-managing direction—and explicit approval—he took similar action.

I sat back in my chair.

"So, what's the reason?" I asked.

"Hey, I don't have to give you a reason. You're fired."

That outburst elicited a glance from the next table.

"I thought you might do me the courtesy."

I stood as I said it, and added, "Got the message." I walked out and drove home.

The word I got from my parents, via my sister, was that I quit—I was the bad guy. My folks knew better. My sister's mind was on its standard different plane.

School received my full attention, and my education again took priority. I resolved to be a full-time student until I had a degree. Most of my life went along swimmingly, if not perfectly. My major was fun and interesting; a challenge well within my ability. I excelled in statistics and the capstone course, as well. I did well enough in my minor concentration and electives, all accounting courses.

My migraines continued with the same frequency, but with increased intensity and duration, usually exceeding one day. Chrisanne found me lying in bed one evening just before dinner with a pillow covering my eyes, shielding me from all light. I begged her to keep our kids quiet; they all knew the routine—I was in agony. Frustrated, she called the nurse next door, and she said she would call her husband, the doctor, who was about to leave for home. Although it seemed hours to me, he only took thirty minutes to be at my bedside. He brought something to inject that he said should make me comfortable. His magic potion did just that—I was paralyzed, unable to move, but I could speak. My head was buried in the pillow so I could not see anything, but I did not care—the pain had vanished. I had a very enjoyable night, frozen in place and listening to a Braves game while my kids crawled all over me. Sleep, which just hit me out of nowhere, was sound. The next morning I awoke refreshed and good to go. I had to get some of that stuff from the good doctor, so I asked Chrisanne about it.

"What'd he give me?"

"I don't know, he didn't say...but he left the bottle here on the refrigerator," she said, handing it to me. "He scared me, Greg. He told me to call him immediately if your heart stopped."

"That boy is such the kidder. We should complain to the State Medical Board," I joked.

"No, really, Greg. He was serious...he was *not* kidding. I checked your breathing all night long."

It was not a concern to me at the time, since I was alive and kicking. Still, I thought he was kidding her until I read the label of the bottle. I had no idea what its contents were, but I did notice it was out of date, as in way past expiration date. I have not let him forget it, despite his assurances there was never any danger to my life. While I do believe him, I still give him grief.

The entire incident got my attention, and I finally sought help. I went to a doctor, many actually. Finally, one advised my blood pressure was nearing the limit above which he would advise drug therapy. He gave me a prescription for a low-dose blood pressure medication; it was a then-new type of drug referred to as a Beta-blocker. The properties of the drug may inhibit my migraines, he suggested—he was right. I have had no further migraines, and my blood pressure levels have remained within preferred limits ever since, albeit with a daily dose of medication, and even after moving to another type.

The classes I saved for my final quarter at Georgia State were not nearly as demanding as prior ones. My world was getting better, and my education plan was finally about to reach fruition. One of the final exams that last quarter was to solve four problems, each phrased in such a way to ensure a student's sufficient knowledge. No surprise. If one knew the material, one would do fine. I knew the material, having done well on the only non-final exam we had in that course, the mid-term. I read each problem on the exam, interpreted, and then solved them. However, my standard luck was with me. I did *not* do even OK; I missed two problems, half the exam. I failed the final, so I failed the course. It was required.

I asked to meet with the professor to plead my case for retest. After looking over my file, he asked two questions.

"You're a veteran?"

"Yes, I am," I responded, taken aback.

"Were you a soldier in Vietnam?"

"Yes, sir, 1st Infantry Division, 1969," I replied, thinking that information might curry some favor with him. It did not.

"I see this is your final quarter…that you're supposed to graduate," he began. "I'm required to administer the test to you again," he said, emphasizing the word "required" with a William F. Buckley-styled drawl. "If you fail the second test, you will not graduate."

Shit, I thought. Here we go again. Right on the cusp of graduation and a problem of my own making rears its head, just like in high school—just like so *many* times in my life. He gave me instructions how to retest. He also said he would *personally* be the proctor. What was his problem, anyway? I needed to pass; he knew it, and I knew he owned it. I kept my ego in check and my mouth closed.

I took his retest mindful I could trip up again. Although he changed the appearance of the problems, the second set of four problems covered the same material as the first set of four—that *was* the material of the course. As he instructed me, I telephoned him for my grade, fully expecting to pass and graduate. I failed once again. The two problems I missed that time were covering the same material as the two I had gotten correct the first time. How? I could see that I did not answer the questions he *meant* to ask, but I did answer the ones he asked. My protests fell on deaf ears; I could not seem to get through to him that any person with command of the material could interpret his problem setup in at least two ways. He finally admitted as much to me but then said I should have had a better understanding of the material. I laughed in his face—he knew that I knew his material. My wrong answers actually illustrated that point.

I told him I had been trained in RTP (read the problem) and challenged him again on his wording. I asked him how many of his students taking those tests missed the same questions that I had, and in the same manner, in either of his versions. True to form, he ignored my question. Perhaps he was considering his response. The second time I asked him he simply replied, "You failed. You will not graduate." It's a professor's privilege. His smile was very patronizing, and I was angered. I held my tongue.

It was another major bummer, yet only a minor life glitch, an inconvenience, so I declined to fight it any further. I registered for the next quarter, the same class, the same room, the same professor—I was on a mission. Since I knew *his* rules, I was determined to beat him at his own game. I went to the first class and picked up a copy of his syllabus and exam schedule. After that first day, I attended only the exams, confirming the date and time with his office. I made certain they knew it was me. When I took the final, I asked the professor when he would be grading. I let him know I would phone for my grade precisely at that time. When I phoned, his assistant gave me the news—perfection. I found it interesting, and quite satisfying, to discover the wording of the problems were no longer ambiguous.

I graduated from Georgia State University, earning my BBA (Bachelor of Business Administration, Management). I lacked only a few accounting courses for that degree, as well.

We tried to visit Chrisanne's family in Virginia at least annually. One of those years was shortly after the Vietnam Wall was dedicated. It was not the attraction that it is today, or even the one it would become, and it certainly was very controversial. I decided I needed to make a visit, and take my own measure of the place. Some veterans had problems with the designer being Asian, others that the design was to be "underground," and others with the design itself. Some even thought it was unpatriotic. I thought Maya Lin's design was excellent, visually implying the build-up and drawdown of U.S. forces and the high cost in American lives. It is my belief that the wall, even were it unadorned by political correctness, does properly memorialize—if not immortalize—those whose names are engraved. I care not one whit who the design was created by or what her ethnicity is. Other than the obvious political correctness added later, I read no politics into it. The wall has never made a negative statement to me, nor do I find any sort of hidden meaning in it.

The wall is the proper memorial to the sacrifice that was our involvement in Vietnam, but is not a celebration of the effort. I would prefer the simplest, understated design, just as the designer had intended, without political additions. I liken modifications to exaggeratedly turning the corners of Mona Lisa's mouth upwards, in an effort to ensure *everyone* knew that she was smiling. Does not her true beauty lie in what her viewers see?

On the morning I chose to make my first visit, there was a misting rain. I decided to go anyway. I took David, thinking that would be a great bonding experience. He was then seven and he would probably soon be hearing a lot about the still too-fresh war in Southeast Asia. I wanted him to be given a more mature and maybe second-hand personal perspective. That was the plan. Yep, that plan had the same problem as most of my other plans—it did not work out well at all. The mist became a steady rain by the time we approached the wall, and we were without an umbrella. I noticed the veterans camping adjacent to the wall had withdrawn inside their tents, but we marched on. (There was not a single visitor that morning other than my son and me.)

Using one of the books provided at the entrance, I searched for names I remembered. I located the panels that reflected my tour dates just left of center. I stood there, wholly engrossed in the moment as I searched for and found names, holding my small son's hand and wanting desperately to share the moment with him. He was only seven and not on his best behavior, crying and whining for his mother. I was frustrated with him and could not understand why he was acting up, so we departed—my visit was cut very short. I had briefly seen the names I had come to see, however.

Author and young son David–1984.

When we returned to our car, I saw what I had done—besides expecting him to share my grief. He was soaked! I was as well, but I had not noticed and, frankly, I did not care at all. I was ashamed I had neglected his need in favor of my own. I was so myopic, intent on finding names and sharing my experience that I was oblivious to his discomfort. I had lost sight of the fact he was seven. *Seven!* Shame on me.

Someday, I hope we can go again as adults, and he can share just a bit more of it with me.

Chapter 22

The Well-Traveled Route

*W*ith a brand new degree in hand, I wondered what use to make of it. I gained useful tools and insights during school: I studied many cases illustrating business successes, failures, methods, processes, procedures, et cetera. It was all standard fare for my major. My academic education should mesh well with my business experience, and, coupled with my military background and leadership skills, I imagined I would make an excellent candidate for employers. The real world awaited my help, or so I thought.

Over a weekend, I considered applying to law school. Monday morning—not being able to get the lawyer jokes out of my head—I put law school onto the same trash heap I had medical school. I wanted to be around my family more. For the previous too many years, my days were extended, only seeing my home after the children were already in bed. Most nights and weekends had been nose-in-the-books time, and there were always maintenance projects around the house when I could get to them. Social life? There was precious little during those years, and Chrisanne and I yearned for it again.

Although my degree and interests were business, I had no inclination toward huge corporations as so many others do. Previously I had enjoyed the short decision cycle of closely held firms, and that is precisely where I wanted to venture next. My mother used to tell me, "You can be a small frog in a big pond, or big frog in a small pond...." There are personality types that mesh well with those large organizations; mine is not one of them. The army was the lone exception. I learned there that when an offered solution is not chosen, I should be a good soldier, offer a sharp salute (figuratively) and get on with the task at hand—as directed.

Surprisingly, my initial job offer came from close to

home and during my final few months of college: Dad needed some temporary project help. To that end, I became aware of microcomputers and their transition from kit curiosity to the personal computer. I was smitten and immersed myself into the technology and its growing application for businesses. Dad saw no immediate benefit to his actuarial consulting business since he was main-frame computing oriented, but did see peripheral possibilities. Before long, we formed two new corporations—a software development-services firm and a publishing company. My roles in each, of course, were not actuarial. Using Dad's software, I developed, produced, and marketed printed tabular products for the publishing firm.

Neither of the new firms would make us rich, but we did attract the attention of a much larger Chicago actuarial firm, and they bought the two newer companies. Given that our new parent company had much deeper pockets, I was able to relax—but not stop—my search for a career home. I wanted to find the best fit for me, not merely the first opening available. I viewed the experience that I was gaining as a high-quality addition to my résumé. It could only help, while I searched.

The Atlanta office closed after the contracts expired. It was expected, even desired. I moved on. My start-up business efforts were rewarded with the repurchase of my stock by the acquiring company, and I was very pleased to do so well in such a short time.

I was again without employment, and there was urgency to my search—I no longer had the luxury of time. A good friend recommended me to a commercial printing firm that he knew. They were an established Atlanta firm that provided printed materials to and for advertising agencies. I liked the sound of it; I was fascinated by advertising and the creative ways of conveying mass messages.

Two brothers operated the business, one their father had purchased when he was a young man. It had historically been a very successful operation, furnishing high-end and high-quality work. I was charged with getting the accounting, finance, and information systems problems resolved. It was evident before I sat down the first day that their company was in total disarray. Dissension turned out to be much worse than had been expressed during my interviews. Accounts were not paying their bills, and, as a result, vendors were not being paid. Yet, with all the turmoil that would bring, the company continued to do expensive work for those delinquent accounts. Curiously, whenever I questioned the practice or wondered aloud what could be done, I was sharply rebuked for encroaching on the marketing and sales effort, but not by the CEO, who was my immediate supervisor. The company had trashed their banking relationships, had serious pension and pay issues with four different unions, and payroll taxes were in arrears. It was insanity.

The challenge was one for which I had been educated and trained; I stood ready. I thought reason, logic, and the force of my personality might win over the warring parties. However, the insurmountable obstacle to my success was the hatred between the brothers. They could not even stand to be in the same room. Although their father sat in the lobby every day, he was only able to keep the brothers from killing each another while at work—the *only* time they were compelled to interact—ever.

There were just four on the management team: the older brother was CEO, and the younger was vice president of sales and marketing. The responsibility for purchasing all the raw materials and services, along with all production operations belonged to the industry-experienced plant manager. My role was as previously described. I discovered an antipathy from union members for accounting and financial management. Where did it come from? Why was it so pervasive?

Company payroll was a responsibility of my department, and I did not relish the inevitable collision of payroll issues with their antipathy. We paid salaries and commissions monthly, and the hourly wage earners, all union workers, were paid weekly. Paychecks were distributed to each wage employee as they took their lunch break, so every Friday at the appointed time there was a mad dash to the bank for cash. Most of the union employees did not trust the paycheck to be any good, even after decades of proof. The mass, frantic exodus was a comical, yet sad, sight.

On the Friday of my very first week, I wanted to prepare payroll myself so I could learn the company's system. Fifteen minutes after delivery of the checks to employees, a woman was standing in my office demanding to know why her check was wrong. She was always paid the same amount she said. She had cashed her check but wanted it corrected. I reviewed the calculations and found that I had made a sloppy error that slipped through my verification, and I apologized to her. I gave her cash (less than five dollars) to bring her take-home to the amount she expected. I told her what I had given her was an advance on her next check. I also said that I would pay her correctly the next week, at which time I would take back the advance. With her Friday cash in hand, she acknowledged next week's process and then went back to work. I gave it no further thought.

The following Friday, only fifteen minutes after paycheck delivery (and after she had cashed her check) the woman was once again standing in my office, this time demanding to know what the deduction was for. I told her of the advance I gave her during the previous week's payroll correction. Then, I also reminded her that she had been paid in full the prior week, having received her standard amount, and that she was paid properly for the current week. She listened but still asked why I was taking money from her check. I decided to illustrate the math on paper. She looked on as I did, but still thought I was taking money from her check. I had a moment of clarity, simplistic clarity.

"What's the usual amount of your check?" I asked.

She said the amount. We each knew it never varied.

I asked her, "Did you get that amount last week?"

"Yes," she said.

"Okay. And did you get that amount this week?"

"Yes." She appeared puzzled, confused.

"Then...what's the problem? You are whole. You have

taken home the correct amount each week. Right?"

"Yes, but why are you taking money out of my check?"

Her concern was only for the new deduction. She would not accept my explanations—there was a deduction that did not routinely appear on her pay stub, and she felt someone was stealing from her. I realized I could never convince her. Then I suggested she take her complaint to her manager, hoping he could get her to understand. I was certain I could not as I was not in the trusted circle of union membership. I never heard anything else about it. Over time, I believe those union folks began to give me a fair measure of trust, after their initially suspicious eye. After all, I was the FNG. Most of the hourly employees came to realize that I was, in fact, fair and honest.

The plant manager held a view of my department similar to union membership. In fact, he actually said to me, "Figures lie and liars figure." He said it when I attempted to illustrate the raw labor cost per hour of running one six-color press. The numbers were not disputable: add the base union rate (without benefits) for each of the three required operators—voilà! The result was the raw hourly labor cost to operate the press. He did not buy the raw rate; in fact, he never accepted any number I presented, advising that since I had never run a press, I could never know how much it cost the company to run one. I mentioned it was *not* the cost to run a press, but was simply the *raw labor rate*—per the union contract he had helped negotiate. He was unmoved. I could never understand his contempt for anything that had not been advanced by a union—any union. He was otherwise a nice guy to me, but he did not trust any numbers from anyone. How can you know where you stand if you do not measure?

The brothers' father died and after they grieved, even greater chaos reigned. Rome was afire and Nero played on. Finally, someone, probably one or both of the brothers' wives, suggested they seek counseling—and they were not teasing. I saw it as a road to possible harmony. *What a great idea*, I thought, *anything to fix the problem*. One of the wives must have arranged for a local business psychologist, because I am sure the brothers could not have agreed on whether to even get one, much less which one. The counseling included all of the management team, at the psychologist's insistence, and we all agreed to attend several retreats as a group. Prior to the first retreat, the psychologist interviewed each of us as individuals, in hopes of gaining insight into the company's core problems.

During my initial interview, I unloaded on him about the brothers. I said my approach was to state my opposing views (if any) openly, supported with facts. I also told him whenever I was overruled I was a good soldier accepting their authority, and carrying out their instructions. He inquired if I had been in the service. Remembering a once not-so-favorite college professor, I guardedly replied, "Why do you ask?" Without any commitment regarding his feelings about military service, he said, "Because I'm curious." I told him where I had served, in what unit, what my training had been, and what my job was. He showed genuine interest.

Before I realized it, we had spent two hours together, one half hour on company business and the remainder about me. I had been crying for most of the last hour. How did that happen? Perhaps someone finally showed a genuine interest in my experience, or that I could talk about my feelings so freely and without judgment. His interest was not the terrible, horrid experiences of war—he wanted to know how they had affected me long term, down at my most basic personal level, and what I felt about them. He dredged it up, and that is what made me so emotional. He never asked me, "How does that make you feel?" Maybe it was already clear to him or maybe he was perceptive enough to read between the lines of my responses—way down there where my innermost thoughts were written in invisible ink.

"I'd like you to consider another chat with me, not about business, but about you. Away from here," he said.

"No. I'll pass, thank you."

No doubt, it would be expensive, and I did not feel at the

time that I needed anything from him. How could he help me?

"You sure?" he asked. "I think it might do you some good to talk to me more."

"Thanks, but no."

I went back to work and forgot about the offer. On his way out of the office that night, the CEO stopped by my office. He usually did, if only to say goodnight.

"Ron came to me and stated very emphatically, 'I need two more sessions with Greg, and you should pay for them.' He said it had nothing to do with business...that you aren't too crazy...fixable, and he would really like you to think more about it. The only thing he said is that it's connected to your being a soldier in Vietnam."

His face showed a pleading concern.

"I was kidding about being crazy, but I'd appreciate it if you'd think about doing it. The company will pay. Happily.

"Wow. This feels very strange to me...weird. Let me think about and discuss it with Chrisanne. I appreciate it no matter what I choose. May I tell you in the morning?"

He said, "Sure. Have a good night. See you tomorrow."

Chrisanne said I would be crazy not to meet with him, and if I did not she would bean me with a frying pan. I agreed to do it, and I am so very glad I did. It was self-absolution. Those few short discussions radically changed my mentality. I cannot put my finger squarely on anything—there was no *aha* moment—but afterward, I was conscious that I was then a changed man, purged of something burdensome. He said it was normal to have been affected by the Vietnam experience. Normal. That was a pleasant thought.

I resumed my flying lessons.

Despite the conflicts of the daily office routine, my home life was much better. Jennifer was entering the final years of her secondary education, and she went to her first prom with a nice young man. Chrisanne and I liked him a lot; he was polite and appropriately deferential. He played football and had won a scholarship to the Citadel, and we wondered if he would be our future son-in-law. I was beginning to size up her suitors for that role; she was coming to that age. Before long, they were no longer an item. No announcement was made at home; she just began to go out with another guy—sort of the anti-Citadel-guy. Actually, the new guy was very much as I had been for far too long—partying, aimless, and drifting. I could relate to that guy, but I did not want him for my daughter.

The corporate retreats had been only temporary fixes. The brothers were irrevocably broken; nothing was going to fix their problems. The plant manager continued to hold any number suspect even when he was doing the crunching. The younger brother could not seem to grasp that his pricing was *always* less than we paid to produce goods—not sustainable in the long term.

"We'll never sell anything," he would argue.

"You will be out of business," I would argue back.

The brothers decided to sell their business, and it was no surprise to anyone. The first suitor showed up with his own audit man, whom I believe was his best friend. Both men were sixty-something, one was the money guy and interested in purchasing a successful business. (I think he just wanted *any* business.) He took charge of the company immediately, which I considered a strange turn of events. After his friend had begun his audit, the brothers did not make a single move that was not cleared through the money guy.

One of my employees, a woman who was remarkable in her ability to collect money past due, asked me for a raise. I had absolutely no reason not to give her the small amount she requested, and a multitude of reasons to give her more. My boss said we would have to check with the suitor. Say what? There was more than I knew to their arrangement. The three of us sat down in the conference room to discuss it. It was a somber mood. The suitor asked me why I wanted to give my employee a raise. I gave him the litany of my reasons and stated her value to the company and to me. After thirty minutes of small-minded questions by him, both about her and about me, he turned to my boss and said, "Go ahead."

As we were leaving the room, I was relieved. The whole process had been unduly stressful—I felt as if I had been fighting targeted intimidation. He made some unnecessary remark to me that I cannot recall, but it was something about our need to be cheap—not frugal—cheap. I responded, almost giddy from the stress.

"I'd give her a million if she asked."

It made no sense to me after saying it, but my comment was only about her worth to me and the company. Of course, I did not mean that I would *literally* value her at that level. It was not until I was out the door and a few steps away that I was struck by his unusual facial expression at my obviously exaggerated remark. By the time I was back in my office, I was thinking no more about it. The next afternoon he came to my office to discuss a minor audit matter. As he was leaving, he stood in the doorway and turned, asking me about my over-the-top comment of the prior day. He wanted to know what I meant by it.

"Nothing. It was probably just a bit of levity on my part."

"There is no place for levity here."

Stunned, I just stared at him as he turned and walked away. Was he serious? My concern was for naught. Two days later, they decided against buying the company. There soon were legitimate pursuers, though. After suffering through two Big Eight accounting firm's audits without any substantial problems, the company was sold. I felt my turnaround work had been vindicated; we were not strong, but there was a slow but good recovery in progress. The people who do the type of work I was doing are often redundant after mergers or acquisitions, and, naturally, I was deemed superfluous to the new owners.

Near the end of the second audit, I realized a perception of Vietnam veterans that I had not known before. One of the audit managers and I were working together one morning and took a break. We began to chat about anything but audits.

"Did you really go to Vietnam?" he asked.

I answered yes, expecting to be called a fool.

"You don't strike me as the type," he said.

I am still not sure what the type is, but I have a good idea a typical veteran is *probably not* a drug-crazed, alcoholic, baby-killing, order balking, homeless, deranged veteran. How is it that most people hear something, correct or not, and make universal application of it? He then engaged me out of his curiosity about an experience I had that he did not. It was very refreshing to discover an educated and reasoned mind in that context. That five minute chat added positively to the good feelings I gained after counseling.

Out of work, I ceased my flying lessons.

There I was, seeking employment yet another time. That condition was distressing and too repetitive. I considered I might be at the time in my life where I would not be easily employable. I was older (forties), and I thought my income level might exclude me from too many openings. It was indeed a very frightening time.

While I was updating my résumé, I looked over my full employment history, both the upside and the downside, and I saw a history of about five years at each employer. Why? What did that say about me? What happened to the plan that would have me at one place for life, retiring with a gold watch and pension at age sixty-five? There were not many instances of that career mentality anymore, at least not that I knew of. I counted on one hand—using only two fingers—the people I knew of who had been employed by one company their entire career-to-date. Those two were not Vietnam veterans.

I saw that there had been a change in our society, our mobility, our technological advances, and that women and minorities were upwardly mobile in the workforce as no time in the past. The world was no longer as it had been back in the days when an employee identified with one organization for life—back at that time when he was the single earner.

I recalled that when I was only fifteen every job I sought required a driver's license. After I had turned sixteen and had my license, the jobs I wanted were calling for a high school diploma. When I graduated from high school, most employers wanted draft exempt status. Once I had completed my service obligation, a college degree was mandatory for any job that I wanted to pursue. After I earned my degree, the jobs I wanted called for an MBA—because they could. I began to wonder if I would ever truly belong, or if my employment history had been the very definition of upwardly mobile. I was not getting interviews as I wanted—quantity or quality—and there was not much interest in me. I thought my world had ended.

Author and teenage daughter Jennifer–late eighties.

Jennifer was in her freshman year at Georgia; David was just a few years behind. He was suddenly a strange man in my house, vying for the attention and affection of my wife. That caused another epiphany—I empathized with my father. I knew then why he had so many troubles with me that did not repeat with my younger brothers. Of course, he had those that had been of own making, but beyond those there were tensions between Dad and me that I did not understand. That is, until David reached the same age and maturity.

Chrisanne and I did not worry about their education; it was taken care of, and if we found we needed more, then we could always convert investments. The "interesting" approach to my own education provided the impetus for us to set up a tuition reimbursement plan for them. It is just as it sounds. We would pay for the first quarter or semester, and thereafter we would make payments on the strength of grades earned, along a sliding scale ranging from full payment for higher grades down to nothing paid. Each class was measured on its own.

Sitting at home and unemployed, I felt useless—I was a dependent. Finally and thankfully, I snagged an interview for what seemed a suitable position offering growth potential, with a subsidiary of a data technology firm in Raleigh. I met with the general/sales manager of the local subsidiary and with the CEO of the parent company. The CEO caught me off guard when he asked what my religion was. After collecting my wits from the illegal and wholly inappropriate question, I responded much as I had to Chrisanne's father. I was polite in my "It's not your business" reply. They hired me anyway. I reported for work my first day a total FNG, with a fever of one hundred and three degrees; some illness had crept up on me during the commute. I remember nothing of that day—not one single thing. Three days later, after recovering from the flu, I rebooted that day. As it turned out, there would have been no difference had I worked that day sick and delirious.

From day one, the office staff gave me grief. I learned I had "stolen" my job from a popular staffer who thought she was in line for it. I was assured she had not been. Within days, I knew the job was not a long-term proposition for me—not at all. The attitude there was toxic. The general manager, a salesman with no discernible business skills aside from an attractive smile and firm handshake, could not manage one whit. He was a throwback to early sixties offices, but the women working there were decidedly not early sixties women.

They ruled, and I stood no chance. My work there was not at all fulfilling. It was too simple—simplistic, actually—and did not challenge me in any way, shape or form. I felt, and I was, grossly underutilized. However, they were paying me well, so I made good use of my time. I returned to my flying lessons.

I did manage to get good things accomplished there, but only after the woman whom I had "stolen" the job from left the company. She was truly poison, and she left a lot behind. In time, natural attrition aided my cause. A few of her good friends also left, and with new hires and her one remaining friend finally beginning to warm to me, I began to feel better about the situation. Yet, I never felt good about that place. As I said, it was toxic; it came from the top.

Without sufficient challenge from my work, I was bored so I seized the opportunity to further my aviation credentials. To my existing Private Pilot Certificate, I added an Instrument Rating, then I earned a Commercial Pilot Certificate, and then I became a Certificated Flight Instructor—Airplane (CFI), and Certificated Flight Instructor—Instrument (CFII). After several years, I added the Multi-Engine Rating to my Commercial Certificate and a Multi-Engine Instructor Rating (MEI) to my CFI Certificate.

With the kids all but moved out, the house was mostly quiet and boring. I had my aviation adventures; I was flying and studying. Chrisanne needed her own stimulation, since the children were not so demanding of her time anymore. She came to me with an idea she had about starting a business. She explained her concept to me and I offered my thoughts.

"You should have fun with that. Might even make some money," I said. "Do you have a business plan?"

"No. Why? It's not like I'm starting General Motors. I don't need money to start it, either."

"Maybe not money, but you do need a plan. I'll support you, but only if you write a plan. That's the only logical way to start a business. It reduces the risk."

"I don't know how to do that. You do it for me."

"Not gonna happen. You do it or I won't support you."

"How do I do it?"

I suggested that she visit a library; the internet was not much back then.

"You will need to incorporate, so read up on that, too. I will do that for you. Um, we *will* have to throw a little money at getting incorporated," I said.

"For what?"

"Materials, stock certificates, minutes' book, corporate seal, stuff like that. The state requires that the corporation be funded. I don't recall how much, and it may have changed. Not a whole lot, though."

"Okay, I'll do that. But you have to help me."

"My fee will be fifty percent of the ownership," I said.

She nodded her approval.

"It's not as if we aren't in it together anyway," she said.

"Not me. My job won't be operations. I'll help you with accounting, advertising, marketing, payroll, banking...but not operations. That's your thing...deal?"

"Deal."

We shook hands.

By the end of her first summer, she had helpers. A few years later, she had dozens of employees. She had made our little business successful beyond her wildest hobby-dreams.

After attaining the majority of my aviation certificates and ratings, I thought about graduate school yet again for about five minutes. Would graduate school be worthwhile for me? I did not have an answer to that question. The point was moot when our parent company sold the subsidiary and I was displaced. Before I arrived home after being cut loose, I had a message from our software provider, a local firm. They offered me a position, which I would have liked, but the money was not there and it never would be. Nor did I expect the work would be satisfying enough in the long-term.

Fortunately, new work for me came much sooner, just a few weeks after I had been displaced. Pay was better than what I required, and there was the promise of ownership. Two weeks in, I knew I had made a *big* mistake. I did not think I would be able to tough it out, all the while hoping that it would improve. I really wanted to bail—and I wanted to right then—but Chrisanne talked me out of it. She suggested that I give my new job until the end of that year, then almost twelve months away, and if I still felt the same, I should leave them and help her in our business. After much thought, I agreed. The non-operations demands of our business had by then grown to the point that someone was needed and soon. That someone should be me.

During our company's first five years, its success offered the possibility of my joining, but I had never even considered doing so until she mentioned it. I always had a very active, although not daily, role in our business. It was capable of supporting both of us, and it had been for years. Even had I thought about it earlier, it had not been the right time for me. It had become the right time.

Chapter 23

It's All Good

Prior to giving notice of my departure, I thought about whether I really should leave at all. After deliberation, and quite satisfied my feelings had not changed in the prior year, I made my decision. Yes, most emphatically yes, I should leave that company immediately—if not sooner. Would it be the most opportune time to join Chrisanne in managing our business? I gave that question plenty of consideration, agonizing over it, wondering if I should search for work again. I was torn—maybe fearful—but I was inclined to work toward achieving the full potential of *our* business.

I gave another look to my employment history, and the self-assessment left me doubtful about my abilities—again. That is, until I stepped back enough to view it all with eyes toward working for my own interest. I did not need to prove a thing to anyone, nor for any reason. I had tested myself in war, in business, and in life in general. I had experienced ups and downs emotionally and financially. My psyche was not scarred from my trip through life, nor was my ego bruised; they had each been emboldened by my life's course. I have been successful by most measurement and in a myriad of arenas. I had proven my mettle well before my introspection, but I had never recognized that I had, and I had always been driven to prove more. To whom did I need to prove *anything*? Perhaps it is the wisdom of age burnishing my past.

> *Upon reflection, I concluded each of my employers had hired me for a specific project need. In reality, I was their in-house (albeit employed) management consultant. My projects were problem-solving efforts where I would solve myself out of a job.*

Because of that soul-searching, I saw I was attempting to live a life that others thought I should be living, probably due to squandering my youth partying and chasing the more gentle gender. Neither of those pursuits warrants criticism from me, though, as socializing and procreation (even the practice thereof) is what turns this planet. I have learned from aviation weather study everything in our atmosphere is a function of temperature change, no matter how minute. I believe the same is true of the activity of life on the surface—everything is the result of the pursuit of sex in some form or fashion. Why will we not admit it?

I gave notice and left that company, never looking back. Thereafter I considered myself retired, yet I work harder for our business than I ever did for anyone else—and I *always* gave my employers much more than they gave me. I turned all my attention to growing our business and to planning its franchising. That was our plan and given our success to that point, we felt our formula was a good one. Based on the numbers I crunched, we were very confident that operations following our model could be very profitable. I had very good experience as both a franchisee and franchisor, so at least I understood the basics and some of the pitfalls.

> *Early in our business, when both Chrisanne and I had full-time jobs elsewhere, we were approached by one of our clients who appreciated the operation and wanted to help us franchise. We thought about it a little but decided to turn down his offer, opting to build our business ourselves.*

After about sixty days of research and planning, Chrisanne and I reviewed the results of my work. I laid out the pros and cons of the prospective endeavor. It was simple to encapsulate—the details of actually getting it done would be formidable. Do-able, but time consuming.

"What would your decision be? she asked.

"It's *our* decision...the business is growing past what we

anticipated it would. We might become modestly wealthy by franchising, but our workload would be an encumbrance to our lives. We wouldn't have much time for anything other than business. And it would mean hiring more people and opening an office."

"We shouldn't be so busy making a living that we forget to live a life," she said.

"And I agree. So...my vote is no franchising. The lifestyle change is not worth it to me. How about you?"

"I totally agree, let's just build one, a *great* one."

Thus, we had decided to make our operation as good as it could be—without franchising. We have not regretted it for one moment. With continuing success, there would not be a reason for us to work anywhere else. Fortunately for us, our business rapidly grew. At one point, there were about one hundred and twenty employees. Fewer now, though, after the Great Recession. Chrisanne has two assistants to help her with office operations. My contribution remains outside of daily operational demands. I am lucky in that the claims on my time are not time sensitive—I can do my critical work on just about any schedule.

I did not accept any of the limitations that plague other small businesses, much as I had experienced over the years working for others. No business management software could provide us the reporting flexibility we wanted. None that was available could store the level of client detail we wanted, nor would those packages allow us to retrieve the information we needed. It was frustrating. Then I remembered the old saw, "If you want something done correctly, do it yourself." I had been there before and had a little experience with DBMS (DataBase Management Software/Systems), so I went for it.

Armed with only a blank paper, I learned to write the requisite code from scratch. I had taken a few programming courses in the past, both in college and for work, so I was not totally without background. I am certainly no expert, and my creation is undoubtedly inefficient in a marketable sense, but the program works great for us. It is far better than good enough. The best part—I can modify it at will. Today we have an operations management system in-house that gives us the information we desire, when we desire, and in the format we desire. If not, we add it.

One of Chrisanne's office staff saw an early version of my project and suggested selling to companies like ours. My ego was stroked, even though I knew it still lacked so much. Nonetheless, I made a cursory check of what the market was and who offered what product. I was very surprised to learn that she was right, and there might have been a need in the industry. After thinking about it and what it would entail, I decided that I needed to make our company our focus. (Yes, it is a recurring theme!)

I have been criticized by some who say I should have pursued that venture (and others), that I would have made a fortune. Maybe. I am not lazy, but I am not about movement for movement's sake, either. Nor am I chasing the almighty dollar—that is not my scorecard. Rather, I have always been one that is much more interested in those things that validate life, its pleasures large and small. What good is a fortune, however that is measured, if you are a slave to the work? I aspire to work to live the life I want, and I refuse to be as so many others are—only defined by my work. Chrisanne need not have worried; we are living our lives.

Another major project I saw the need for was a website. On two separate occasions in the mid-nineties, I outsourced the design and the coding of a one-page website, and later a multi-page website. I was not impressed with the results from either of those so-called experts, and I thought I had been robbed. I resolved to learn to do it myself, and I did. Again, starting with a blank sheet of paper, I learned to code, and I have built our website just as we want and need it. As with the database manager, I can modify it as we wish or need. We now have a site with several sub-sites, each incorporating multiple pages and interactive forms. It is very client-friendly, employee-friendly, and mobile device friendly. I am proud of my work, but again, I am not an expert, and it is not nearly as efficient as it might be—I could never earn my living as a software programmer. Yet, it works well for us.

I also get to do other fun things, and one of them has been flight instruction. I am not the type to sit idly by for very long, so I began to teach flying on a heavy part-time basis at one of the local flight schools. For over a decade, I gave flight instruction to students at all levels of pilot certification and experience levels—including airline pilots, a few former and future military pilots, corporate pilots, and general aviation pilots. Most flight instructors are young and teaching only to build time. I was not, so given my age and experience, older pilots sought me out. A few pilots who had flown in WWII and who were no longer legal to be pilot-in-command have asked me to ride along for safety and legality. They had not lost the love of the sky and just wanted to get some stick time. I have learned a lot from them. As a sometime student of WWII and military history in general, I truly enjoyed the enlightening and interesting discussions we had.

The airline and military pilots I worked with usually only needed a refresher in simpler flying. Due to the complexity of aviation technology, many of today's airline pilots are systems managers more than they are stick-and-rudder pilots. When they fly unsophisticated (by their standard comparison) much lighter aircraft—and have not done so for some time—they seek an experienced instructor to help them in the transition to much lower and slower aircraft. The issue usually is only one of their visual perspectives and recalling what they had long ago forgotten through disuse.

Through a connection with a couple of airline pilots, I have flown Boeing 727 and Boeing 767 simulators. After only five minutes in the 767 simulator, I departed with one of its two engines failing on takeoff. First time—fail. I crashed the airplane (simulator), and killed over two hundred (simulated) passengers. I gloriously (in my non-airline mind) succeeded on other failed-engine takeoffs. I rolled the B767 (simulator) over Texas Stadium. What a hoot. I had not hankered to be an airline pilot for some time, but I did finally answer to my satisfaction the question every general aviation pilot riding in an airliner has pondered—"Could I land this thing if I had to?" Yes, I could. I shot a half dozen instrument approaches (with one engine operational) down to approach minimums (simulating low overcast) and landed uneventfully. I freely admit that I crashed on my first attempt—but the rest of my landings were successful. Bragging aside, I am fully cognizant that I am far below the competence level required of airline pilots to routinely fly that refined an aircraft. Although—with no other pilot on board and one on the radio talking me through it—I might just manage it. Just sayin!

When I pursued my aviation certificates and ratings, I briefly considered again trying to catch on with an airline. I was still at an age that I could have gone that route and flown for fifteen or so years, until the then-mandatory retirement age of sixty. I rejected the idea because I did not want so drastic a pay cut. Naturally for my standard luck, as I was about to turn sixty, the FAA changed mandatory retirement age for airline pilots to age sixty-five. That put the U.S. in sync with the rest of the world. I still could not get things right, could I? After all, I am that guy who joins the shortest line only to find it becoming the most time-consuming line. Builds character, I say.

Flight instruction gives me enjoyment by allowing me to help aviators at all levels gain and/or improve their flying skills. What could be better for a guy who simply wanted to fly, than to be the go-to guy for other pilots? I have been greatly rewarded watching some of my students embark on careers in aviation. Today, former students of mine are flying for airlines, governments, corporations, charter companies, the military, and many just for their own pleasure. I enjoy helping pilots and rating aspirants achieve standards that are stricter than the FAA's by guiding them to their full potential.

Flying an aircraft is exhilarating most of the time, and sometimes it is terrifying; it can be humbling, yet it is so very rewarding. It is a fun physical, emotional, and intellectual challenge. Perhaps for me it is that long absent and often sought after adrenaline rush that makes it so.

An instructor can only try his best to prepare students and instill good judgment. There are personality types that no one can help; they will do as they see fit and sometimes that is costly. There have been a couple of new pilots that I have known, or known of, who arrogantly exceeded capabilities, theirs and the airplane's, and hurt people. There are always students who, as successes in life, are of the attitude that all they need is an instructor to rubber stamp their awesome skills. Most of those are marginal talents. I try to avoid them, preferring someone who is receptive to what I might offer.

One negative example is a student who approached me to complete his training for the Private Pilot certificate. He said he was ready, with only a few cross-country hours that remained to meet the requirements. He was dead wrong. He was incompetent and dangerous when flying beyond the local training area. He had little of the knowledge that is required to fly cross-country safely and successfully. I told him as much after a ground and flight lesson, and he did not hear me. I was trying not to crush his ego; maybe I should not have been so empathic. During the next flight I thought that pushing him past his limits would show how much more work remained. Afterward, he told me he was ready, that I did not know what I was talking about. I informed him I would not be recommending him until he could show me that he could exceed the *minimum* standards. I was happy when he moved on to another instructor. He was curious: a lawyer and judge who could not read and interpret regulations.

It is most interesting to me the man's father, who was in his eighties when I flew with him for a BFR (Biennial Flight Review) in his high-performance and complex airplane, is one of the three best pilots with whom I have *ever* flown. That man truly was a damn good pilot.

Similarly, a student whose instructor left in pursuit of the airlines came to me to finish his Private Pilot certificate. He had soloed recently and was anxious to move rapidly through the rest of his training. He was of the impression he was the greatest pilot around. After our first flight, I advised him he needed more work, and I would not be allowing an airplane's dispatch to him until he corrected a few minor things (which could bring him major hurt). He did not like that I challenged his greatest pilot standing. I suggested he would probably be better served with a younger instructor, one that he more readily identified with. He found one. A week later, he was flying alone—his new instructor authorized him to solo—and he stalled the plane while landing. He hit the runway hard, destroying the airplane—he was lucky he only broke his nose. The propeller, complete with bent tips, hangs over my fireplace.

A student asked me to be his instrument instructor in his own aircraft. It was a high performance, complex airplane and an excellent instrument-training platform. He was one of those who listened, questioned, and learned fast. I was not surprised; he was former military. He did well and moved through his training quickly and thoroughly. A few months later, he telephoned to let me know about a trip he had just completed. I thought I had previously impressed upon him to avoid *any* convective (thunderstorm) activity.

"I was flying out over the gulf...the weather clear, when the controller advised there was a level-one cell ahead."

(Simply put, it is the smallest thunderstorm.)

"And...?" I asked.

"She said I could have ten degrees either way whenever I wanted it. I could see the damn thing. It was nothing more than a small but tall cloud."

"No brainer, right?"

"Damn right! That's exactly what I thought as it spit me out the other side."

"Really? You dove in?"

"I thought I would wind up in the drink. It really scared the living shit out of me."

"Lucky. Gonna try again?"

"Never. I should've listened to you. I'm a believer."

Aviation is full of such stories.

Another instrument student had recently trained with me using his airplane that had several instruments driven by a vacuum pump. That was the standard in those days. Since vacuum failure was a possibility (things *can* get ugly, quickly when flying blind), instrument rating students often train "partial-panel," where the unexpected failure of a vacuum system is simulated, rendering the pilot's normal instrument references unusable. It is a challenging event for all students initially, but on their check ride, they must demonstrate a minimum level of competence. Comfortable in training maybe, but with the hope that should a real world failure visit, their training would come to the fore—and they would not panic. (There is rule number one again.)

That former student was one who detested partial-panel training, and he experienced a real-world vacuum failure while in actual instrument conditions. It really happened to him. He told me he settled right in, no panic, and then called air traffic control to inform them, just as required. The air traffic controller asked what his intentions were, standard stuff. By then, he had gotten so comfortable with his real-life partial-panel, that he said he would continue on his way home—three hundred miles. I was disheartened. Partial-panel is considered to be an emergency procedure and meant only to get the aircraft safely on the ground. That former student credited my instructional skills and suggested that any future student I had complaining about my partial-panel training should give him a call, and he would set them straight. I said all I did was help him learn and then said a few words about safety and decision-making, but I took the compliment.

As small business owners, Chrisanne and I work harder and longer than ever before. We work strictly for ourselves and answer only to ourselves, governmental entities aside. We have excellent employees, a testament to screening, training, and management skills Chrisanne has learned over the years. Our decision cycle is very short, made without committee or multiple levels of approval. Today our company provides us a good living, surpassing all of our early expectations, even the most improbable. The down side, if there really is one, is we are together almost around the clock, so we must give one another personal space from time to time. After decades of marriage and working so closely for so long, our individual space is a mutually welcomed respite. That said—it has been a special trip we have made together.

Best family ever!

I have been very fortunate throughout my life—but many times not so smart. I have great kids, children-in-law and grandchildren—two boys and a baby girl (and hoping for more). Could I love them any more? Hell, no. What have I done to deserve this good life? Dunno. I am not aware of a single thing, and one may reasonably make an argument I do not deserve everything I *have* realized. I am not surprised, however, that I have always landed on my feet—recall that I arrived onto our beautiful blue orb a breech birth.

That is my story, the one I tell here—both the crude *and* the delicate. Rehabilitation began with encouragement from Uncle Sam, after which I completed my education and more, while trying my best to follow the standard crowd, traveling the well-worn path. The earlier coarseness that I encountered while moving from my adolescence to adulthood contributed mightily to the reconstruction; the delicate has continued to nourish and sustain me. My large appetite for life and its atypical adventures remains, albeit with a more measured pace and sometimes even deliberation. I remain spontaneous, but today with a keen awareness of consequences.

I determined a long while back that my problem was the routine, well-worn path—that it was not the correct path for me. Not everyone must conform to convention or expectations of others. I know now that I am the arbiter of measuring my achievement.

Whenever I meet someone new, their inevitable question is, "What do you do?" I would prefer they ask me, "What have you done?"

> *Two roads diverged in a wood, and I—*
> *I took the one less traveled by,*
> *And that has made all the difference.*
> *—Robert Frost*

Epilogue

While I was in "The Nam" I used many terms applicable only to the military and to armed conflict, and most of them have little or no use in civilian life. However, I think there were three expressions commonly used by servicemen in Vietnam that I believe do translate directly to regular life. The first, "there it is," indicated much the same as the currently vogue "it is what it is." Neither expression really says anything, but they do express futility. The second, "(it) don't mean nuthin'," was uttered when someone might feel the powerlessness of his position or when insanity was prevalent. Those nearest would say it to indicate the ineffectiveness of getting agitated about it. The third, "What can they do? Draft me and send me to The Nam?" The speaker has made a decision that might result in personal woe. (I used it earlier in dialogue.)

For what it is worth....

Don't Mean Nuthin'

In the early eighties, prior to my "business" counseling, I got up early one Sunday morning and turned on the television to keep me company before Chrisanne and the kids got up. The TV was on VH-1, at the time a new cable music channel. Not having a remote control back then, I went over to the TV to change the channel. Billy Joel had just begun a song, and I recognized him, but not the song. Then I heard the chop-chop of a Huey lead-in to the song. It hooked me. I sat down right there on the floor in front of my console TV. While he sang "Goodnight Saigon," in the background was a slideshow of veterans' personal pictures from Vietnam. I was stunned—mesmerized by those images and my memories. Chrisanne, by then awake, came over to me just as the song finished. I was holding my knees tightly and rocking back and forth, in full-on bawling mode. She softly placed her hand on my shoulder and asked if I was OK. When I looked up at her, I could not speak and neither could she. We did not know what to say. I know that I had an edge way down deep inside for well over twenty years; it was not until receiving counseling that those tensions began to abate. The sessions I had did wonders for me. So, too, has talking and writing about things I previously could not or would not talk about openly. We do not lament in war—that waits until we are home, safe, and reflective.

I knew I came home with new perspectives. Chief among them was mortality. We all know from childhood that we will die someday. Awareness comes in a myriad of ways, usually through our parents or religious teachings, and those are usually shrouded in euphemism. We learn about death in an academic sense. When we mature and begin questioning the world, embarking on life and career, we tend to ignore our personal mortality; we have no time. We are too busy with life, or it is too far in our future—like when we are old. We do not usually consider our life as the gift it is. Others may teach us it is a gift, but again, we are too busy to be concerned. Most of us do not much dwell on our own mortality until we get older, when we are awakened to it by the loss of a close relation or a close friend. I said most of us.

The fragility of life is visceral for combatants. Suffering a traumatic, life-threatening event brings personal mortality to the fore. Combat veterans from any war, on any side and in any time, generally understand *and* accept their mortality the first time they see someone vanish in an explosion, or bleed out, or hear a friend's death rattle. It occurs when they are young—that is who bears the true burden of battle, the young. Their experience is extreme, and it hits them hard—indelibly so. The acceptance of their own mortality and the preciousness of life thereafter remain for their entire lifetime.

How could it be that any young man would continue in harm's way toward the possible loss of his life? It is not for Mom, not for apple pie, and not even for flag and country, although those very things may have started his march into danger. He continues for the guy next to him—his buddy. They fight among themselves as siblings when the common foe is not before them, and they join forces in concert for the common good when they are; they protect the guy they do not like. What compares to that? Family!

Merely being in the service is risky; being in a theater of war increases the risk multi-fold. Most FSBs in Vietnam were probed and attacked on a regular basis, but being truly out "in the bush" was constantly dangerous. The field was home to my unit and those units like us (cavalry and armor) and for extended periods. There was no roof, no bed, no mess hall, no shower—not even a two-holer—often for many weeks at a time. We maneuvered every day, all day, openly subjecting ourselves to enemy fire, mines, and booby-traps. The very tip of the spear has a finely honed edge. That said, REMFs also served. Despite all the remarks I have made, they should be respected as well, and I thank them for their service.

In battle—out of necessity—there is trust; it is a trust like no other. (Bonds of firefighters and police are kissing cousins.) Some would say competitive sports and fraternities offer a similar bond. Seriously? Are their lives in constant danger and for protracted periods? There is tremendous value in those organizations, and there definitely is bonding, but the connections were not formed under the daily risk of their imminent death, traumatic dismemberment, or grotesque bodily disfiguration. Ask *any* former combatant.

Who is it that says a combat veteran does not want to talk about his experience? (I suspect it is the proverbial "they.") Some vets may be too busy moving through life, and some may have an emotional or sentimental inhibition. It is my view that we just do not have an appreciative audience. When the Vietnam vets I know get together, we reminisce of Vietnam—good and bad. I realized soon after I returned home that there is just no way for us to convey our experience to anyone who has not seen combat; to understand it is to have been in those moments. (All mothers know that only another mother really gets it. Their shared experience provides their understanding.) I have tried to bring others to my experience without success—Chrisanne being chief among them. I do not blame her or anyone else. I did not get it until I experienced it. For years, I routinely kept people at a distance due to that divide. I am told that is not unusual for a veteran, but it is for me—I am, and have always been, very social.

*Rear: author, Doc Witwicki, Jack Tinsley;
Front: Richie Guerine, Terry Valentine.*

I am not a unique veteran in that a day does not pass when I am not reminded somehow of people or events from my Vietnam experience. Trust and closeness have eluded me since; I am unable to blindly trust those I do not know well, or to become close friends readily. Unexpected, loud, and sharp noises continue to rattle me. Two Quarter Cav friends have disability attributed to Agent Orange. Others have an assortment of cancers, heart concerns, and other maladies, each occurring too frequently and at too young an age. Some survived their military service physically unscathed and have since died well before their time.

The guys that I spent the most monumental year of my life with never said they had my back, but they certainly did have it—all day, every day. If I asked them, they still would. I recently had the chance to thank a few of them. In the late summer of 2013, several former Quarter Cav troopers made a stopover en route to the annual 1st Infantry Division reunion. Wayne "Doc" Witwicki (medic), Jack Tinsley (platoon leader), Terry Valentine (tank crew), and Richie Guerine (ACAV crew), and I visited for a few days. We slipped back into our young selves and took a trip down to visit the new Infantry Museum at Ft. Benning. (Interesting twist for me—embracing infantry.) I forget who it was, but one of the guys said, "The last time we were together people were shooting at us." Yes, they were.

Several years earlier, Jon Laird (Jungle Pig) was in town and we connected. He was the first Quarter Cav trooper I had seen since leaving the service. Reminiscing with Jon put me in a very good place, enhancing the counseling I received years earlier. I am grateful.

I am so glad I got to spend time with all of them.

I did not know anything about it until about 1999, but....

In 1988, a U.S. Army NCO in Germany by the name of Clyde Lee Conrad was arrested for espionage. He was later found guilty of spying for the Hungarians and is said to have ultimately given up more planning information to the Soviets than any spy during the Cold War.

Why is this pertinent? Conrad had been recruited by Zoltan Szabo. Yes, the very same Zoltan Szabo I had known in Vietnam in 1969. He had been a spy for the Hungarians since 1967—two years before I met him. In the early 1970s while he was stationed in Germany as a sergeant, reduced in rank after the war ended, Szabo recruited many U.S. Army soldiers into Conrad's ring of spies. Szabo was the one who had recruited Clyde Conrad into the spy network. The book *Traitors Among Us: Inside the Spy Catcher's World* by Stuart

A. Herrington gives readers an account of their devastating espionage. It is an interesting read.

I recall reading in the Atlanta paper back in 1966 that a cavalry trooper serving in Vietnam sacrificed his life to save his crewmates by jumping on a grenade. I remember it so well because I was incredulous. While in Vietnam, I learned a Medal of Honor was awarded to a trooper from Quarter Cav three years earlier. The man I read of in 1966 was the Medal of Honor recipient from Quarter Cav.

SGT Donald Russell Long was posthumously awarded the Medal of Honor for his actions on 30 June 1966.

My mother never understood why I never got angry about draft dodging. While some received a jail term for their refusal to serve, others left our country. Then there were a few who went underground—wanted by the law and living in fear of discovery by the FBI. Who knew Jimmy Carter would grant them a pardon, or that they would ever be pardoned at all? I was not upset at their pardon—they paid the price for their stand. However, I respect only their commitment to their beliefs. They talked the talk *and* walked the walk. Too many talkers do not do any walking.

Vietnam veterans became veterans at a time when being one was not cool. Perhaps that was because of a few bad acts by a few bad actors. They are popular with the media and its audience—they are inherently more interesting. Certainly, there *were* bad acts and bad actors in Vietnam, but they were few, and I make no excuse for them. Mostly, it is the faddish derision and disdain of warriors fueled by media exaggeration that failed veterans upon homecoming. We know that now, at a time when veterans are rightfully praised for their service.

If you are one who demeaned or actually caused harm to a returning warrior, shame on you. You should be forgiven, though. I long ago forgave those who agitated me, and I am much better for it. If you have come to realize that one can support the warrior without being a warmonger, that you can both hate war *and* respect the warrior, then you—finally—understand what is just. Nevertheless, you have arrived late to the party, and good manners require that you refrain from espousing your new position so obnoxiously. *Never* bogart that patriotism, my friend—it is unseemly.

There It Is

My plan to stay out of the infantry, out of combat, and away from Vietnam failed miserably—at least when measured by the standards I set for myself in March of 1968. Looking back at the four-plus decades since, I accept and embrace that my non-standard experiences molded my future. It is not the idyllic future I envisioned in my youthful dreams of reaching for and securing the stars within my sector of the heavens. My adventures and misadventures molded the future that was meant for me. Why did I not see it all along? I was too busy moving down the road less traveled to understand how busily traveled that road actually is—I thought I was alone. Plenty of people have taken that road, and many are veterans.

    I seek sympathy from no one. I am much richer for the path I have taken. I am not offended when my path is referred to as the "error of his/your ways." A non-standard path does not an error make—it can make a very exciting adventure. My life-trek has provided experiences a relative few can claim. As a result, I am generally more tolerant, empathic and open to ideas, and with less of an ego than those who have not had a similar experience. I certainly know the value of this life, how very precious it is, how fleeting, and how fragile. That is why I shake my head at those with no clue, those who think they have answers after having done little except to follow everyone else down the common path, claiming it uncharted. Those types of people tend to make me much less tolerant, and I think of them as I do exploiters, opportunists, bullies, social and career climbers, blowhards, and bloviators.

I said earlier that this book is not a war memoir. It is not, but my take-away from my service cannot be ignored. It has affected everything I do, every day. I have recognized that fact since my counseling and instead of trying to erase it, out run it, hide it, or overpower it, I have learned to embrace it. I am in a fine place now. I hope you are, as well, veteran or not. It took me some time to grasp that I could not conquer very much until I first conquered myself. Lesson: Only after you find yourself will everything else find its home.

I submit that the course I took was a better route for me because it taught so much more than I could ever have learned another way. I do not regret my past—I am able to reconcile my actions with reason and common sense, forgoing emotion, fad, and politics. I was served well by the army and by Vietnam. Where was I headed before I enlisted? Who knows? The army gave me self-discipline, and the war steeled me. I have always had enough confidence in myself that should I choose to do something it would get done, and well; if I did not know how, I would learn how. Fortitude comes from within, not as others grant it. I have not had a concern that others see me as a success, as smart, or even as a good man—not for a long time, now. That validation comes from me and me alone.

Never a hunter, I was raised where hunters were in the majority. When hunting is *not* merely wanton killing, or where it is *not* weighted mightily in favor of "hunters," I appreciate the tradition and the sport, especially when non-endangered animals are tracked in time-honored ways. After Vietnam, though, where our prey skillfully hunted us right back—often successfully—I have never had the inclination to hunt.

I have consciously sought excitement, however. Maybe it is the adrenaline rush caused by the pronounced excitement of battle that I miss. (I do not wish to revisit combat.) Maybe it has been my personality type all along—a craving to feel alive with my blood flowing freely. To that end, aviation has been my personal go-to support satisfying most of that need.

Throughout my post-Vietnam business life, whenever I

was told or asked to do something with which I disagreed, I took the good soldier approach. I would respectfully state my case without equivocation, and when I was unable to alter the course, I accepted my instruction and got the job done, just as directed. I was never asked in Vietnam, nor have I ever been asked in civilian life, to do anything immoral, illegal, or unethical—only illogical, and there has been plenty of that.

One day in 1966, my mother and I were discussing my dating activity. OK, it was not a discussion. She questioned me, and I was not forthcoming, acting very much the teenager I was. I think she was merely trying to get a glimpse at what was going on in my personal life. After probing without much success, she finally accepted my minimal responses as proof that I was playing the field.

"You'll probably remain a bachelor all your life, just like my brother," she said with a little frustration, "You'll never get married."

Thence came wisdom from on high. From behind his newspaper, my father added his opinion, his voice carrying more than a hint of resignation.

"Of course he will, Helen." Dad paused for effect. "Four or five times."

Fooled 'em! I married only once—in 1974—and I am not about to go anywhere since I am just about house broken. In the last few years when Chrisanne and I have met people for the first time and they ask how we met, my response is, with a grin, "I stole her from her starter husband...yanked her right out of her practice marriage." I kid about that, but the truth is that I regret what happened with my new friend Russ way back then. However, I recognize that it was not because of me. My kidding about it aside, their breakup was because of, and between, the two of them—but I benefited.

I was ashamed of my service for some time and, after those initial false starts and rude people, avoided almost any discussion about it. Then for years I was neutral, still hiding everything about my Vietnam past. For some reason, since that time I have become proud. I do not know at what point I stopped wanting to forget about it, or when I embraced my personal history (including those periods prior to and after army service).

Someone asked me once when I had been to Vietnam. I said, "I visit every day." Today those visits are not so dark. However, when I have as few as two drinks I get sentimental, and that may lead to my becoming misty-eyed. I admit there are times that I do not even need alcohol. Do I cry for my lost friends and acquaintances, many of whose names I long ago forgot, and most whose names I will never know? Do I cry for the wounded, many of whom were permanently disfigured—those we never heard from after they left the battlefield? Do I cry because I was deep down scared shitless each and every second in Vietnam? Do I cry because my fun-filled youth is ancient history? Do I cry when I am reminded of family and friends who have predeceased me? Do I cry in fondness when recalling all the special moments I have had during such an experience-rich life? The answer is abundantly clear.

"YES…YES…*HELL*, YES!"

Appendix

Readers may find the following books of interest. Each was written by a veteran of the 1-4 Cavalry in Vietnam.

Colonel (Ret) William C. Haponski
1-4 Cavalry Commanding Officer

Danger's Dragoons
First Division Museum at Cantigny Park, 2014.

One Hell of a Ride
Booksurge (Amazon), 2009.

Hugh L. Mills, Jr.
1-4 Cavalry Aero Scout Pilot

Low Level Hell
Presidio Press, 1992.

Colonel (Ret) Paul D. Walker
1-4 Cavalry Platoon Leader

Jungle Dragoon
Presidio Press, 1999.

www.ingramcontent.com/pod-product-compliance
Lightning Source LLC
Chambersburg PA
CBHW021847090426
42811CB00033B/2169/J